Body & Mind Transformation

The Ancient Way...

well-being. Treating just one aspect does not lead to true healing at the core level of the health issue.

... be the Messengers of ...

... imagine that frequent cold and allergies ... with cancer. The simple logic is that cold and cancer are caused due to weak immunity, and due to high ... and acidic state of the body. However, modern medicine ... the idea of weakening immunity to manifest ... someday unless it actually happens!

... Secondary Disease While Treating the Primary

... been prepared to believe ... disease in the bargain of one.

... Not Considered ...

... we would have caught these diseases, we would have been in a much better position because our body is well equipped internally to fight off anything that is caused by external factors. That's why we have been blessed with an immune system. Since modern diseases are not caught but are developed ...

Body & Mind Transformation

The Ancient Way...

Dr. Deepti Sehgal
(Macrobiotic Health & Wellness Consultant)

My Books Publication

First Published in March 2017

by

my Books

Think | Create | Publish

My Books Publication
publish@my-books.in

ISBN: 978-93-86474-05-6
eISBN: 978-93-86474-06-3

eBook & Cover Design
DigiConv Technologies

Firstly, this book is dedicated to my family, friends and all people for whom liveliness, positivity, health, happiness & wellness is of prime importance & a way of life. However, this book is all the more dedicated to people who seek to be healthy & well, but do not understand what health & wellness is all about. It is also dedicated to all people who follow the best diets ever & follow an exercise routine come what may, yet, do not feel & perform to the best of their potential. Most importantly, this book dedicated to all diseased people who continue to live under the shadow treatments in a hope to achieve fake levels of health by investing their life, energy & resources on external treatments versus focus on internal healing.

ACKNOWLEDGEMENT

This book is an outcome of a lot of things coming together, including my interest & passion into the wonderful world of holistic studies specifically Macrobiotics & Traditional Chinese Medicine, the diseased world, the will to find health solutions the natural way, sickly lifestyles of people that are dragging them towards health disasters and wish to spread awareness about how the lost art of holistic health and living well is costing us our body, mind & soul.

Heartfelt thanks to all the people who contributed in their own ways towards the completion of this book. Special thanks to my family including my parents (Mr. Arun Chugh & Mrs. Manju Chugh), my husband (Mr. Anurag Sehgal) and children (Diya Sehgal & Aliya Sehgal), who helped in their own small ways to make this book come live. Days and nights of writing, without bothering about home chores and children would not have been possible without their contributions. Not to forget my domestic help who has been handling the home responsibilities quite dedicatedly & efficiently to ensure that this word goes out! Thanks to my sister (Nandini Chugh), uncle (Mr. Arvind Chugh), aunt (Mrs. Neeru Chugh, Mrs Sunita Chopra), cousin's (Anurag Mehandiratta, Pallavi Mehandiratta, Sandy Chugh, Kshitij Chugh & Vashu Chugh) who by choice or by chance kept living a Macrobiotic lifestyle and sharing their transformational experiences.Thanks to all my friends who have been an inseparable part of this milestone through discussions, suggestions, contributions and help whenever required. Thanks to 'Smriti Bhatia', for always being encouraging and boosting my confidence to be able to complete this book in 4 months. Thanks to all those who kept practicing what I kept learning and discussing during my studies, and kept showing the positive results that has always been my confidence booster.

I am thankful to my Macrobiotic instructor Mr. David Briscoe, who helped set-up such brilliant concepts about holistic health & wellbeing in such a simple understandable way and instilling the confidence to practice the learnings without any doubts. My ex-neighbors, Sahay's, who have always been encouraging and excited about my holistic health studies. Also thanking them for practicing and adopting what I learned through this wonderful journey.

Kudos & thanks to my clients who trusted themselves and me and adopted a healing path towards a better physical and emotional health.

'To be healthy & well in body & mind, each person must know how their body functions. However, you need not study biology or chemistry for years to know yourself. Rather, in ancient times biology or chemistry never existed! Years ago, ancient healing sciences such as Macrobiotics, Traditional Chinese Medicine (TCM) & Ayurveda observed the patterns of nature to understand human body functioning. The observers concluded that, like nature our body also goes through various seasons. Different kinds of energies in nature form us internally, where, 'Air' represents breath, 'Water' represents blood & other body fluids, 'Fire' represents metabolism & digestion, 'Earth' represents our structural components like cell wall & 'Metal' represents various elements of body functioning. Our body functions exactly as per the patterns that exist in the nature. Precisely, this also means that our body & its internal functioning gets activated when the sun rises & it becomes slow as the sun sets. That is the reason that we feel fresh as Sun in the morning and become sleepy & off at night. If we understand & follow our synch with the nature, no force can make us sick ever!'

ABOUT THE BOOK

This is a revolutionary one-of-its-kind book that looks into the dietary & lifestyle patterns of people in modern times and relates how people with modern lifestyles are birthing their diseases themselves each single day. Time-to-time, it discusses health excerpts from ancient litratures of 'Macrobiotics,' 'Traditional Chinese Medicine' & Ayurveda. This book puts across a strong message and will make you think:

While the world is progressing brilliantly in all aspects of life, is the world eating, living & thinking right for their health & well being?

If yes, why are health disorders becoming a norm in modern lifestyles?

Is there any aspect of health & well-being that we are missing in modern times?

If we begin to understand the science of life, the human body unfolds as an amazingly integrated mechanism. We are naturally blessed with all internal mechanisms to become healthy, beautiful, happy, energetic and peaceful, yet we run pillar to post to find solutions for our agonies, diseases, and pains. Ironically, we seek solutions for diseases that we have created for ourselves. We keep disturbing our body balance with our hazardous dietary and lifestyle practices and become diseased over time, it is as straightforward and logical as that! However, irrespective of any lifestyle disorder that we may suffer from, we can begin healing ourselves at any stage by shifting our focus from external treatments to inner holistic healing.

This book is all about self-investigation and self-discovery. It will forever change the way you look at your foods, diet, health, well-being, diseases, beauty & yourselves! It will help you begin your transformation towards natural health & well-being by empowering you to understand yourself inside out. Without any need to study biology & chemistry, you will understand your body functioning & it is holistic connect with nature. This book also empowers you to be knowledgeable enough to take a right dietary & lifestyle approach to health & well-being. After reading this book, you will understand:

- ❑ You possess all the power to live through the day energetically and with positivity, irrespective of your daily duties and responsibilities.
- ❑ You carry a face & body that speaks the story of your internal health.
- ❑ Your outside appearance reflects a state of your internal health. You need not depend on pills, cosmetics or a beauty clinic to look and feel beautiful.
- ❑ Your health is nothing to do with any particular diet type. It is to do with consuming right foods as per your body type and eliminating the rest.
- ❑ Your physical well-being begins with a healthy mind and by living by your dreams and beliefs.
- ❑ You can rediscover a new realm of energy by focusing on right diet & lifestyle.
- ❑ Your healing for any health state begins with a healthy gut and proper digestion.
- ❑ Your smartness, beauty, intelligence, peace and calm are a lot to do with the foods that you eat and the way you live.

Through this book, I take you through the inward journey of knowing yourself biologically and to healing yourself internally. You will understand why everything including health, healing, energy, beauty and happiness begins in the kitchen and not at a doctor's clinic, a spa center, or a beauty salon.

This book explains why health and well-being are more a matter of choice than fate. How through awareness, right decisions and realistic changes, your body can be brought back to balance. As your body begins to attain balance internally, you automatically start to attain a healthy body & sound mind. Your skin automatically starts to get radiant, your health issues start to fade away & your energy starts to enjoy your company the whole day. Your body starts to get into shape healthily, and your mind starts to focus on positivity, all by itself!

Precisely, this book talks about:

- ❑ Daily routines of people which manifest into diseases.
- ❑ Ancient concepts of human body functioning.
- ❑ Holistic connect of humans with nature.
- ❑ Face & body traits that speak your health story.
- ❑ Nature-intended ways of eating, living & thinking right.

DISCLAIMER

The sole purpose of this content is to educate and spread awareness about holistic ways of living life. Though you can use this content alongside medical treatments to support healing, this information is not intended as a substitute for use in the diagnosis, treatment, cure or prevention of any disease. This content is not a substitute for medical therapies. If you suffer from any severe acute or chronic health concern, please consult a trained health professional who can fully assess your needs and address them effectively. Neither the author nor the publisher shall be responsible or liable for any loss of damage allegedly arising as a consequence of your use or application of any information or suggestion contained in this book.

CONTENTS

PART 1

This section takes you through the lives and routines of people living modern lifestyles, where you will find reflection or direct connect with your life & your health state. It explains in detail how your health issues keep becoming bigger & bigger as you live through the day daily. It empowers you to understand yourself and your body functioning inside out. It emphasizes why it is important to know yourself before beginning a diet plan, before starting an exercise routine, before deciding to live and work late nights, before starting to have fun with gadgets & before deciding to go for treatments every now & then. It focusses why transforming your diet & lifestyle is the only solution to lasting health & well-being.

INTRODUCTION - IN MODERN AGE, WHAT'S WRONG WITH OUR HEALTH & WELL-BEING?

'Nature always intended our body, mind & soul to be in a natural state of harmony, happiness, health & well-being; Nature provided us with all means to be so!'

It is an internet age and we have easy access to any health information that we need. We are more informed today, highly educated, eat healthily, go gymming, do yoga, and meditate, only to realize that our sufferings are rising by the day. The more we try to live healthily, the more alarming health statistics we get to see in research studies.

What's wrong with our health and well-being? Why is every other person diseased today?

There was a time when people used to die due to external influences like virus and bacteria. However, today people die of their wrong habits, diets, and lifestyles! Lifestyle Disorders, as the name implies, are, 'The Maladies Created by Humans Themselves,' and, I insist that we all reaffirm this statement until we begin to believe that no third element is the cause of our suffering, pain or life-threatening disorders including diabetes or cancer. It is our own body that starts to work against us because we fail to provide it with the right means and resources to function well.

Let's change perspective and understand how we create our diseases. If the name, 'Lifestyle Disorders' implies that our way of living is the cause behind our health issues, does it make sense to rethink how we live our lives today? Does it also make sense to realize that only treatments are not enough to put a stop on the gripping epidemic of lifestyle disorders because we still keep feeding the roots of our diseases by continuing to live a similar lifestyle that caused the disease? Does a treatment for Parkinson's disease, for example, leave you constipated as a known side effect? And so, does it mean that 'side effect' is a safe term used for acquiring one disease in return of another! National Cancer Institute openly accepts that the cancer patients are prone to treatment side effects; it's an accepted bargain to either die of a life-threatening disease or live with yet another persistent but non-deadly health issues.

The health statistics from across the world:

- ❑ The probable age of developing diabetes has come down to 13 years.
- ❑ Every 1 in 28 women develops cancer in her lifetime.
- ❑ Incidences of cancer in Indian women aged 30 years and above are expected to rise in future.
- ❑ Every 1 out of 6 adolescents in India is overweight.
- ❑ Puberty rate in girls has come down from 16 years to 6 years in the US, 7 years in South Africa and 10 years in India.

Today there are best treatments available, and hospitals outnumber schools and parks. Medical infrastructure is getting better, yet the world is getting sicker.

So, the million dollar question is, why our health and well-being is under threat? Who is making us diseased?

And, the million dollar answer is we ourselves are making us diseased!

Let's dig deeper into our habits, diets, lifestyles, our beliefs and thinking patterns to understand this. Our social conditioning is such that we have been convinced to believe that at the age of 50 or 60, an individual is bound to suffer from ill health and some fatal disease. Our belief system accepts that progressing years are meant to be diseased. With that understanding emerge our actions of giving up on our efforts to maintain health for years. Following a convenient path of popping pills has become our lifestyle. However, we realize nothing gets better, and diseases keep getting worse overtime, even after taking medications.

However, this was not the case a few years back. The ancient healing systems including Macrobiotics, Traditional Chinese Medicine, and Ayurveda had a different take on age. Ancient wisdom states that with age we are supposed to become wise, strong, flexible, full of life and energy, contented, calm, knowledgeable and happy. It further states that progressing age is no reason to accept diseases, sadness and pain. Earlier people used to die of old-age, today people die of diseases. The medication culture has made life convenient, and conversely, has deviated our focus from healing to treatments. The advancement of medical science, in a way, has made us lazy enough to be able to think of the root causes that made us diseased and sick and to act upon them promptly. With the handy convenience of medication, we never think what led us to a state of disease. For example in the case of diabetes, insulin vaccinations do help control blood sugar levels, but internally the blood sugar spikes still happen with any external triggers & the biochemical processes involved in body's normal functioning are still in a disturbed state. Despite the treatment, a diabetic patient is still prone to obesity or a heart disease or any other metabolic disorder such as thyroid.

Having said that, the advancement of any disease is a clear indication of the damage done inside the body. And so, treatment may be required. But treatment is not healing. Treatment is all about curing symptoms. Healing is about correcting the causes of diseases, and these causes & triggers could be as raw and straightforward as our daily dietary factors, our routines, our way of living and our thought process. For example, in the case of diabetes, treating means insulin vaccinations, whereas healing means focussing on controlling the factors including diet & others that are causing metabolic disruptions or blood sugar spikes. For example, a high refined carbohydrate, fat or protein lunch is enough to trigger blood sugar spikes within the body. If we keep creating this disturbed state for our body, it is bound to give up some day resulting in a diseased state.

The most disturbing trend is to see our younger generations suffering from lifestyle disorders. Let's look into some statistics in case of younger generations. With the trend of both parents working, food & eating habits have gone quite liberal. Additionally, marketers are doing a brilliant job in influencing children to buy chemical-laden, sugary & trans-fats containing delicious food products. The children today are often seen having disturbed behaviours, irritability, bloated tummies, seasonal allergies, flu, cold, cough, hyperactivity, nutritional deficiencies & sudden mood swings. Most often we tend to associate these symptoms with weather changes, environmental changes or with any other convincing reason. And some of us just consider such health issues as normal side-effects of growing up in an urban set-up. Like never before, the children of today struggle with high-pressure lifestyles & end up in a state of physical & emotional mess. Our perspective of handling this mess is to get our children treated through medications. However, what nobody talks about is, when a child's health begins to deteriorate, the very first symptoms show up as weakened immunity causing frequent cold, cough, allergies, flu, respiratory issues, irritability, emotional upsets, sensitivity and other minor health concerns. Statistics reveal that the puberty rate has gone down drastically & does not give a child's body enough time to adjust to the side-effects of puberty including hormonal changes and physiological issues. A child's body is too tender to be able to handle such matters & may end up in disturbed emotional state & ill physical health. Ultimately our next course of action is to seek professional help without realizing that the roots of such issues are hidden in our daily routines including convenience foods, anti-nature lifestyles, high exposure to gadgets, polluted environment and excessive usage of chemical-laden health & beauty products. Alternatively, with professional help readily available, we prefer to treat our children with medication, rather than working on the root causes behind their health states. As per nature's design, a child's body is the purest & cleanest from inside. And so, a child's fate must not be to suffer from allergies, low immunity, colds & flu, ear infections, sore throats and other health issues.

Few ironical facts about the dietary consultations that we seek for ourselves & for our children:

- ❑ More & more people are seeking nutritional and dietary consultations than ever before.
- ❑ More & more people are consuming commercial food products than ever before.
- ❑ More & more people are getting into dedicated exercising routines.

And yet, more & more people are becoming diseased, dangerously obese and emotionally upset than ever before. More and more people are on drugs and going under the knife for treatments. This had never happened before in the history of health and well-being. The trend only points to the fact that modern ways and perceptions of diet, health, and well-being are somewhere missing on some other important aspects of life.

The Fortune magazine clearly points out that we are losing the war on cancer! According to National Cancer Institute, deaths in millions will happen in the coming years due to the cancer epidemic. By the way, do you wonder why am I quoting cancer time and again? It is because cancer is the state of highest toxicity within the body. In simple terms, when the body gives up on its war against toxicity, it manifests into a cancer. And since we live in a diseased and highly toxic world, cancer has the apt environment to strengthen its roots on the human race.

The bottom line is, though it is hard to find a truly healthy person in current times, with awareness and knowledge we can begin to live right, eat right, think right and create a healthful environment for ourselves that will give ensure that our body's internal environment functions right. With that rightinternal environment, the probability of developing a disease goes to a minimum. From a foundational perspective, the root cause of any disease may be one of these:

- ❑ Toxins trapped inside the body.
- ❑ Highly acidic internal state of the body.
- ❑ Nutritional deficiencies or malabsorption of nutrients.
- ❑ High exposure to electromagnetic chaos.
- ❑ Emotional and mental stress.
- ❑ Energy imbalances.

Today, the only saviour of our health & well-being is awareness and changes in dietary and lifestyle habits. Let's explore in the sections below, how your day-to-day routine may be contributing towards your disease causing factors & what can you do to help yourself.

CHAPTER 1 - CONSUMING FOODS DEVOID OF VITAL LIFE-FORCE

Nutrition & energy are the twin daughters of a single mother – Food. Nutrition is the set of recognized elements that build our body, help us grow & perform our biological functioning. Energy is the unseen vital force that keeps us alive & regulates our existence. Today, we consume the most nutritious foods, yet we are the sickest breed amongst all life-forms on earth. This is because our total focus today is just on one aspect of food which is nutrition. The other aspect that is 'life-force' or energy is lost amidst science's total focus on nutrition. Despite of consuming best foods, we are still creating imbalances within our body because our foods lack vital life-force, 'The Energy', the neglected sister of nutrition'

Scenario

Ayra, 14, is a young teenager who enjoys eating out and is fond of junk food like all teenagers in current times. Her parents are working, and their house is full of readymade healthy commercial eatables such as corn flakes, muesli, canned juices, vitamin drinks, etc. In breakfast, Ayra consumes whole wheat multigrain bread & often a glass of cold coffee. Her mother is convinced that at least Ayra eats healthy breakfast & dinner. Her quick snacks are multigrain biscuits, and in dinner, the entire family consumes home-cooked meal consisting of chapatti or rice with lentils and cooked vegetable. Ayra often complains of indigestion. So, to conclude Ayra's meals contain a substantial portion of processed, chemical-laden foods, artificial flavours, and preservatives. Ayra is 14 years but looks like 18 years old. She entered puberty when she was 9 years. She is lazy, a TV addict, does not have any daily activity routine such as playing out, cycling, etc. Ayra stays most happy with her iPad playing games, listening music videos and doing other time-killing activities on her gadgets. She is fond of fragrant toiletries and cosmetics just like her mother. She does not have the energy to cope up with her daily activities and gets tired quickly. For quick energy, she banks upon ready-made juices, chocolate drinks such as Milo and a few multi-grain cookies. Ayra is attention deficit and minor dyslexic for which she is seeking professional help.

Food For Thought:

Doesn't this sound like the story of every teenager? Are you convinced with Ayra's mother's reasoning that Ayra eats healthy? If Ayra eats healthy, why does she feel tired, exhausted and irritated at such a tender age? Do you approve of Ayra's eating habits? Most importantly, do your children possess similar dietary habits?

Case Analysis:

Ayra's routine, body state, and eating habits are worrisome. She consumes so-called healthy lifeless foods in her daily routine. She is a technology addict. She entered puberty at a tender age, and physically she looks much older than her biological age. Since a child's body is too young to be prepared for hormonal changes and the associated emotional ups and downs, many children today face emotional issues without knowing what's happening to them. The readymade foods may contain fortified nutrition, but at the foundational level, these foods disturb body chemistry, create digestive issues, weaken immunity, and keep us devoid of vital life-force that balances our integrated existence i. e. 'Body' and 'Mind. 'Ayra is also fond of cosmetic products, most of which research suggests are hormone provoking! Quite possible that Ayra's cosmetics and toiletries have a role to play in her fast-forwarded growth cycle, and hence she hit puberty early. As a holistic health and wellness practitioner and after analysing Ayra's dietary and lifestyle patterns, it is no shocker for me that Ayra suffers from emotional, digestive and other 'so-called' negligible health issues. Seen from a holistic health perspective, the impact of her incorrect diet and lifestyle pattern has already started to show up as laziness, digestive issues, mood swings, and emotional ups and downs. Worst still, no one is bothered about the root cause of Ayra's issues. She still eats foods that contain preservatives, additives and probably growth hormones, specifically dairy products. Her mother already assumes that she eats healthy most of the times and from emotional health perspective her counseling sessions are successful in treating her. Probably, Ayra does not complain of any health issues at this point. Thanks to her relatively young body that is still in a naturally healthy state, and so she may have a good scope to digest whatever she eats, while not showing any visible deteriorating physical health signs. However, the net effect of her diet and lifestyle is culminating into minor health issues for now and over the years may make her body prone to further health deterioration if she continues with her ways. Her mother thinks she is all ok as minor health issues keep emerging in today's times. However, look at her routine, and you know her nutritional needs are not being met daily. Just think, does our body give up on its biological functioning? No, it doesn't. It still performs its functions without its essential elements and in the process leaves us 'Imbalanced' – the foundation of all health issues! Ayra's body and mind have already started to show subtle signs of exhaustion, laziness, tiredness, lack of energy, mood swings and irritability. This is how her body is interacting with her and conveying her that she must feed herself right stuff, give her body the right resources to function well and realize her body's needs in time before any disaster strikes!

Our Beliefs:

Being on a diet has become a global craze. 'I am on a diet' is the most used phrase on this planet today, yet maximum diets fail for so many people!

So, is there anything wrong with our nutrition system?

Our belief on modern foods has strengthened over years as it is a science-based system to measure the nutritional requirements of our body. Though the modern nutrition system does have positives in terms of understanding our foods better, the problem with this system is the narrow approach with which foods are looked upon and utilized today. Nutritional science has its 100% focus on nutritional elements and ignores the concept of its step sister – Energy!

The modern dietary approach works on a 'one size fits all' formula. Constitutionally, each individual is unique. What may be a remedy for someone may be disastrous for someone else. Assume that you have diabetes and your spouse doesn't. Now, healthy foods specifically high glycemic index foods such as pineapple may not be recommended for you but may prove good for your spouse who is suffering from a seasonal cough. Unfortunately, modern nutrition does not consider a person's constitution (what you are blessed with in your genes) and condition (what you suffer from) as primary factors when putting together nutritional approach. It goes with a single-minded approach about the importance of all nutritional elements while ignoring its applicability on individuals. The nutritional sciences' approach is based on Food & Drug Authority (FDA) recommendations on calorie counting system or protein to carbohydrate ratios and other government guidelines. These guidelines fail to take a holistic approach to nutrition.

Modern nutrition recognizes the value of each food in terms of carbohydrates, proteins, fats, vitamins and minerals. It works on a calorie system, where each food has a particular numeric value associated with it called the calories. So, as a human, your purpose is to consume those many numbers of calories in a day and burn them right to be healthy. For example, for an average female, nearly 2000 or more calorie count is considered the ideal number to be consumed in a day, irrespective of her constitution and condition. If you analyze the nutrition and diet industry today, you know this is what is being followed in the diet rat race, and we are still getting unhealthier! The importance of whole and natural foods is quite under-estimated. With industrialization, we started breaking our foods and separating them from their vital parts such as husk, bran, and flour. We then began marketing the importance of joining these parts for complete nutrition. For example, wheat porridge is already a whole food. But many times we come across marketing campaigns and doctors' advice that recommends adding bran to flour for all nutritional benefits. This is a significant gap that modern nutrition does not considers. Our ancestors ate whole foods; we eat 'broken and rejoined' foods. Our ancestors were much healthier despite of lesser food varieties; we are much weaker and sicker despite of consuming 'broken and rejoined' foods from the world over. Do you get the point? Breaking and rejoining foods back with its parts changes the entire chemistry to foods and so no one knows how it may be impacting us. There could be a probability that we are sicker due to this! Modern nutrition also does not consider the concept of energy when researching or recommending certain foods. Energy may be unseen and so not recognized by science, but it still holds a lot of power. Had the energy not been there, we would not have been falling sick eating lifeless foods!

Facts:

For a moment just think:

- ❑ Is it normal for a child to begin showing fast signs of growth?
- ❑ Do you think early hormonal changes in Ayra are normal?
- ❑ What should a child aged 8 – 10 year be like, look like & behave like?

If we consider how nature intended us to perform, we know that an 8-year-old child is supposed to be chirpy, energetic, full of vital force, unaware and inexperienced of chemical imbalances and non-bothered about the how we begin to get sick. Sadly, deterioration of body at a younger age is what our younger generation is experiencing today. Especially the pre-teenagers and teenagers are the most affected lot who consume the worst foods ever on earth. Their dietary patterns are highly influenced by the modern view of food and diet. It is no secret that the growth hormones are injected to livestock's to meet meat and dairy requirements. Moreover, with fast food chains being a trend in youngsters, the consumption of non-vegetarian foods has seen a tremendous high.

In recent years there has been a drastic decline in puberty age. Hormonal issues that once arrived at the age of nearly 16 years, now affect 7-10-year-olds. Ultimately, all the chemicals, growth hormones, preservatives, artificial colors and additives used in dairy, livestock or processed food industry are getting into our bodies. With each food choice at each meal, our bodies are either getting nutrition or toxins and slow poisons that are making us sick and mature before age. Too much of such foods are inversely affecting our hormones, immunity, sanity, radiance, vitality, health and our whole existence.

Holistic Perspective:

Though modern medicine does not recognize the concept of vital life-force and its role in one's health and well-being, the TCM and Ayurveda ancient sciences consider this vital life force as the primary force behind human existence. Today, our foods are fortified with nutritional elements, but vital life-force cannot be fortified in foods. It just exists, like in sprouts, where some unseen force makes them grow. By the way, does your bread grow? No!!! 100 calories from sprouts will make you feel alive and vibrant, whereas 100 calories from a slice of bread will make you feel dull and exhausted. That's where you experience the life-force!

Life force is the essence of our being, and this energy flows through different aspects of our body including our physical, emotional, and spiritual bodies. Similar to the unseen electricity current that traverses through dedicated power grids & lights our homes & offices, the unseen energy or life force system works within our bodies on virtually laid out energy channels called 'Meridians' in TCM & 'Nadis' in Ayurveda. Acupuncture is a science that balances the flow of this unseen energy through the use of needles that unblock the flow of energy in the meridians. The primary reason why medical science does not believe in the concept of life-force is that there is nothing tangible about it. Energy cannot be touched or seen, yet, it is something so powerful that lights up our entire existence!

Take Away Thought:

'I follow a diet plan; still, I do not lose weight…' I often come across this statement from a lot of people who are following some diet plan. My first response to their concern is, if you are eating healthy and exercising right then why do you think you do not see the good results? And, the answer that I get is 'I do not know!' The answer is…

…The life-force or 'Chi' in TCM & 'Prana' in Ayurveda gets activated primarily through air and food. Unfortunately, the air that we breathe is highly toxic today. Additionally, our breathing patterns are too shallow, and so we do not take in enough life-force through the air medium. We spend most of our day indoors away from fresh air and away from green oxygenated areas. We keep re-breathing the artificially circulated air in closed chambers. Our foods are devoid of life-force as we majorly consume processed foods. The quality of our foods has degraded due to the use of pesticides, fertilizers and other chemicals. We no more thrive on whole and natural foods diet. It's all chemical-laden and processed stuff that our body majorly deals with on day to day basis.

To conclude, our two core sources of essential life-force i. e. 'air' and 'food' have become artificial. In such a scenario, any diet that we pursue will create fundamental imbalances. Unless this balance is restored, health & healing in the real sense cannot be achieved.

CHAPTER 2 - DRIFTED FROM NATURAL RHYTHMS OF NATURE

'Technologically we may have become much advanced, however, when it comes to the internal operations of our body system, we are still very traditional, very very ancient in terms of body functioning. Rather, our body functioning is still the same as it was during early mans' times. Interestingly, cavemen of stone age & new born baby of today function similar internally! Till date, no human could ever develop a technique or a filter to parse the wrong intake without it having an impact. What we consume affects us, each single bite! The way we choose to live & eat creates us. Since we are not putting a stop to the abuse on our bodies done in multiple dietary & lifestyle ways, & our body is continuing to function traditionally, that is the reason that our body & mind systems are getting weaker by the day & we are becoming diseased despite of superb technological advancements!'

Scenario

Shrene, 47, feels that discomfort is her way of life. Since long now, she keeps lying awake in her bed & her mind keeps racing in the dark. She wakes up at 9 A. M. She eats her breakfast at 11 A. M. and bathe's by 1 P. M. Lunch timings vary anywhere from 4 P. M. to 5 P. M. depending when she feels like consuming food. After her meal, Shrene takes a nap of 1 hour and wakes up at 6 P. M after which she prepares dinner. Dinner time begins at 8. 30 P. M. & by the time she winds up all, it is already 11 P. M. By the time she gets into the bed it is already 12 P. M. Her sleep is already gone by that time. She keeps awake with a racing mind until sleep blesses her by 1 P. M. During daytime, specifically after breakfast, Sherne experiences digestive distress, gastric issues, and acidic body issues. She does not feel like waking up early and doing things. She does not feel enthusiastic about things and herself. Though there is nothing so serious about her condition, she admits that she does not feel very well through the day. Dullness, unknown sadness and lost feelings keep haunting her for no particular reason. And she feels that's how she is and is used to herself now!

Food for Thought:

Do you think there is anything wrong with Shrene's routine? Do you think she can ever feel better by lying awake in bed every night? How might her lack of sleep be affecting her? Why do we feel fresh in the morning? Why are we supposed to sleep at night? Why are we meant to work during the day time? Do we know how we must operate as per the laws of nature? Do you think our daily activities are tied to some unseen internal clock?

Case Analysis:

Shrene recognizes herself right; she is lost & her body & mind is confused! She is living life totally opposite of how nature operates within us. Lack of proper synchronization with her internal biological clock is creating a mess in her physical and emotional health state. Starting with her waking up timings, till her meal schedules and then sleep timings, she is totally out of sync with nature. Her lack of sleep at the right time, meals at ungodly hours and daily routine activities at inappropriate times like sleeping at 6 P. M. is throwing her internal clock cycle totally out of balance. She experiences the impact in the of low moods, unworthy and dull feelings and a lost sense of being. It is important for Shrene to realize that our biological clock functions differently at specific times of the day. It is critical to synchronize our activities as per this internal functioning.

Our Beliefs:

Today we live in a 24/7 culture. Technology has connected the world so brilliantly that physical presence in geographies does not matter anymore, specifically for work purposes. Business operations can be kept going day and night, geography to geography. People travel to different geographies quite often & in an entirely opposite time zone where their body cycle gets disturbed. Individuals who have faced the consequences of overnight travel understand how miserable if feels if our day & night cycle gets disturbed even for a day. At the biological level, there happen various other unpleasant consequences within us if we drift away from our natural internal sleeping cycle.

Today, Our Disturbed Body Clock & Our Routine Life Looks Like This!

- ❑ At night when we must be sleeping, but we are either eating or watching TV.
- ❑ During midnight when we must be in deep restful state, we often end up struggling with sleep issues.
- ❑ Early morning when we must be waking up, we are in a deep sleep.
- ❑ In the morning when we must be cleaning ourselves internally (bowel cleansing, brushing) and externally (bathing), we are either sleeping or reading newspaper or having morning tea.
- ❑ In the morning when we must be having breakfast, we are still struggling with our daily cleansing activities and getting ready for work.
- ❑ Later in the morning when we must ideally be focusing on work, we are having breakfast.
- ❑ Early afternoon when we must be consuming lunch, we are working.

...Likewise, through the day we keep living a jumbled routine that our internal clock does not sync with. The chemical operations in our body work haphazardly due to this internal and outer confused body state. And so, the internally jumbled state of the body behaves like this:

Ideal Activity	Our Activity	Probable Negative Impact on the Body
Sleeping early at night	Entertainment/ Eating/Reading/ Working	Disturbed hormonal & chemical activity, rejuvenation function impacted
State of deep sleep by midnight	Preparing to go off to sleep	Liver function impaired, overburden on kidneys and heart
Waking up early morning	In deep sleep	Dullness, low moods
Having early breakfast	Preparing to wake up, have tea or reading newspaper	Gastric issues, digestive problems, blood sugar irregularities, nutritional deprivation
Beginning work early	Getting ready for work, bathing or eating breakfast	Disruption in internal body functioning, decreased alertness
Having lunch	Deeply focusing on work	Gastric issues
Relaxed later in the afternoon	Having lunch	Burden on digestion
Enjoying outdoors in evening	At work indoors	Fatigue, headaches, tiredness, overworked body
Having early dinner	Returning from work/going to gym/watching TV/going out	Disrupting rejuvenation that happens during night time

So we see how ultimately our activity times and our daily routine begins to make us diseased internally each single day. Our way of life may someday manifest into blood sugar irregularities, hormonal problems, weakening organs, tired body, deprived body, and imbalanced body organs.

In a study on American individuals, it was concluded that Americans' 24/7 lifestyles are chocked with work, commitments, pressures, e-mails and other distractions. Their lifestyles demand to compromise on sleep to be able to perform well in their respective areas of personal, professional and social commitments. And the result is devastating. For a relaxed sleep, today we juggle with work shifts, jet lags and day and night artificial electric lighting surrounding us. As our body has limited capacity, we try to increase our ability and induce relaxation artificially by consuming coffee, alcohol and other nervous system stimulating items. Without even realizing we see our body changing negatively. And then the 'pill-culture' takes over our senses! And we see, what begins as a matter of common daily choices between our daily activities, manifests into a 'pill' treating what we created ourselves!

Facts:

Interesting Facts About Our Internal Body Functioning Timings!

- ❑ According to a study performed by the American Journal of Preventive Medicine, it was found that women who work in night shifts for nearly five years have greater chances of premature death and heart disease. Another study published in the Occupational and Environmental Medicine Journal reported that shift workers are likely to suffer from cognitive impairments such as taking longer to process information and having trouble with short and long-term memory. The brain aging fast-forwards in people working in shifts for more than a decade. Canadian researchers also caution that shift work may act as a probable carcinogen and may increase the risk of breast cancer in women.
- ❑ According to a report by United Kingdom's Health & Social Care Information Centre, it was found that people who work outside 7 A. M. to 7 P. M. timings are more likely to suffer mental-health problems, decreased alertness, obesity, and diabetes.

- ❑ An interesting study suggests that blood pressure medication can be most effective during early morning hours. This is because the changes in the heart rate and blood pressure during morning hours could somewhat account for the increased risk of heart attack or stroke in the morning.

Our Body's 24 Hour Internal Activity Cycle

A 24-hour internal activity cycle operates within our body. This 24-hour activity cycle operates differently at different times of the day and gets regulated by natural light and natural darkness. This daily cycle is so regular that irrespective of our activities, choices, or any external influences such as jet lags due to night travel, it still works as it must without any compromises.

Latest research now reveals that there exists a tightly regulated dependency between our internal functioning, metabolism & cellular functioning & sleep. This Internal activity cycle must be reset everyday by following the day and night cycle and by performing daily activities as per the sun cycle. Melatonin, an internally produced antioxidant, helps in suppressing harmful free radicals in our body and slows down the production of estrogen. More production of estrogen is related to cancer in women. In the case of disrupted internal functioning, our body's hormonal system gets disrupted, and less melatonin may be produced. This means lesser defense against cancer! Further, any kind of stress including fatigue-related stress, diet-related stress or work-related stress, leads to the release of negative hormones such as 'cortisol'. These negative hormones increase heart rate and blood pressure, making muscles tense and impacting digestive activities. At the brain level, the chemical chemistry moves towards negative state and such a state for a prolonged period leads to avariety of health problems. There have been numerous studies that indicate a direct link between disturbed internal activity and depression, headache, indigestion, obesity, diabetes, high anxiety, heart disease, high blood pressure, insomnia, and cancer.

Our internal clock evolved hundreds of years ago, & since then it has been operating with the rising & setting of the sun. By default, this internal clock assumes that we must sleep at night and work during the daytime. Not just our sleep-wake up cycle, but our internal body functioning is also very closely coordinated with this sun cycle. For example, the liver performs its cleaning work in the state of rest at night when we are done with ingesting toxins throughout the day. Kidneys relax at night, and their action slows down during night hours. Even heart activity slows down its pace during night hours. This is how we are designed to function. And aligning our day-to-day activities with these internal activities keeps us in the best state of health. If we fail to align our daily activities with this internal activity cycle, we confuse our body, the chemicals operating within us, the hormones, the organ functions and all other activities. Such conflicting signals to the body make it work differently than what nature intended us to. Few internal body activities that rely heavily on the internal clock include:

Internal Body Functions	How and At What Time Internal Clock Functions?
Sleep-Wake Up Cycle	Sleep-wake up cycle in humans and animals is directly related to the cycle of the sun. We automatically begin to feel sleepy as we approach towards the dark time of the day. Mornings though make us feel alive and active. Our brain receives the waking or sleeping signals from our internal clock that operates in sync with the sun cycle. When it comes to the chemistry behind sleep-wake cycle, this internal clock releases the hormone 'melatonin' during naturally dark hours of the day that makes us feel sleepy. Respecting this naturally induced sleep cycle can save us from a lot of other issues that may arise by disrespecting natural sleep.

(Continued)

	That also explains why we do not fall asleep easily later at night or in the morning. Our body operations comprise of a series of internal chemical reactions that make us feel sleepy, hungry, sad, happy, and anxious or anything that we experience and feel on the outside. Going against this chemistry initiates premature deterioration and aging of body cells leading to harmful effects in multiple ways.
Rhythm and Moods	Does it ever happen to you that you experience sad, happy, and anxious or any other feeling in a regular pattern at a particular time of the day? It is because our moods tend to change with the internal clock activity. It has been reported in various studies that people experiencing emotional highs and lows, bipolar disorder, mood swings or seasonal affective disorder (SAD) have a disturbed internal clock cycle due to sleeping too much or too little, eating at odd hours, overeating or any other disturbed external activity. Interestingly, the brain chemical 'serotonin' adjusts automatically with natural sun cycle. During natural light or daytime, the serotonin levels increase, while in the dark or during night time serotonin levels decrease. With a disturbed sleep-wake up cycle the chemical balance gets disturbed, probably giving rise to emotional ups and downs.
Exercising	It is proven in the research studies that exercising in the morning yields better results for our mind and body. This is again due to internal clock at play indicating that during peak morning hours our spiritual energy is at its peak.

(Continued)

	That also explains why early morning meditation is recommended versus meditation at any time of the day.
Stress	Our internal clock controls the production of stress hormone 'cortisol' and helps us get into a relaxed state. Night shift workers are especially prone to stress as cortisol gets impacted with opposite sleep-wake up schedules of people.
Eating	Our hunger cycle begins early morning, and our stomach is in a better state to digest food during morning & afternoon hours.
Hormone production	Our internal clocks tightly control hormones. For example, hormone 'melatonin' peaks at night, 'cortisol' peaks during stress hours and daytime and impacts metabolism and immune system regulation.
Body Temperature	Our body temperature also follows the internal clock and fluctuates through the day in a particular pattern. For example, our body temperature in the evening may be one degree Celsius higher in the morning as compared to the night-time temperature.
Cardiovascular system	Studies report that more strokes and heart attacks occur in the morning hours than at any other time of the day. Even blood pressure has a tendency of rising in the morning. These activities are closely tied to our internal clock.

Lifestyle Disorders & Our Connect With the Internal Clock

It is interesting to know how our health issues are so closely related to the disturbed internal clock. Studies show a direct correlation between diseases and upset internal clock.

Lifestyle Disorders	How Internal Clock is Connected
Cancer risk	Changes in hormones like melatonin due to disruption of internal clock may have a significant impact on cancer progression. This hormone is produced during sleep in a deep state of rest and is known to suppress tumor development.
Short term memory	Alterations in the ideal sleep and wake up cycle interfere with the release of certain neurotransmitters in the brain. If the internal clock is confused, an excess of 'Gamma-Amino Butyric acid' (GABA) amino acid that acts as a neurotransmitter in the central nervous system, gets released. This amino acid is responsible for calming nervous activity. An excess of this may affect the ability to retain new information and lead to short-term memory problems.
Immune system	The release of certain hormones during sleep at the right time contribute immensely towards a stronger immune response.
Weight gain/loss	Disturbed internal clock mainly due to lack of sleep at the right time has shown to affect levels of two hormones. These two hormones are responsible for appetite and eating behavior. If you are sleep deprived, the production of hormone 'leptin' decreases. This hormone is responsible for communicating to the brain when to stop eating. Lack of this may make you eat more. Additionally, another hormone 'ghrelin' triggers hunger, which gets produced in the absence of 'leptin' ! Needless to say, sleep deprivation or lack of sleep at the right time may make you gain weight.

(Continued)

Diabetes and heart disease risk	Diabetes is closely related to internal clock and sleep deprivation. It may get triggered both ways; either due to lack of sleep or excess sleep. Less than 6 hours of sleep or more than 8-9 hours of sleep is likely to trigger diabetes and heart disease symptoms.
Menstrual cycle	The menstrual cycle is also very closely related to our internal clock. Disruption of hormone 'melatonin' is associated with the disturbed menstrual cycle.
Infertility	Consider the relationship between 24/7 working culture and the rise in infertility cases! Night shifts are now being termed as 'infertility shift' and seem to be impacting conception directly. Research studies suggest that women working late night or in a night shift culture are highly susceptible to irregular menstrual cycle. These findings are also in line with the fact that human body operates differently in natural light and darkness, and produces specific hormones in the daytime and at night. These hormones work best at their particular times of production which is regulated by the day and night cycle. When we play around with the natural way of living life, we create imbalances and disturbances within our body that further leads to physical and emotional problems.

Holistic Perspective:

'Dincharya,' is an Ayurveda routine that was devised years ago after the early saints realized the importance of internal clock as an important pillar of our health. Dincharya is about performing various customary activities each day at certain times of the day as per the sun cycle. By following daily regimen (Dinacharya), one can take a positive step towards their health and well-being.

Though Ayurveda suggests practicing a series of 'Kriyas' or activities for complete rejuvenation of body and mind, at the bare minimum level, the structure of one's 'Dincharya' must necessarily consist of the following activities:

Daily Activities	Dincharya – How to Live Daily Life According to Internal Clock
Waking Up	Ayurveda's concept of following a 'Dincharya' suggests waking up 2 hours before sunrise. It is considered to be an ideal time of the day to strengthen the power and energy of mind through yoga and meditation. Our body and mind are in a state of calm and rest during this time and are away from worldly noises.
Drink Water in the Morning	Drinking warm water in the morning is believed to wash off the gastrointestinal track and flush the kidneys. Warm lemon water is considered to stimulate peristalsis, which is the intestinal muscle movement that helps in evacuation of the bowels.
Evacuation	The way we clean our house in the morning, similarly our body system must be cleaned internally and externally before beginning the day. The bowel and urinary evacuation activity must ideally be performed on waking up. However, we must not be straining ourselves for the waste removal movement and give our body time and right means to get into this habit of evacuation. Sitting or squatting pose is considered to be the correct postures for evacuation as it straightens our evacuation route for complete cleansing.

(Continued)

Cleaning the Teeth	Teeth must ideally be cleaned using astringent, pungent, and bitter toothpaste. Better still is the traditional Ayurveda way of dental floss that uses a 'Neem' tree stick that is bitter in taste and removes the fine food particles making teeth strong and healthy. Other ancient tooth cleansing options include licorice root sticks, roasted almond shell powder, a green twig of the margosa tree or mixture of salt and mustard oil are a better substitute for cleaning the teeth.
Exercise	Regular exercise is an important aspect of body and mind soundness. Yoga is considered to be a complete body and mind rejuvenating tool that provides strength, beauty, flexibility, endurance and better circulation. It freshens and calms the mind, and helps one relax, improve digestion, remove toxic body waste and sleep well.
Pranayama and Meditation	After exercise, few minutes must be dedicated to pranayama and meditation. It creates a rejuvenating effect on the mind and prepares one well for the day ahead.
Bathing	Ayurveda suggests bathing twice a day. Bathing must be a rigorous activity of stimulating body through oil massage and cold/hot water to activate the internal functioning.
Meals	Ayurveda prescribes consuming two or three meals per day depending upon physical labor. Breakfast must be consumed early, and dinner must be eaten by 7 p. m.
Sleep	Sleep in Ayurveda is of utmost importance. Sleeping early is the best activity that one can do for themselves. At least 6-8 hours of sleep is a must for a healthy body and sound mind. Sleep regulates hormonal activity, rejuvenates us, restores our energy back and has and supports ideal body functioning.

Take Away Thought:

Our internal clock is real and regulates our internal activities. It directs all internal body processes and works differently at different times of the day. It determines the right functioning of our body including sleep, waking up, digestion, blood pressure, organ functioning, cellular functioning, etc. It ensures all individual and coordinated activities happen at the correct time of the day. This internal process highly influences hormonal activity. Some hormones get released at night while some get released during the day time. That explains why some activities are better performed during day time and some are better done at night.

The choice to choose is a great human power, and we must use it to do right at the right time! We have been blessed with the power to choose to eat when we want, drink when we feel thirsty, exercise or not exercise, sleep or keep waking and hundreds of other choices that on each single day decide our health fate. However, ironically our power of choice does not apply to our internal body functioning. We cannot direct our blood sugar metabolism to hold until we feed ourselves! Neither can we choose to stop our hormones from getting disturbed due to some trigger that is based on our choice of activity, food or time! We cannot even direct our cells not to accumulate extra hydrogenated or trans-fat when we choose to eat a pizza or a burger! We must utilize this power of choice wisely to align our activities with nature. Doing activities as opposed to the internal clock can have a disastrous impact on body and mind health.

Connect and catch-up with the rhythms of nature for a drastic change towards better health!

CHAPTER 3 - EATING, DRINKING AND BREATHING TOXICITY

'What we choose to eat, drink & breathe, either nourishes us or makes us diseased; There is nothing in-between!'

Scenario

Alisha, 28, is a corporate professional working in a cosmopolitan city. Her work profile is hectic. She is required to meet the company clients often due to which she ends up eating out quite often. Eating at home is about quick readymade stuff such as brown bread, corn flakes, garlic bread or some other fast food. Apparently, she keeps a lot of ready-made and junk food at home as a quick munch. In her office, home or at client meeting venue, she spends her entire day mostly in an enclosed air conditioned environment. She is a very active professional and likes to invest in her interests and self-care after work. Swimming or gymming keep her busy in the evenings. Alisha is a luxury lover, and she quite often indulges in branded wardrobes, shoes, perfumes, cosmetics and other self-care range including fragrant bathing products, moisturizers, lip balms, lotions, body butter, etc. She has recently moved into her new apartment which has been recently painted before her shifting. Alisha is very particular about home cleanliness and ensures she uses the best home cleaning products such as bleaches, toilet cleaners, and other home cleaning products. Her new home is situated in a developing area where mosquito menace is a huge problem. She has to plug-in a mosquito repellent for a peaceful sleep & sometimes through the day to keep mosquitoes away. Over weekends, Alisha goes for outdoor fitness training in a nearby lush green park which is enclosed in a traffic-heavy area.

However, the park where she goes for a jog is lush green in the midst of dusty developmental area. Health-wise Alisha is doing fine except a feeling of unclear bowels. She feels her bowels do not get clear properly. She also sometimes experiences indigestion, which she thinks is due to her eating out during client visits. On enquiring, Alisha's take on the probability of her being toxic, she justifies that most of the day she stays indoors in the air conditioned environment, and so there is not much scope for accumulating toxicity. Regarding food, she mentions that she does not suffer from any health issue and exercises regularly, so hopefully, her system is working fine. She believes that she is already taking right measures for her health and well-being.

Food For Thought:

Did you find anything toxic about Alisha's diet and lifestyle? Where all do you think she is absorbing the toxicity from?

Case Analysis:

Alisha lives in a city where due to development and pollution, one cannot escape toxins. Now, if you ask me where all Alisha is accumulating toxins from, my simple answer would be, from everywhere!

Alisha is accumulating toxins due to:

- ❑ Indigestion and unclear bowel activity.
- ❑ Radiation as her profile demands her to use laptop & cellphone quite frequently.
- ❑ Inhalation of toxic gasses and metal particles from her indoor air conditioned environment that releases toxic particles.

- ❑ Preservatives, chemicals, and other additives through food sources.
- ❑ Colas and ready-made beverages.
- ❑ Room fresheners, mosquito repellants, and other chemical-laden products.
- ❑ Swimming in the chlorinated water.
- ❑ Self-care products, cosmetics & perfumes.

Our Beliefs:

A few years back, a very dear friend called up to inform that a prestigious beauty product company is offering some tempting offer on its newly launched flagship 'nutrition for skin' product. She was super excited with the thought of getting a better skin through this therapy and was informing all friends about this deal. Though it was a brilliant deal, do you think I should have gone ahead with it? Well, I did not!

Let's dig deeper and look at few examples to understand what makes us buy the toxic deals!

What We Are Made to Believe	What Perceptions We Form
A beautiful woman in a beauty product advertisement appears to promote the product by relating it to her incredible skin transformation.	We perceive that changing skin tone, texture, aging and becoming radiant is a one-product magic.

Reality: Hope and a beautiful dreams are sold in such commercials! However, in the whole drama, there had been no mention of toxic elements that the product carried. Few elements that it contained were:

- ❑ Dimethicone – Suspected cause of tumors and mutations in clinical experiments.

- ❑ Disodium EDTA – Suspected to draw chemicals into the bloodstream.
- ❑ Petrolatum – Contains two well-known cancer-causing agents Benzo-A-Pyrene and Benzo-B-Fluoranthene.
- ❑ Methylisothiazolinone - Suspected neurotoxin and known human immune system toxicant.

What We Are Made to Believe	What Perceptions We Form
Celebrity endorsement for diet cola or a vitamin drink is surely the solution to our weight issues and vitamin deficiencies.	We perceive that the solution to weight issues is a diet cola & for nutritional deficiencies, the vitamin drinks suffice. Since celebrities endorse such items, there is a level of trust and a sense of achievement associated with our beliefs.

Reality: Carbonated sodas, colas, and other such beverages contain chemical sweeteners & loads of toxicity. Most of them block calcium absorption.

What We Are Made to Believe	What Perceptions We Form
Ready-made fruit juice is shown to be a perfect solution for our nutritional needs. It saves time, it is convenient, it is readily available, and most importantly it is a healthy option as compared to other beverages.	We believe juice is juice, & how does it matter whether or not it is real. It contains vitamins and other healthy elements.

Reality: Ever thought what happens to the stalest fruits that no one buys!!! Yes, you indirectly buy it as juice. The juice processing goes through genetic engineering to become a tasty product. However, it is living natural enzymes are destroyed by the time it reaches the commercial market for selling. The natural life-force of fruit is lost. Filtration process and sugar addition are mentioned as a safe sweetener on the juice label. Finally, a stale natural fruit gets converted into dead, sugar-laden, human-made processed juice, to represent the goodness of real fruit. The truth is still hidden that it is tainted with toxins!

What We Are Made to Believe	What Perceptions We Form
Luxury cosmetic brands compete to find space in people's lives. Top-class cosmetics get endorsements by top celebrities with revolutionary promises in skin care. And, believe it or not, at least half of the women force goes ahead & use all cosmetics.	We actually think that beauty is sold on retail shelves & must be acquired by spending on chemical-laden products.

Reality: Toxins enter our body through our skin as well. Just imagine how does sweat come out? So, if sweat which is the internal toxin comes out through the skin, why can't external toxins get in! Our body absorbs whatever we feed it, be it an esteemed beauty product or an oil massage, all goes in and mixes in our bloodstream within a few minutes of application. Often we are informed by the marketers that external products contain chemicals and must be used for external use only. But no one tells us that what we apply on our skin gets in too including chlorinated water, toxic air, perfumes, creams, lotions or any other product.

Facts:

Research points to some worrisome 'Toxic Facts':

- ❑ A newborn baby's body contains 300 different chemicals on an average immediately after birth!
- ❑ An American 16-year-old teenager girl's body is exposed to 167 different chemicals in a day just through the use of self-care products.

- ❑ Most of the chemicals used in self-care products are hormone disturbing, which maybe one of the primary cause of early onset of puberty in pre-teenager girls.
- ❑ There is a range of over 15,000 toxic chemicals that are allowed to be added to foods without being listed on the label.
- ❑ Added ingredients in foods have been shown to cause depression, and many of them are addictive in nature.
- ❑ Added sugars make a person get fatter even if they don't eat much. The commercial food strategy goes like this; you eat addictive foods, you get fatter, the fatter you get, the more you crave that food, and that's how you create cravings for such foods.
- ❑ Five most common ingredients in sunscreens are carcinogenic, a Swiss study concluded. We are not sure if the sun causes skin cancer, but sunscreen products have surely been tested to be carcinogenic!
- ❑ Even swimming is toxic! Research suggests that our skin absorbs chlorine from swimming water and increases the risk of developing allergies or asthma, especially in children. In adults chlorine absorbed from swimming water increases the risk of for coronary heart disease.
- ❑ You are not toxin-free under the shower either! Under the shower, you not only absorb all toxins through the skin, but you also inhale volatile and dangerous gases created by the steam.
- ❑ And I bet you do not know this! Heavy metals such as mercury and leads get absorbed from water, tooth fillings, cosmetics & processed foods.

Though the presence of toxins in the sources mentioned above is a much-dreaded reality, our biggest source of toxins still remains our food. The chemicals, preservatives and all other additives being added to our foods are unnatural, toxic chemicals. They breakdown the defense mechanisms of our body. They suppress our immune system making it more susceptible to diseases. They make us age quicker. They transform the internal state of our body from alkaline to acidic, which means we become more prone to cancer, heart disease, diabetes, allergies, etc. They fill our body with toxins & spoil our skin. They start chemical fluctuations within our body & impact our emotional states leading to anger and irritability. In short, toxic body state keeps us alive but takes away our sense of liveliness! Toxins are everywhere, and the bigger truth is that all our senses absorb toxins. Mouth absorbs toxins through foods. Nose absorbs toxins in the form of fragrances, polluted air, metal particles, dust and any chemical-laden fragrances. Ears absorb toxins in the form of noise, abusive language, disturbing, unnatural & loud frequencies & vibrations. Eyes absorb toxins in the form of aggressive, fearful, vulgar visuals. Skin absorbs toxins in the form of cosmetics, topical creams and self-care ranges. Mind accumulates and processes the absorbed toxins from all senses. It all culminates into a consolidated toxicity working against you both at physical and emotional level. All these toxins in the material form or otherwise have an enormous impact on our total health and well-being.

Holistic Perspective:

Ancient healing sciences including TCM & Ayurveda focus on the fact that removing toxic elements from our body and replacing them with healthy, nourishing elements must be our way of life. The idea of detoxification in these ancient healing practices is about incorporating various detox methods in daily routine. Rather, these sciences focus on adopting a life approach that is detoxifying on a regular basis. Cleansing or detoxifying oneself helps rebalance the body through alkalizing foods & other holistic practices. Any safe detox program needs to be done for several weeks and should include specific therapeutic and supportive supplements to ensure proper removal of toxins through the two stages of the process.

The human body is designed in a manner that it is capable of keeping itself clean from inside through a set of internal processes. Our body design consists of a nose that is supposed to breathe out toxins in the volatile form i. e. carbon-di-oxide. We have been blessed with skin to sweat out toxins in liquid form. Our primary elimination system – kidneys and bowels must be kept in good working condition so as to ensure the removal of solid and liquid wastes from the body. Regular detoxification must be approached in a systematic way that includes:

- ❑ Stopping the source of toxins & minimizing the exposure to toxic environments.
- ❑ Adopting detox approaches break the deeply set-in toxins and pushing them out of the system.
- ❑ Adopting a routine that supports regular detox on a daily basis. This includes ensuring proper bowel action, sweating, and correct breathing pattern.

Ideally, the internal cleansing is the first step towards healing. It helps you unclog your arteries, melt the fat hanging around your intestines, repair body organs and revert disease symptoms. Detoxification is often promoted as a physical process. However, it is equally important to detox your mind of fear, anxieties, aggression, anger and other emotional issues. Emotional baggage is unseen non-physical garbage that must be vented out for a holistically healthy and well you. Emotional detox includes approaches and activities that help create a positive ideal environment for our senses. You must learn how to vent out emotions at the right time, channelizing your aggression and anger in a positive direction, pursuing some passion or activity that keeps you in astable state of emotional health.

Take Away Thought:

So, again a million dollar question.

How are we supposed to live in such a toxic environment? Is there a way to avoid toxicity in modern times, when it comes from everywhere?

It is a very logical thought, and frankly, the answer to this is not very straight. We live in a world where toxicity is at its peak. We all are at equal risk. However, what makes a healthier person differ from a sick one is how clean, clear & optimally working your body is from within. Regular daily detox measures can only help us achieve and maintain a healthy body and mind. Most people that I counsel do not understand or comprehend the amount of toxicity that they eat, drink, breathe and absorb each single day. Our health awareness is just limited to foods, exercise, drugs, and medications. The number of toxins that we consume each day & the destructive ability of these toxins is quite underestimated. Rather, it is never talked about. We are just made to see & believe the rosy picture about our foods & other products. I have covered the approach to daily detoxification in detail in the sections below.

CHAPTER 4 - DISTURBED SLEEPING CYCLE AND NO REST

'Nidra, an ancient term for sleep in Ayurveda, is nature's own way of helping us self-restore & self-heal. Disrespecting or delaying this essential activity of life is bound to manifest into a body or mind issue!'

Scenario

Sachi, 38, regularly works at night till 12 P. M. or 1 P. M. Some days her work demands her to work late nights, while other days she keeps waking by chance. She finds difficult to fall asleep at night and the specialists have termed her condition as chronic insomnia. Sachi realizes that her insufficient sleep is adversely affecting her daytime activities. She feels tired, fatigued and irritated through the day. She is suffering from insufficient sleep for a few years now. She even tried medication to cure insomnia but experienced severe side effects of medication that she mentions were even worse than insomnia. She finally discontinued the medication. For quite some time now she is practicing meditation and yoga, which did help her condition slightly. She goes gymming after work to get physically exhausted in a hope to sleep well at night. Her daily consumption of coffee is nearly 4-5 cups that keep her awake and active at work. Sachi does not have any fixed sleeping routine. She tries to catch-up with sleep when possible. Due to her disturbed sleeping routine, she ends up sleeping till very late in the morning. She ensures to have 6-8 hours of sleep a day in the daytime, if not at night. Sachi's social life is disturbed, her state of health is disturbed, and despite being a promising young woman, she is not able to perform to her best potential in personal as well as professional life. Not to forget, Sachi is diabetic and turned obese recently. She recalls that specifically after the onset of her sleep trouble, she has been gaining pounds regularly year after year.

Food For Thought:

Do you think Sachi's body is in a state of mess due to her sleep trouble? Do you think there could be a direct correlation between lack of sleep and Sachi's physical and emotional state of health? Do you think that any person compromising on sleep may also go through similar symptoms like Sachis' ? Do you tend to stay up till late at night? Do you think there is any difference between sleep at night and sleep during morning hours or daytime?

Case Analysis:

To summarize in a single sentence, Sachi's life & her entire biological functioning is in a confused and messed up state! The chemicals in her body are creating havoc, ranging from disturbed moods to probably her diabetes! Yes, studies suggest a direct correlation between sleep disorders and sluggish metabolism. Diabetes is a metabolic disorder! Her obese condition may be adirect consequence of her insufficient sleep, as the hormones regulating satiety and hunger get severely impacted by sleep disorders. This leads to overeating, weight issues & obesity. Sachi's irritated moods may be less to do with her daily frustrations of life and more to do with her sleep troubles. Further, caffeine is confusing Sachi's body by temporarily stimulating her nervous system and keeping her active for a while through the day. Sachi manages to complete 6-8 hours of sleep daily thinking that ultimately her daily sleep quota is being met. However, facts are very different from what Sachi presumes.

Our Beliefs:

In the midst of 24/7 wakeful environment, we find some reason or the other to compromise on our sleep. During peak sleeping hours we often end up catching on some work, fun or excitement. And then we tend to catch up on those 6-8 hours of sleep later in the morning or sometime during the daytime. Rest and relaxation have become our last priority, even if we feel miserable, tired, overwhelmed, stressed and sick. And we believe, as long as that cup of coffee or a sugary treat can keep us active, awake, focused & alert throughout the day, sleep can be taken for granted.

Sachi's problem is her insomnia due to which she cannot sleep easily. However, for those of us who do not suffer from insomnia, suffer from a modern epidemic called 'Sleep Procrastination' ? It is a new epidemic defined as an intentional failure to go off to sleep at the intended time, while no external circumstances prevent a person from doing so. Just imagine how many people you know who procrastinate sleep with no important reasons to be up & wakeful? I know many! And such people either rely upon external stimulants such as coffee, sugar, etc. to be active through the day because the impact of lack of sleep shows in the daytime activities.

We believe that we must complete at least 6-8 sleep hours daily. That's it! In the 24 hour day and night cycle, most of us manage to achieve those many sleep hours by either sleeping till late mornings or by catching up on sleep during the daytime. Further, the only consequence that we know of insufficient sleep is a little fatigue & under-eye bags & dark circles. We further think that these side effects arising due to lack of sleep can be well managed with a few cups of coffee in the daytime or by applying any under-eye cream respectively.

Let's explore what happens when we self-create our sleep timings.

Facts:

It is 10 p.m., and you are done with your daily chores. Your body is communicating signals of tiredness & you do not have any justified reason to be awake. Still, you do not want to sleep. You are ok watching anything on TV or being up aimlessly but will not go off to sleep unless the clock shows 12 a. m. This is a reality of our lives today. And if this sounds like your story, you qualify being a 'Sleep Procrastinator'. You believe there is more to the day and nowhere you think that you are compromising on sleep because you think you will cover up the sleep debt the next morning or over the weekend.

According to a study performed on people receiving flu shots who were sleep deprived the next night, the results indicated that they did not create the antibodies required to protect them against the flu. Dr. Jordan Stern, founder and director of the BlueSleep Centre in New York City, states, 'As soon as I see the first signs of an upper respiratory infection, I try to sleep for 10 hours'. He further states, 'If you're chronically sleep deprived, you're more likely to develop recurring infections. '

Shanaya, 45, a real-time bed procrastinator after 20+ years of bedtime resisting and chronic sleep-deprivation defines her state of health as exhausted, fatigued, cranky, depressed, anxiety-prone, constipated, troubled skin, mood swings & cloudy thinking. For all her symptoms Shanaya ended up trying all except focussing on her sleep.

Few 'Sleep-Disturbing' Facts!

- ❑ Statistics reported by the Centre for Disease Control and Prevention (CDC) reveal that nearly one-quarter American adults suffer from some kind of sleep disorder. One-third of adults do not sleep well, and only one-third of high-school students get a good night's rest.
- ❑ Research suggests that only 5-6 hours of sleep may increase the risk of high blood pressure by 350% to 500%.
- ❑ Sleep disorder or insufficient sleep can be an active contributor to the conditions like diabetes, cardiovascular diseases, obesity, depression, memory problems, high blood pressure, irritability, irregular hormone production, weight gain, decreased concentration and weakened immune system.
- ❑ Research suggests that delaying going to bed may be a direct indicator of an individual's incapability to resist temptations and adhering to their intentions in all walks of life.

- ❑ About 90% of sleep apnea sufferers go undiagnosed. Sleep apnea is a condition where an individual stops breathing at night for few seconds. Snoring is an indicator that one might be suffering from this condition.
- ❑ Sleep has high restorative powers and repairs all damaged body cells during deep sleep.
- ❑ Untreated and ignored sleep disorders have an adverse effect on moods and behaviors of an individual. It may further lead to strained work and family relationships and hampered productivity and physical health.
- ❑ Growth and development in children gets hampered due to poor sleeping habits.
- ❑ According to the Harvard Medical School's Division of Sleep Medicine, sleeping less than 6 hours at night may lead to a higher body mass index (BMI) leading to obesity, and increased mortality risk by roughly 15%.
- ❑ The most dominating factors that cause distractions to sleep are technology, electrical gadgets, work commitments and 24/7 entertainment industry.
- ❑ Insufficient sleep and rest have recently been labeled as a 'public health epidemic' because statistics report high numbers of traffic accidents, occupational misdemeanors and inability to perform daily tasks due to sleep deficiency.

What Goes on Inside Our Body When We Sleep?

Repairing & Detoxification: Sleep repairs & detoxifies our body each night. It heals the body after whole days' hard work performing digestion and other biological activities. Sleep helps generate new cells, heal injuries, perform toxin cleansing activity, rejuvenate muscles, and strengthen vital body organs & brain. Research suggests that the people who do not sleep well, their rejuvenation, restoration & detoxification process is not as efficient & it shows in people's health issues & moods and behaviors the next morning.

Strengthening of Immune System: Sleep helps produce antibodies to fight against infections. Sleep is the single-most influential factor that can give our immunity the much-required boost.

Rejuvenation of Brain & Organizing of Thoughts: Sleep gives our brain a break and helps it organize thoughts. Whenever we go off to sleep with a problem in mind, we wake up with a direction, feeling better and grounded. An old age saying puts across this capability of sleep just perfectly, 'Sleep over your problems, and you' ll be better when you wake up' ! Sleep helps solidify memories & forget useless information. Sleep specialist Christopher Colwell at UCLA School of Medicine states, 'We take in all information all day long, and most of it is luckily forgotten, if you remembered everything, it would fill up your brain, so a sorting process takes place during sleep. '

Balancing Hormones: Sleep balances ovulation, appetite and metabolism hormones. Research suggests women who do not sleep well are prone to hormonal problems. A woman requires an average of 8-10 hours of sleep to maintain hormonal balance which further regulates menstrual cycle and ovulation.

Regulation of Breathing Patterns: Sleep positively impacts our breathing pattern making it deeper, relaxed, diaphragmic and regular. During the day we unknowingly breathe irregularly owing to different emotions, postures, and other factors. Relaxed breathing during sleep is one of the important factors that help us wake-up calm and energized. People suffering from sleep apnea generally do not wake-up fresh even after 8 hours of sleep due to their irregular breathing pattern at night.

Focus on Night-Time Physiological Activities: Sleep slows down many physiological activities to carry out rejuvenation & detoxification activities efficiently. We produce less urine at night which is an indicator of slowed kidney function at night. This also means kidneys get much-required rest after a whole day of liquid waste processing. Growth hormones get active when we sleep.

This is the reason that a newborn baby sleeps for almost the whole day and seems to be growing quickly.

Regulation of Cardiovascular Activity: Sleeping is the best way to slow down & put the cardiovascular activity at rest.

Holistic Perspective:

According to Ayurveda, 'Nidra' is an important supporting pillar of life. However, Ayurveda suggests that a good restful & fulfilling sleep must be taken at the right time for a sufficient number of hours. Quality sleep is an excellent rejuvenator for both the body and the mind. It helps us work to the best of our potential through the day. Even the most powerful medicine fails in its effects if our sleep foundation is weak. Ayurveda describes the importance of sound sleep by associating sleep with the following terms: 'Sukha' or pleasure, 'Pushti' or nourishment and growth, 'Bala' or strength and immunity, 'Vrishataa or potency and sexual vigor, 'Gnaanam' or knowledge and intellect, 'Jeevitam' or good lifespan and longevity of life. The lack of sleep at the right time is associated with the following terms: 'Dukha' or grief, 'Karshyam' or consumption or emaciation, 'Abalam' or loss of strength and immunity, 'Kleebataa' or impotence and sterility, 'Agnaanam' or ignorance and idiocy and 'Ajeevitham' or death.

Ayurveda recommends sleeping latest by 10:00 p. m. Nature works in such a fashion that by this time the environment naturally gets slow, stable and dull. As nature and our body and mind are tightly integrated, this dull impact is not just limited to the environment but affects our body and mind also. The dullness at this time makes it the most favorable time for sleep. Sleeping after 11 p. m. makes us enter naturally hot, sharp, light and intense environment and has the same impact on our body and mind. This explains why most people find it difficult to fall asleep easily at midnight. Rather, by midnight we tend to feel energetic, ready and motivated to do anything but sleep.

Take Away Thought:

When we are sleep deficit, under eye bags and the tired look is what shows on the outside. Sadly, our understanding is just limited to what shows on the outside. However, the lack of sleep is much more and intense than what shows on the outside.

Just think:

- ❑ Does our body delay digestion and retain food if it knows that next day we may not have time for lunch?
- ❑ Does our body ever give up its biological functioning such as making urine or digesting food?
- ❑ Do we have any control on the internal functioning of our body such as eliminating body wastes?
- ❑ Is there any system fitted inside the body that can absorb the impact of wrong food intakes, while not causing any harm to us?

The answer to all these is NO!

There are some important biological activities that our body performs during night time only in the state of rest. Failing to catch-up on sleep will lead to imbalances in the body, surely. Research suggests that there is 3 times more risk of a heart attack in individuals who slept less than 5 hours a night.

Health always seems to be our focus area in life. However, we rarely think of working on the fundamental pillars of health. When it comes to health and well-being, our total focus is diet and exercise, while sleep is the most under-estimated health requirement of our times. We do not want to go to bed in time & still want to feel refreshed and rejuvenated all the time!

CHAPTER 5 - ACIDIC BODY STATE

'Acidity is a much bigger demon than a feeling of pain in the abdomen. It is not just limited to the chest pain, indigestion, bloating or acidic taste in the mouth. It is the cause of change in our entire body chemistry. It is a poison that we produce, that eats up our body from within. It is a demon that changes form to become osteoporosis, arthritis, heart disease or even cancer. It is highly dangerous, as it easily escapes eyes! Worst still, it keeps playing foul under the wraps in the shadow of lifestyle disorders!'

Scenario

Sophie, 58, is a non-vegetarian food lover and a great cook. She suffers from osteoporosis which is a medical condition associated with weakening of bones. She is a fun loving lady and has a wide circle of friends. However, pain in her knee joints does not let her live a healthy life. She has been diagnosed with an inflammatory condition and is on medication. Her left knee is on the verge of complete deterioration, and she has been prescribed a knee surgery by her doctor. She is trying her best to regain her bone density by consuming milk 3 times a day along with calcium supplements. She has also been on steroids for her condition for quite some time now. She complains of heartburn, indigestion, acidity and antacids are her best buddies. She also keeps trying any home remedy that she comes across. However, her condition has worsened over the years. Nothing seems to have improved despite all her efforts.

Food For Thought:

What might be the cause of Sophie's osteoporosis? Do you think acidity is anything to do with her condition? Do you think her non-vegetarian food style may have a role to play in her health condition? Do you think milk consumption and calcium supplements may be doing her any good?

Case Analysis:

Sophie suffers from an inflammatory condition, and her non-vegetarian dietary habits have a strong role to play. Non-vegetarian foods are concentrated forms of nutrition. Such foods give our body a hard time. Their digestion & elimination from our system is tough for our body. Sophie is on medication which is helping her suppress the osteoporosis symptoms. With medication, she manages to live her everyday life with ease, but looked upon from a broader perspective, her health issue never took a U-turn. Rather, it is just growing. The toxicity of drugs is further adding toxicity to her inflammatory condition. The world's favorite remedy to deal with calcium deficiency – drinking milk and calcium supplements, is her favorite remedy too. Her stomach and digestive issues are continuously giving her clues that she is constantly feeding herself acidity. Sophie seems to be making all efforts to get better, except listening to the subtle signs and feelings that her body is communicating!

To conclude, Sophie is successful in delaying her deterioration through medication, milk, calcium, home remedies and certain other efforts. However, she is continuously feeding her ailment with the same old lifestyle & dietary patterns. Further, her total focus is external treatments. She is doing no effort to heal herself internally.

Our Beliefs:

When we get detected with cancer, arthritis, heart disease or any other inflammatory condition, our first reaction is treatment and medication. Rather, this is what we know that we need to do when any lifestyle disaster strikes. For most of us, the course of action goes like this:

Step 1: Visiting a doctor.

Step 2: Geting diagnosed and geting all tests done.

Step 3: Discussing report with the doctor.

Step 4: Obviously, begin medication the same day!

Step 5: And, we seem sorted with our health issue!

For few aware people, few other steps follow. This sequence of additional steps may either be based on personal choices or what out 'neighbors and relatives' suggest, such as:

Step 6: Beginning home remedies, anything and everything that one comes across.

Step 7: Beginning yoga or any other exercising routine.

Step 8: Meeting a nutritionist and beginning a diet plan.

Step 9: Beginning walking while chatting!

Step 10: Beginning supplements or increasing the consumption of special foods as highlighted in newspapers or by the media, like milk & calcium like in the case of Sophie!

Step 11: Venting out our sufferings by talking to all near and dear ones.

And this action marks the end of all efforts that we can do for ourselves!

Now, read carefully what we never do – the actual steps to inner healing:

- ❑ Self-reflecting, rewinding our life and finding clues that made us sick over time.
- ❑ Consuming real life-force containing foods.
- ❑ Giving up similar lifestyles, routines, and habits that made us sick.
- ❑ Detoxifying our body & mind through right techniques regularly.
- ❑ Breathing fully through our diaphragm.

- ❑ Following our heart & intuition.

Facts:

Milk-related facts:

- ❑ Milk is an acidifying animal protein.
- ❑ Scientific studies show that milk increases the risk of fracture.
- ❑ Childhood consumption of dairy products has been reported to be associated with an increased risk of hip fracture in old age.
- ❑ The connection between dairy consumption, calcium supplementation & bone health has been reported to be almost non-existent in studies.

Acidity & the Human Body

Acidity is not just what you feel in terms of gastric & digestive issues. It is true that at the physical level we feel acidity symptoms in the form of these problems, but the term 'Acidity' is the foundational cause behind all our health problems. Acid inside the body could be a consequence of shallow breathing pattern or could exist due to too much intake of acidic foods. It could accompany stress, or can just arise due to consumption of chemical laden foods, cosmetics & other products. Irrespective of the form in which acid enters your body, it can ruin your body fully if you keep taking in acid through various sources. Too much acid enters the fluids running in your body & changes their chemical composition. Once acidic, our body fluids impact cell functioning and our body cannot function optimally. The impact could be:

Gastric & Digestive Issues: The only feeling that we relate to when we talk of acidity.

Inflammatory Conditions: For example arthritis, cancer & heart disease.

Weakening Mineral Reserves of the Body: Osteoporosis and lesser bone mass is the consequence in this case.

Weakened Immunity: Seasonal allergies, flu, cold, cough, respiratory issues & headaches are the prominent symptoms in this case

Other manifestations of high acidic state includes fungal infections, foul breath (where mouthwash is not the solution!), foul body odor (where deodorants are not the solution!), unexplained aches pains & headaches (where prescription drugs are not the solution!).

Scale to Measure Acid-Alkaline State Within the Body – The pH Level

The pH level is the numeric measurement to verify whether our body chemistry is acidic or alkaline. The count of 7. 4 indicates the ideal pH level for the optimal internal working environment of our body. Even the slight fluctuations in this pH number mean high acidity which may also indicate a state of cancer.

If you are high on acidity, the symptoms show up as frequent cold, flu, low immunity, fatigue, tiredness, allergies, skin rashes, etc. These minor negligible symptoms keep breeding inside & overtime may manifest into diabetes, arthritis, heart diseases, cancer, inflammatory conditions, etc. At this stage, if you begin treatments and precautions, but do not keep a tight check on what you eat, your health issues will keep progressing subtly even after medications. This is because you still hold on to your old ways of eating and living that had made you sick! And it becomes a vicious circle of diseases one after the other!

Diet & exerciseis the best way to keep our body alkaline. Unfortunately, in our fast-paced lifestyles, we have no bandwidth for mindful healthy eating. We do follow diets which are nutritious, yet our diets are not healing. The majority of our foods today are either acidic or get converted into acid as soon as they are ingested.

Holistic Perspective:

The holistic approach to dealing with body acid must be practiced at the following levels:

- Consuming a variety of natural foods.
- Eating in moderation.
- Mineralizing ourselves through fruits & vegetables.
- Keeping our body functioning well through exercise.

Take Away Thought:

With the progression of modern food industry, the health hazards of modernistic and convenience foods are quite visible. Disturbed behaviors, irritability, bloated tummies, seasonal allergies, flu, colds, hyper activeness, sore throats, nutritional deficiencies, crankiness, lifestyle disorders and sudden mood swings are what defines a modern human being. However, we often end up associating such symptoms with weather changes, environmental changes or with any other convincing reasons. Despite consuming the best modernistic foods, our sufferings are at an all-time high! In the case of any disease, the way to real healing begins with alkalizing oneself and working towards maintaining ideal pH balance.

CHAPTER 6 - ATTITUDE OF ACCEPTANCE TOWARDS ROUTINE HEALTH ISSUES

'Accepting a disease may help us embrace treatments positively. However, our acceptance without self-realization of disease causing factors, deviates us from thinking what caused the disease! The only route to healing begins by self-reflecting the causes that left us in a diseased state, and not by popping pills for convenience!'

Scenario

Ashiya, 35, is an IT professional who frequently suffers from sinus and allergic issues, the only hindrances in her career! Three times in a week she has a running nose, and her desk is full of tissue boxes. Often she returns back from work tired and exhausted. She complains of frequent headaches, and for quick relief, she consumes strong coffee, tea and medication in the worst case. She does not mind taking anti-allergic medication if need be. She does get better for a day after taking medication, only to return back with worsening symptoms when next episode happens. When asked what is she doing to get rid of her problem, she replies that she suffers from allergies and cannot do anything about it. She considers her minor but routine health issue as a natural state of health. She simply states that a lot of people suffer from the similar condition and in current times this is normal. Now, since the majority of people tend to suffer from minor health issues & since it has become a community phenomenon, Ashiya has developed an acceptance attitude towards her consistent health concerns.

Food For Thought:

Do you think Ashiya's acceptance towards her minor health issues is right? Do you also think the same about your minor health concerns? Do you believe it to be normal to accept your condition and continue life with symptomatic relief medications?

Case Analysis:

If you carry the same attitude like Ashiya's, I insist think again! Even though medication helps Ashiya deal with her symptoms and provides her quick relief, internally her body is in a state of mess. Her body is in a confused state as she is continuously suppressing the signals that her body is conveying. On the outside, Ashiya does create an illusion of healing, yet internally everything is the same, rather deteriorating. Every time her body raises signals, she suppresses them with medications. Frequent headaches, bloating and sinus symptoms are the subtle signs that imbalances have occurred within the body. Further, medications are adding their own toxicity and side effects to her condition. Additionally, Ashiya's daily routine, diet, lifestyle, and habits are still the same. So, at the foundation level, she is still feeding her disease, though she is treating the symptoms externally with medications. The larger picture is that her body is getting weaker & it is not able to handle the normal pressures of daily life. With each new episode of health issues, her body's immune responses are getting weak. However, since Ashiya's everyday life is not hampered majorly, she continues to neglect her condition. Slowly such imbalances may manifest into something bigger and disastrous. It's a practical scenario happening to all of us slowly and unknowingly. At the core level health begins to get disturbed, deteriorated and we realize it when the disaster is done!

Our Beliefs:

How many people do you know who are perfectly healthy, who do not suffer from any allergies or seasonal issues, who are blessed with clear sinuses, who do not feel fatigued and tired, who have not fallen sick for years irrespective of external influences, who do not complain of bloating and stomach issues, who do not complain of unexplained aches and pains, who just do not suffer from anything including emotional lows and highs? I hardly know of anyone!

How many of these people that you just counted are conditioned to believe that minor health issues are ok and acceptable as per modern standards of living? I bet all of them carry the same attitude!

Our changing health perceptions towards health and well-being, the intervention of medical facilities and the medical convenience has transformed us to believe that minor health issues are a natural phenomenon of our modernistic lifestyle.

Believe me, it is not!

Facts:

Medications for routine ailments are very effective in providing symptomatic relief. However, on the outside medications help you feel better, while on the inside they just quick fix your ailments. Further, such drugs add toxicity that shows up as side-effects in many cases. For example, a headache medication provides you immediate relief, but in some cases, it causes stomach issues & nausea. Failure to take the ownership of our own health has led to a rapidly growing culture of aliment acceptance. The consumption of quick-relief drugs is continuously on a rise. We seldom realize that the quick symptom relief is followed by a bigger demon – the medication side-effects, that may range from upset stomach, dry mouth, nausea, drowsiness, noticeable mood swings, changed sleep patterns, gastric and digestion issues, increased irritability and more.

Holistic Perspective:

Accepting our health issues while not taking action and responsibility for our health is making us more diseased. Minor health concerns are nothing but a communication channel that indicate the internal state of health. If we keep accepting them as the side-effects of living in modern society, we will keep getting diseased. Listening to the subtle body signs and acting upon them in a natural way can go a long way in helping us maintain our health.

In recent years there has been a drastic shift in the way medical science looks at physical diseases. During my doctorate convocation, I got a chance to attend a conference on alternative healing practices. To my surprise, nearly 80% of medical specialists who read their research papers in the conference had a focus on mind and meditative techniques. 'Body, ' 'Mind' and 'Soul' represents the oneness of our existence. With each positive or negative thought or experience, our body triggers a series of chemical reactions that may support or go against our healing process respectively. When we begin accepting our health issues, and 100% rely upon medical treatments, healing never occurs.

Take Away Thought:

Do you know of anyone suffering from cancer, heart disease or any other lifestyle disorder? Did you ever try to realize that all these conditions did not develop in a day? If you analyze closely, you will realize that anyone suffering from chronic ailments, did experience or complain of minor health issues at some point during their journey towards a bigger disease. The trend clearly indicates that as we have begun to accept minor health concerns, the bigger devils start creating a space for themselves automatically.

Health and wellness seem to be deteriorating continuously for each one of us including our children. Acceptance of our conditions in the name of fate and current lifestyle standards will only take us a step closer towards health disasters. Healing does not begin with symptomatic treatments. It starts with the understanding of the root issues that caused us diseases. And these issues are as basic as what we eat daily, how we live daily, how much we understand your body, how we think and react to situations daily, what activities we perform daily, how much do we relax daily and how balanced life we lead daily.

CHAPTER 7 - IMPROPER ELIMINATION OF BODY WASTES

'What goes inside the body must come out in some form or the other. Holding on to anything at either physical or emotional level will create internal imbalances & this is the undeniable law of nature!'

Scenario

Kuhu, 36, has been suffering from Eczema for a decade. She has undergone numerous treatments and tried steroid-based medications for years. Despite of taking best skin treatments, her skin allergy has gotten worse over the years. Her skin problem has been so chronic that it has had a psychological impact on her life. She avoids wearing clothes of her choice as her skin gets inflamed easily. She avoids meeting people due to low self-esteem. Kuhu often feels fatigued, dizzy, nauseous and gastric. She is highly allergic to various triggers such as the sun that literally burns her skin. Even hot foods create rashes on her face & body. Due to excessive use of steroid-based topical medications, her skin has become dry and sensitive. Kuhu continuously suffers from constipation and has frequent skin breakouts, abdominal discomfort and bloating. She keeps practicing self-treatments and home remedies such as laxatives which are of no use. She has a weak immunity & she is bound to experience allergic reactions to weather changes. Sinus congestion is one common allergic reaction that she experiences frequently. She also feels swelling in joints, heaviness, and reduced appetite. Her skin is dull, lusterless, acne-prone & blemished. She complains of foul breath and smelly sweat. She wakes up tired even after a good night's sleep.

Food For Thought:

What is wrong with Kuhu? What could be the cause behind her health issues? Is Kuhu able to get rid of her body wastes sufficiently? Is there anything else apart from bowel cleansing that Kuhu must work on?

Case Analysis:

Kuhu's health state is a direct indicator of high body waste accumulated within her body. Eczema & sinus issues are direct indicators that Kuhu has a weakened immunity. Her steroid-based internal & topical treatments seem to be impacting her internally and causing her inflammation due to which her joint pains are emerging. Not sure if topical medicines helped Kuhu with her eczema, but it definitely has made her skin sensitive to the sun & other factors. The worst part is, Kuhu has spent money, time and effort to cure her skin but her problem is just growing over the years. It has not just impacted her physically but emotionally too. Kuhu has become prone to other allergies. Along with her skin condition, Kuhu also complains of various other health issues related to stomach, bowels, sinus, foul breath, and sweat, tired feelings, etc. If we consolidate Kuhus's symptoms, it is a clear indication that Kuhu's body wastes are not getting eliminated.

Our Belief:

When it comes to eliminating body wastes, our target area is just our bowels. The term 'Constipation' rules half our life and our total focus is to have a regular motion. About 99% people that I counsel have all their energies directed towards ensuring optimal bowel health.

An interesting elderly man that I know is quite aware of the importance of eliminating body wastes. He consumes fibrous foods, salads, laxatives and even medications to keep his bowel activity regular. His purpose of life after retirement is to have clear motion every day! He consumes enough water throughout the day & is very particular about his daily walks. However, even after all efforts to keep bowels clear, he suffers from heart disease, his weight is just increasing, he is bloated and gets tired and fatigued easily.

When we talk about body wastes our entire focus shifts to consuming adequate fibrous foods & liquids. We become serious about exercise, take laxatives and sometimes take medications too. However, in most of the cases, bowels still remain unclear!

Facts:

After digestion, elimination is the next biggest function of the human body. Our body makes all efforts to get rid of all wastes that it accumulates. There are 7 channels of elimination that purge waste and toxins from our body. On confronting toxins or foreign substance, one or more of these 7 channels get involved in cleaning the system. The key to excellent health is to keep these 7 channels in optimal working condition.

The primary elimination channels include:

Colon (Large Intestine): Colon is undoubtedly the most important elimination channel of the human body. It purges the solid wastes out of our body. However, it is the only elimination channel that is the most talked about in the health world. Rather, some people are only aware of this channel for exit body wastes. The fact it that our colon just eliminates nearly 28% of body wastes. Further, we are unaware that even if we have one elimination a day, it is quite probable that our colon still is unclear. We may still be holding toxic wastes that can eventually lead to a chronic condition. Symptoms such as fatigue, allergies, nausea, bloating, etc. can be a direct indication of high toxicity. Fibrous diet, hydration & consumption of whole & natural foods are the keys to keeping the colon working properly.

Kidneys: Kidneys are responsible for filtering liquid wastes by producing urine. Every one in 10 people are susceptible to developing kidney stones. Dehydration is one of the main causes that leads to inefficient kidney functioning. Proper hydration and an alkaline diet is the key to keeping kidneys working optimally.

Skin: Our skin is fully involved in the elimination process. It is an important elimination channel that releases toxins through sweat. Further, our skin has the capability to absorb whatever we apply on our skin. The best way to help our skin perform its elimination process properly is by getting rid of all chemicals, preservatives and natural fragrances from personal care products.

Lungs: One of the most underestimated elimination channel – the lungs, eliminate 70% of our body wastes in gaseous form through the breathing activity. Lung and breathing disorders are highly on a rise today due to our sedentary lifestyles. Additionally, we inhale a lot of carcinogenic elements in the form of smoke, polluted air, automobile and industrial exhaust, pesticides, chemicals, scents in personal care products and other artificial fragrances every day. People today mostly breathe toxicity and do not move their body. A sedentary lifestyle makes our lungs weak impacting our breathing capacity. This is one of the leading causes of lungs and breathing disorders today. The best way to keep lungs in best condition is to perform exercises that activate our lungs and breathing, by not smoking & deep breathing fresh air for at least 15 minutes a day.

Liver: Liver is a hidden elimination organ, yet, the most integral part of our body's detoxification system. The liver is responsible for cleaning and metabolizing everything from food, preservatives, chemicals, fats, sugar, residues and alcohol. In its healthy state, the liver performs more than 500 essential functions inside the body. Some essential liver functions include removing wastes from the blood, storing nutrient reserves, filtering toxins, converting ingredients into body-usable substances, metabolizing excess sugars & fats, building chemicals that our body needs to stay healthy, breaking down harmful substances like alcohol and other toxic chemicals, etc. To naturally detoxify the liver, we must eat plenty of antioxidant-rich foods & minimize the alcohol consumption.

Other two important elimination channels include:

Blood: Blood is considered to be the transporter that provides nutrients to all parts of our body. It also carries waste products to be transported to kidneys for filtration. The quality of blood is highly dependent upon the foods we eat. Blood detoxification can be achieved through a healthy diet, sweating, hydration and regular exercising routine.

Lymphatic System: The Lymphatic system is the drainage system that removes toxins, wastes and other unwanted materials from the body. The lymphatic system must regularly be activated as it is a major source to remove body toxicity. It plays a major role in fighting infections and absorbing excess fluids, fats, and toxic waste material from the body. Few factors that make lymphatic system sluggish are a lack of exercise, iodine deficiency, and digestive imbalances. A clogged or blocked lymphatic system may contribute to various health issues such as a heart disease, arthritis, cellulite, headaches, colds, sinus infections, fatigue, cholesterol, skin problems, digestive disorders, etc. The best way to keep the lymphatic system in perfect order includes avoiding processed foods, eating whole foods, body massage, exercise, and sauna.

What we often consider as minor health issues could be our body's signal that body wastes are accumulating and need cleansing. If you notice the signs and symptoms such as eczema, cysts, psoriasis, painful or swollen joints, unexplainable aches, lethargy, fatigue, heaviness, dull skin, reduced appetite, acne, lack luster, flatulence, bloated stomach, white coating on tongue, foul body smell and sweat, constipation, lack of mental clarity, sinus congestion and breathing difficulty, sticky smelly and bulky stools, it is quite possible that you have a lot of accumulated body waste. For relief in such cases, it is recommended to clear your system through right dietary approach and detox efforts.

Holistic Perspective:

Ayurveda describes body wastes as 'Ama –The creator of diseases in literal sense.' Ama accumulates as a result of impartial or improper digestion.

Ideally, the foods that we consume must be fully digested. Half of the digested food must get absorbed into the body as nutrients, and the rest of it must be expelled out of the body as waste product. Ama is a result of half-digested food that is not metabolized. This impartially digested food keeps circulating in the body as toxins. In case our body contains ama, it is only one-third of foods that get fully digested and absorbed as nutrients. The other third gets expelled as wastes, and the remaining one-third food gets stagnated in the stomach in a partially digested form. As our system does not recognize this half-digested state of food as either nutrient or a waste product, it is neither absorbed nor expelled out.

It is important to know that before we develop a disease, we go through a disease development life cycle. The first stage of disease life cycle is the accumulation and circulation of wastes or 'Ama' in our digestive system. Ama shows up as a white sticky substance that clogs our body channels and organs. As there exists no easy exit channel for Ama, it keeps getting accumulated in the digestive tract, bronchi, lungs, arteries, liver, and kidneys. Ama forms a white sticky lining on the intestinal wall and slowly spreads to other parts of the body. Bacteria and fungi thrive on Ama leading to body inflammation, weakening of digestive system, high cholesterol, cysts, tumors, diarrhea, asthma, joint pain, hair loss, weight problems and other issues. On waking up, ama can be seen on our tongue as white coating. On teeth, Ama accumulates as plaque.

The causes of ama could be:

- ❑ Weak digestion and lowered metabolism.
- ❑ Consumption of foods that cannot be digested easily such as processed, fried or hard to digest foods.

- ❑ Consumption of foods that are against our body type.
- ❑ Consumption of foods during the times of stress.
- ❑ Consumption of cold foods and drinks that weaken digestion.
- ❑ Overeating or eating frequently.
- ❑ Partially digested foods.

Take Away Thought:

Your recurrent health issues may have their roots in accumulated body wastes. Holistic healing practices consider ama as the beginning of a disease life-cycle.

In today's times, we live a sedentary lifestyle and follow unhealthy dietary practices. We do not realize that our choices and habits cause Ama to form, accumulate and circulate within our body. Though Ama is not a disease in itself, if left untreated, it may manifest into other serious illnesses.

Healing ourselves requires a close communion with our bodies. It is ironical that we know the functioning of our cars more than our own body functioning. The first step to healing in case of any health issue is by stopping the accumulation of wastes inside the body. Holistic cleansing practices are naturally crafted to work and detoxify all elimination channels. Few such holistic practices include dietary changes, herbal cleansing programs, colon hydrotherapy, exercising, nutrient supplementation, saunas & steam baths & body massage. Detox or waste elimination is not limited to bowels only. It requires a holistic approach to cleansing the entire body.

CHAPTER 8 - COMPROMISED PHYSICAL ACTIVITY

'Body movement is the second nature of human body after food, water, & air, & so exercising is not a choice but a necessity. Ancient exercising techniques describe body movements that aim culmination of body, mind & soul!'

Scenario

Tarush, 45, a large man with 5 feet 8 inches height & 98 kgs weight, has been explicitly told by the doctors that he must do some physical activity or else he may continue to add weight. Tarush has been gaining weight consistently over last 3 years. He mentions he is fond of eating & considers his eating habits as the prime cause of his obesity. Tarush suffers from high blood pressure, high cholesterol, and diabetes.

Food For Thought:

What are your notions about exercise? Do you think it is only the diet that makes one obese? Do you think that if Tarush begins exercising, he can recover his health? In what ways do you think that Tarush can be benefitted by exercising?

Case Analysis:

Tarushs' case is straightforward. His weight is already very high. Most importantly, Tarush is aware that his eating habits are making him obese. However, what he does not realize is that lack of proper body movement is adding on to his obesity. Looking at Tarush's medical history, it seems like a clear case of sufferings owing to wrong dietary habits and lack of exercise.

Our Beliefs:

Exercising for a majority of people is more about a set pattern and professional guidance. We do not understand exercising as a biological necessity. While exercising for some is a part of their daily routine, many of us get into an exercising routine only when a health disaster strikes & our doctors recommend it. Some people just keep thinking about the right time to begin exercising, while some are active fitness-freaks, so much so, that sometimes they end up injuring themselves.

Our perception of exercising is limited to what we have been told by our doctors or fitness experts. Our beliefs about the purpose of exercising just revolve around building body, maintaining fitness or disease management. Though all these goals are important, there is much more to exercising that just focusing on these mentioned goals. Building body should not be our ultimate goal, rather building both body and mind, and expanding our consciousness should be the exercising goal. When focusing on fitness, health must be the priority, as fitness does not necessarily mean health. Exercise for disease management is an essential part of healing and must be emphasized, similarly as medication is emphasized.

The world knows that physical inactivity increases the risk of many diseases. However, not many know that body movement in the right way is as essential as breathing, eating and drinking. It is necessary for the optimal physiological functioning of our body. Any disease that occurs is majorly because we fail to provide ourselves the ideal functioning environment, and exercising is an important element of this environment.

For ages, exercising has been encouraged by experts. The significant gap, however, has been that most of the times we are just advised to exercise, while not focussing on what happens inside when we begin to exercise. What we are generally not told about exercising is:

- ❑ Why exercising is such an important pillar of our health, as necessary as breathing, eating and drinking?

- ❑ How exercising supports and activates our internal body functioning?
- ❑ How it helps our organs perform optimally?
- ❑ How it enhances mental health, cognitive performance, coordination, memory and enables us in decision making?
- ❑ How it reduces insulin resistance and inflammation?
- ❑ How it stimulates the release of various hormones and helps balance them?
- ❑ How can it be one of the best remedies to ward off emotional issues due to changed neurotransmitter levels such as cortisol - the stress hormone?
- ❑ How it balances the pH levels in our body thus reducing body acid levels?
- ❑ How it helps muscular and skeletal system by enhancing more frequent muscle contraction, increasing muscle temperature and blood circulation?
- ❑ How can it increase the width and density of bones & reduce the incidences of bone-related injuries?
- ❑ How can it stabilize and improve the flexibility of joints by improving the strength of muscles, tendons, and ligaments?
- ❑ How it oxygenates the body which is crucial for internal body functioning?
- ❑ How does it help to increase the size and strength of our heart muscle?
- ❑ How it strengthens the diaphragm and intercostal muscles which are the two most important breathing related muscles?
- ❑ How it increases our vital life-force by forcing the removal of the volatile toxic waste of the body (carbon-di-oxide) through forcible exhalation after a deep breath?

Facts:

There are a host of exercise types that we are aware of including gymming, yoga, walking, jogging, aerobics, swimming, tai chi, qi gong, etc. However, the basic premise behind each of these exercises still remains the same. The purpose of every kind of activity boils down to one single fact - body movement!

Nature always intended humans to move their body as an essential part of being alive. However, due to the rise in modern conveniences, the body movement has hugely got impacted. We spend majority of our day sitting at our office, in front of the computer or watching TV. In the name of body movement, we complete the ritual by completing our walk or gym activity for an hour or so a day. However, many of us shy away from completing even this ritual. Research suggests that people procrastinate exercising due to lack of time, laziness, family obligations, lack of resources, spending time watching television or in front of laptops or overwhelming lives.

Few research-based facts about exercising:

- ❑ According to a study done at the University of British Columbia, the aerobic exercise that activates heart and sweat glands boosts the size of the hippocampus - the brain area that is involved in verbal memory and learning.
- ❑ The Daily Mail newspaper reported that inactivity is as deadly as smoking. It stated that the lack of exercise is causing as many deaths as smoking across the world.
- ❑ Researchers estimate that the lack of exercise could be responsible for around 1 in 10 cases of heart disease.
- ❑ Studies suggest that the two most successful ways to maintain a healthy heart are physical activity and avoidance of high-fat foods. Exercising has a cumulative effect on various activities of the body including improving blood circulation, improving cholesterol & fat levels, reducing inflammation in the arteries, keeping blood vessels flexible & open.

- ❑ Analysis based on national health survey results suggest that inactivity is a bigger obesity contributor than high-calorie intake.
- ❑ A sedentary lifestyle is likely to surge the risk of developing high blood pressure by 35% as compared to people who are physically active. Regular exercise helps keep arteries elastic, thus ensuring good blood flow and normal blood pressure.
- ❑ Studies indicate that the part of brain that controls thinking and memory has greater volume in people who exercise versus people who do not exercise. Dr. Scott McGinnis, a neurologist at Brigham and Women's Hospital & an instructor in neurology at Harvard Medical School, states that regular exercising of moderate intensity for over six months may lead to an increase in the volume of selected brain regions.
- ❑ Studies indicate that 4 out of 5 teens are not performing enough physical activity, thus posing a high risk for chronic disease later in life.
- ❑ Dr. William Evans and Dr. Irwin Rosenberg of Tufts University have documented that doing regular exercise can reverse many key biomarkers of aging by improving muscle mass, bone density, strength and aerobic capacity. It is one of the most powerful ways to stay healthy, relieve stress and reverse the aging process.

Transformational Experiences of People After Adopting Exercise as a Routine:

'I know for sure that exercise helps in many ways, both mental and physical. When I stop running from my regular routine, I notice my mood isn't as positive, and physically feel I have less energy to take me through the day' - Mary Johnson

'We know that exercise has significant benefits for our heart, but we rarely think about the advantages for the human brain.

Exercise is becoming a therapy for those afflicted by this condition!' - Glotzer

Holistic Perspective:

Unlike modern view of exercising that is purely based on improving body strength, physical beauty, and body functioning, the core premise behind ancient view of exercising was the mind and body connect. The ancient texts in Ayurveda, Yoga, and TCM originated after an apparent understanding by sages that human body is designed for physical activity. We are typically designed to move, breathe and circulate our vital life energy in this specific order! The ancient texts have given a lot of importance to exercising for health and longevity. A 5000-year-old text written by master Ayurveda physician Charaka states, 'From physical exercise, one gets lightness, a capacity for work, firmness, tolerance of difficulties, elimination of impurities & stimulation of digestion.'

Ayurveda theory emphasizes that 'From physical exercise, one obtains lightness, capacity to work, elimination of impurities from the body, firmness of the body, efficiency of digestion, and balance of metabolism.' Our body craves for exercising, and it is very clearly indicated in our body language, for example, the urge to stretch on waking up in the morning is a body's signal for its urge to move. It is a natural, healthy impulse that we must nurture. Before becoming a modern fad, structured physical movement always enjoyed a prime slot in Ayurveda routines in the form of Yogic postures. Ayurveda texts mention that at the body level exercising eliminates digestive impurities, enhances digestion, gets rid of heaviness and stiffness, dissolves impurities in the tissues, creates flexibility, improves firmness and endurance, creates balance, enhances immunity, banishes fatigue, stops early aging, retards weight gain, burns calories, increases muscle mass, improves flexibility, coordination, breathing, posture and strength. At the mind level, exercise creates self-awareness, mental agility, improved self-image, and self-sufficiency. It helps us know ourselves better and to truly connect with ourselves. As per the Ayurveda's tradition of exercising, the focus must not be on future goals such as weight loss or fat burning, rather, the focus must be on tuning oneself with right breathing techniques, being aware of physical responses and trying to get into the zone of well-being through meditative states.

Even TCM holds a similar viewpoint about exercising. Orientalists believed that exercising helps the body to regulate itself and to stay in harmony. The continuous flow of life energy and blood throughout the body is important in sustaining good health, especially given the turmoils of the daily lives. The ancient Chinese people believed that active life is essential for good health. Traditional Chinese exercises are a part of Chinese culture for past 2000 years. Even today in China, the elderly population aged 80 and 90 years can be seen practicing daily workout of stretching, strengthening and breathing exercises and acupressure and self-massage techniques. Li Ting, a sixteenth-century Chinese physician stated, 'Everyone knows that prolonged walking and standing can cause excessive fatigue, which is harmful to good health, but few people mention the damaging effects of lying down or sitting all day. 'Ancient Chinese texts suggest that the key to health is to maintain the right balance between rest and activity. And it is kind of interesting to know that if we listen to our body, it communicates this balance of rest and activity to each one of us. However, the right level and type of exercise and rest may vary from person to person, similarly like right foods for people may differ. Traditional exercising forms are an important aspect of healing in TCM. They are known to improve body functioning including sleep & digestion, boost the cardiovascular fitness, strengthen the body tone, relieve the joint and muscle pain, balance emotions, boost energy, enhance circulation, deepen & regulate breathing, increase flexibility, calm disturbed mind & maintain good health and prevent illnesses.

Take Away Thought:

So now what should we do? Start exercising obviously!

When beginning to exercise for the first time, walking is a good start. However, any kind of exercising activity that you start with such as yoga, tai chi, qi-gong, aerobics, cycling or swimming, it has the power to transform the body and mind if done in the right manner. It is important to like your exercising routine to do it regularly, so choose the exercise form that appeals you, benefits you and that you believe in. Avoid flowing with the flow of modern exercising fads. Take up yoga if you believe in it, or join a gym if you can carry on with it passionately. The idea is to engage in a physical activity that you can look forward to, that helps you banish stress & following a routine that you can prolong without getting bored. Enjoying your exercising routine will create a happy mind & fit body. It is equally important to respect your limits. Too much exercise can be damaging. Fatigue, lack of glow on the face, the strain on respiratory and cardiovascular systems may be the side-effects of too much exercising. Learn to listen to your body and understand when it tries to stop you by giving fatigue signals. Modern research confirms that too much exercising can create free radicals and damage the body. Degenerative diseases and premature aging are a result of excess free radicals. Further, too much reliance on modern conveniences is hazardous specifically when it comes to conveniences that restrict our body movement. Earlier, people used to walk to work, today people drive to work. Countries like China, Germany, Sweden, Netherlands, and Denmark have adopted an eco-friendly trend of cycling to work. The bottom line is to move your body regularly & not exercising excessively to the extent that the body breaks down.

CHAPTER 9 - COMPROMISED SELF-CARE

'An old saying goes like this, 'Empty vessel cannot serve anything to others.' Your uncared self cannot care for others whole-heartedly. The art of self-care is a nature's way of making us love ourselves unconditionally. Self-care is not selfishness. It is about valuing and respecting oneself. Self-care is a medium to showcase self-love. Self-care beautifies the body, satiates the mind and heals the soul. It is a medium to fill oneself with love, care, affection, satisfaction & the with the feelings of giving back.'

Scenario

Mitali, 35, is a homemaker & is a mother of 2 children. Mitali is ambitious & wants to do something. Before children, Mitali had been very particular about her self-maintenance. However, today her family responsibilities have taken over & she is even devoid of basic self-care. She mentions she does not get much time for herself. She meets her friends occasionally. Her daily routine revolves around her children and husband. She wakes up at 5 a. m., prepares lunch for children and gets them ready for school. She gets over from children's chores by 8 a. m. and then gets involved in husband's office preparations till 10 a. m. Mitali eats breakfast after her husband leaves at 10 a. m. She goes out for grocery shopping or any other pending tasks between 11 a. m. to 2 p. m. In the afternoon she is available for children's activities.

Mitali has a desire to have a life of her own too, but family responsibilities keep her busy. She often experiences irritation, exhaustion & does not want to be bothered by any additional responsibilities. She is seeking some self-time for herself to plan things that she wants to achieve. She is piling up weight, has a blotchy skin, she is out of shape & has graying hair. She has convinced herself that once her children grow up, she will find time to take proper care of herself. Apparently, Mitali is seeking self-care & time to fulfill her aspirations.

Food For Thought:

What is it that bothers Mitali? Is it some deep desire that makes her feel miserable? Is Mitali just obeying her family duties or is she doing that whole heartedly? Does Mitali share a harmonious bond with herself? Can you imagine how the lack of self-care and self-attention may be costing Mitali and her family in terms of quality of life, disturbed emotional moods, and happiness in life? Is Mitali becoming an empty vessel? What does self-care mean to you?

Case Analysis:

Mitali is totally disconnected with herself. Mitali seems to have some innate unfulfilled desires that appear to be dying due to her family responsibilities. She rarely takes care of herself and keeps juggling between family, children, duties and responsibilities. Mitali has given up on her true self, her wants, needs, and desires for her duties. Her responsibilities have taken the front seat, and her own self has gotten lost in the background.

Mitali feels that finding time for herself is hard. She is struggling with her own self which is making her feel exhausted, irritated, tired & stressed at a sub-conscious level. For Mitali the concept of self-care does not exist. As her physical appearance is impacting her self-esteem physically & her aspirations are bothering her emotionally, Mitali must self-reflect & come up with an action plan that caters to her needs at physical & emotional level. For physical transformation, Mitali must begin with changing her dietary habits for good & starting with some exercising plan to shed extra weight.

This will definitely boost her self-confidence & her will to achieve her goals in other areas. Next, she must plan her day well & ensure that her free time after personal responsibilities is dedicated towards her aspirations. Taking initial steps will help her regain confidence in her abilities. Mitali must work on physical & emotional self-care techniques that can be accommodated in her daily routine. She must begin taking better care of herself in terms of diet and self-nurturing techniques. She must exercise, meet friends, pursue her passion, foster creativity and have fun along with her daily responsibilities. She must spend time outdoors in the nature that she can easily accomplish by accompanying her children to a nearby park. Mitali must self-reflect & try to understand herself better. As far as lack of time is concerned, Mitali must plan her day well. For example, Mitali cooks everyday, and so she can spend time experimenting healthy meal plans for herself during that regular cooking time. Mitali bathes everyday and she can incorporate skin cleansing, activation, and detox activities while having bathing. Mitali can also join an activity class with her children such as dance or music.

Overtime, with proper self-care and by scheduling her own self-revival time, Mitali can get to know herself better and will develop respect for her own needs. This will ultimately lead her towards self-satisfaction. Becoming a full vessel then will help Mitali spend quality time with her family versus just continuing to perform her duties and responsibilities as a mandate.

Our Beliefs:

The concept of self-care in modern times has got externalized. For us today, self-care is all about:

- ❑ Visiting a spa or a salon.
- ❑ Consuming supplements & other medications for body and skin care.
- ❑ Getting yearly medical check-ups done.

- ❑ Following a dietary pattern.
- ❑ Joining a gym for body maintenance.

However, self-care is a highly integrated activity of mind, body, and soul. Where our total focus is on physical self-care in a modern way, the term has much more in store. In ancient times self-care was very much a part of daily routine. And so we used to see elder generation so particular about oiling and following other self-care rituals such as taking steam etc. The tradition of regular daily self-care is lost in the hustle and bustle of routine life. Frequent oil massages have been replaced by chemical-laden treatments. Ancient bathing techniques have been replaced by indulgence in chemical-based cosmetics and fragrances. Self-care routines have been replaced by professional spa set-ups. Skin treatments, anti-aging solutions, radiance products rule the self-care world today. Extreme solutions such as surgeries and medications are readily available & one can buy beauty rather than acquire it through internal bodywork. Additionally, self-care for emotional health is not considered as an essential practice for our well-being.

Self-care is quite devalued and takes a back seat in comparison to our duties and ambitions. We keep catering to worldly expectations such as working extra hours, keep pushing ourselves hard and continue managing things at the expense of extreme stress. We act unjustly to ourselves all the time, do not listen to our body & often suffer from 'overload burnout'.

Self-care is the most underestimated activity of modern times. Love for self is not looked upon with dignity by many individuals. Moreover, motherhood, work, job and family priorities disconnect us with ourselves. However, it is important to develop a positive mindset towards self-care and consider it as a good stewardship of the only gift that one can gift oneself to remain happy, healthy and well.

Self-Care Myths:

Myth - Self-care means putting myself first. How can I do that!

Fact - The thought of putting ourselves first versus our family, work, responsibilities and children is quite unacceptable and uncomfortable to us. However, have you ever wondered what would happen if you and any of your dear ones are drowning? You will save yourself first and the latter later. Because protecting self is the natural human instinct. It is only when we save ourselves that we can save others. But since out daily situations are not emergencies like the drowning case, we often tend to forget our natural instincts. We need to save ourselves first by taking proper care of ourselves. Many of us struggle with the idea of buying themselves a gift or pampering themselves or listening to their own needs. Being a part of reputable society, we have always been taught to put others before ourselves and ignore our own needs. And it is quite visible in the households where women give up their careers to another significant milestone in their life – marriage. A lot of women forget themselves after the birth of their children, and the society considers it as an ideal step. However, that's absolutely unfair because as said earlier 'Empty vessel cannot fill others.' It is important to keep ourselves happy to spread the happiness wholeheartedly.

Myth - Affording self-care is an expensive affair!

Fact - Self-care today is more associated with the commercial product and services industry. Spa treatments, salons, cosmetic surgeries, beauty pills have captured the majority of self-care market, thus, changing the perception of self-care. However, though all modern facilities constitute a part of self-care industry, the actual concept of self-care as per the ancient texts is that self-care is an important pillar of health and well-being. It must be a regular self-initiated practice versus going for occasional self-care services. Self-care must begin at home and be a part of one's daily habits and routines.

Myth - Self-care is being selfish specifically if it involves sparing time at the expense of my responsibilities!

Fact - We have been made to believe that self-care is selfishness. However, thought from an individual perspective, self-care is a medium to fill oneself with contentment, love, happiness, care, respect and satisfaction. Accruing these traits is highly dependent upon realization of one's expectations with oneself. Self-care strengthens us from within and imparts us will and energy to serve others whole heartedly. Serving others with depleted energies or half-heartedly or with frustrations does not do any good to anyone. Though quite underestimated as a stress-relieving therapy, self-care can act as an antidote to the stresses of life. It helps build resilience to cope up with the challenges of daily life in a positive way. Self-care is not a selfish act and an absolute must to be able to connect with oneself.

Myth - Responsibilities are important, self-care is not!

Fact - It is true that responsibilities are important, but compromising self-care in the name of duties is not right. Quite often we recuse ourselves and compromise with our wishes. While caring for others, we often give up on ourselves. While performing responsibilities is important, listening and attending to our own needs is the most important task for each individual.

Myth - My care is others' responsibility!

Fact - We all have expectations. The only gap here is that majority of people expect attention from others versus taking care of themselves. One's care is one's own responsibility and nobody else's. What you can do for yourself, no one else can.

Facts:

Ernest Hemmingway, the author of 'Men Without Women' mentions, 'The most painful thing is losing yourself in the process of loving someone too much and forgetting that you are special too.'

What is Self-Care?

Self-care refers to making our physical and mental health a priority. It is about developing a mindset that puts one's health and happiness at equal priority as one's responsibilities. It involves performing a set of activities and rituals that lead to a happy state of mind and stable health. It must be practiced as a daily ritual, and our ancient texts have laid special emphasis on the importance and techniques of self-care in daily routine. The scope of self-care includes both physical & emotional self-care. The self-care approach includes:

- ❑ Following a healthy diet and regular exercising routine along with adequate rest.
- ❑ Learning to say 'No' without guilt for situations that are against one's value system.
- ❑ Treating oneself with kindness and compassion while on a journey to realizing one's goals.
- ❑ Practicing mindfulness.
- ❑ Listening to self & prioritizing one's needs.
- ❑ Demanding help when in need without hesitation.
- ❑ Setting right expectations and boundaries in the family and with friends.

Self-care can help you get back on track and to refocus. Taking a break from stressful situations is a great way to promote an attitude of self-care.

The Case of Recovery Through Self-Care:

Jenny, 26, takes care of her disabled father and younger sister, does house work and prepares meals for three of them. Between her job and family needs, Jenny has no time to relax, enjoy leisure activities, or even sit down and eat with her family. Jenny began to lose weight; feeling exhausted and was irritable at work quite often. Luckily, Jenny soon realized that her mood is impacting her performance at work and her ability to take care of her family at home. Jenny decided to see a therapist who made her realize that she is doing too much for others, and for her to maintain a state of emotional well-being, it is important for her to spend time with herself. The holistic healing therapist helped chart out a plan for Jenny that included self-care techniques at three levels:

- **Body:** Included techniques to relax and beautify herself.
- **Mind:** Included yoga, meditation and pursuing creativity and passion.
- **Soul:** Included techniques to connect with her own self, to develop fulfilling relationships and to consider her needs as important as others.

Very soon, after working out her way to incorporate the suggested plan, Jenny began to spend some time with herself, and her moods improved drastically.

The bottom line is that we must intentionally make time for activities that help us rejuvenate. If we take care of ourselves, we are more independent and less needy of seeking attention or affection. We become more capable of truly connecting with other human beings. As a bonus, self-care rituals beautify you, lend you good skin, lustrous hair and shiny nails. It improves energy levels and makes one feel better, and function better.

Holistic Perspective:

Ayurveda has laid special emphasis on daily self-care rituals. So much so, that it specifies a set of self-care techniques to be incorporated into everyday routine. Ayurveda also correlates true beauty with simple acts of reverent self-care activities. It states that when we undertake our daily health and hygiene routines with the knowledge that each one of us is precious to ourselves, we develop a unique manifestation of life-force energy within ourselves.

The Importance of Self-Care in Everyday life – The Ancient Perspective:

Self-care is an art to be chosen to practice in the daily routine. With that satisfaction of caring, love, and affection for self, our bond with ourselves gets strengthened, and we connect with ourselves better. Being mindful of self-care can be a great tool to help shape our decision, help us handle daily stress with clarity, be clear about our choices and be able to nurture healthy relationships. Self-care is a powerful technique to understand oneself and drift away the mind from all stressors of life. For example, practicing belly breathing as a self-care routine has the power to calm oneself versus chest breathing that causes more anxiety in times of stress. Self-care imparts a radiant beauty inside out, it makes our skin clear and glow from within, it makes our hair get shinier and most importantly, it lends us self-confidence & strengthens our belief in ourselves. Self-care is not unaffordable, it is all that you do to yourself with the means that you already have. You just need to prioritize and plan your time for yourself in your daily routine. For example, you may still complete all your daily tasks by reprioritizing them, so that you make time for yourself, you may cut down on your TV time or wake up a little early to pamper yourself in multiple ways at physical, emotional and soul level. If housework seems overwhelming, hiring a domestic help may serve your purpose. When it comes to affording self-care, it is a myth that you must bank on professional services. In our daily set-up, we already have means available to care for ourselves. Do not get overwhelmed by advertising campaigns that play around with our mindset that self-care is a luxury. Ancient self-care techniques are powerful and free of cost! What you just need is making up your mind and get started.

Self-care can drastically enhance the quality of life. It helps drain away toxicity in all possible ways. Self-care gives you a chance to respect yourself for what you are and taking it ahead from there, versus admiring someone and aspiring to be someone else. It can significantly shape up your personality your way!

To summarize, the Ayurveda self-care methodology is just a drop in the ocean. There is alot more to self-care. More details on this topic are covered in the sections below. My intent of referring self-care as a part of Ayurveda is to spread awareness that self-care was always a part of our ancient culture, and must be revived in each single household. Ayurveda self-care practices have been designed to support the healthy functioning of our body. Moreover, it makes you look at yourself as a divine manifestation of life itself. When you honor yourself and your body in this way, no matter what your age is or how you look, the natural vitality, grace, and generousness shines through you.

Take Away Thought:

So, does a bright person appeal you even if they are dressed simply? Is it vitality & vigor that you long for? Do you get attracted towards people that exhibit ever lasting energy? If yes, then self-care is the way to go. Just imagine will you ever feel brightened up from within if your skin shows signs of aging, blotching, acne or cellulite, even if you wear clothes and make-up from the best brands? I bet no because what cannot be reflected from inside cannot be created outside. The charm of looking good and feeling good is different when you radiate from inside. Ever wondered how someone with beautiful skin beauty, shiny nails, and lustrous habit radiate from within and appeal even if dressed-up in simple attire.

Few Facts About Self-Care:

- ❑ Self-care begins at home & needs minimal resources. However, it has been commercialized to an extent which makes it look like more of a professional service.
- ❑ Taking care of yourself empowers you to take care of others whole heartedly without any grievances.
- ❑ Self-care is not selfishness. Rather, it is loving, knowing, understanding and respecting oneself for who you are and being compassionate towards oneself.
- ❑ Having a self-care routine is not about hiring professional services.
- ❑ Self-care can be easily accommodated in one's routine.
- ❑ It is important to be consciously present for ourselves and to appreciate our body for being healthy and working hard everyday.

- [ ] Self-care applies at all levels of mind, body & soul. Begin self-care from somewhere & treat yourself well, that's the ultimate key to loving yourself!

CHAPTER 10 - LOST MIND-BODY CONNECT

'Each physical action has an impact on mind & each emotion has a physical impact. Foods that we consume not just nourish the body, but our mind too! Thinking & behavior not just impact our mind but our body too. Positivity or negativity in mind originates equally with good or bad body experiences. And so, mind & body are the two sides of the same coin & a part of the same ecosystem –The Human Body. Body heals with activity, mind heals with peace, soul heals with self-connect & joy. If you connect the dots, ancient wisdom on Yoga perfectly offers healing for this combination of body, mind & soul!'

Scenario

Sophie Sabbage, 50+ years, was diagnosed with lung cancer and had developed multiple tumors at several sites including her brain. Her doctors declared that she did not have much time to live & she was recommended steroid treatments & surgery. The thought of living a paralyzed life and being under treatments with deteriorating quality of life made Sophie think of dealing with her miseries in a different way. And something shifted. Suddenly, her will to live became stronger, she gathered all the courage to take charge of her health & the thought rose up her tumor- ridden spine like an electric charge. She mentions that she never took steroids and they never irradiated her disease. She took a bold step of not going ahead with treatments. She empowered herself with knowledge, resources & will to heal herself the natural way. She trusted her own intuition above any expert recommendations. Five months later after taking charge of her health, Sophie's brain was cancer free. Her doctors consider hers as an exceptional case of healing with a strong will and adhering to the right ways of eating and living.

Food For Thought:

Do you believe that Sophies' will & transformed thoughts may have led her to reverse her cancer state? Do you believe that emotions have an impact on your physical being? Have you ever experienced physical suffering due to disturbed state of mind or vice versa? Does it ever happen to you that your body wants something and your mind wanders somewhere else? Have you ever experienced a mind-body disconnect?

Case Analysis:

With the change in mind, Sophie Sabbage transformed her disease, her body, and her life. She overpowered her physical condition through the power of the mind. Sophie is the author of the inspiring book, '*The Cancer Whisperer*' , where she talks about how cancer made her transform for good at mind, body and soul level. She mentions how she chose not to give-in into the never-ending sufferings associated with treatments. She rather chose to strengthen her mind and heal her body through will power, courage and with intent to change. She transformed her ways of eating, living, and perspective towards life. As a part of her healing journey, Sophie worked on uncovering the secrets to total wellness at physical, emotional & spiritual level. Her attitude and reaction to her situation made her recover from her miseries. She reaffirmed, 'I am going to live, ' and convinced her body to believe in her belief. Having said that, Sophie worked upon herself to face the facts about her health, learn about her illness and take the right course of towards her healing in a natural way.

Sophie's story is a story of the power of mind and how taking control of one's life can make miracles happen. Today, Sophie helps others recover through right attitude and right ways of thinking, living, and eating.

Our Beliefs:

Global boundaries have shrunken, and technology has made it possible to connect with anyone in the world anytime of the day. However, the more connected we have become with the world globally, the more disconnected we have become with ourselves. Today, our lives demand too much from us. We live in a frenzied world amidst job pressures, family responsibilities, desire to present ourselves well, high competition and demanding work life. Our sense of achievement is defined by the wealth that we accumulate, the properties that we construct or the fame that we acquire. Realization of passion, satisfaction driven by winning hearts and growing in the areas of interest are some of the self-contentment traits that have lost their value over time. We abide by the fake markers of achievement today. These false markers defined as fame, power & position demand too much from us & leave us disintegrated with our own selves. While living life on a fake plane, we make our body work extra hard, and our mind thinks endlessly. We do not pay attention to the stress signals that our body communicates in the form of frequent illnesses such as low immunity, cold, cough, flu, skin problems, falling hair, allergies, etc. Also, it is not just our body but our mind too that suffers from our habits, thoughts and thinking patterns. Stress, emotional disturbances, low moods & depressing thoughts. Ultimately we tend to lose our health and well-being partially due to our wrong dietary and lifestyle habits and partly due to the disconnect between our body and mind. When such disconnect manifests in the form of real symptoms in the body and mind, we do everything except trying to connect with ourselves. The classic example in this case is to see the achievers who earned fame & power, struggling with some health issues or the other.

In our daily lives, there are times when our body signals tiredness, but we let our mind ignore such messages. There are times when our emotions are causing a havoc, and our body is reacting to such thoughts in the form of fluttering gut or localized aches and pains. Yet, we ignore the importance of our connect with ourselves. We overlook the fact that every action, thought and behavior triggers some impact on both the body and mind.

When it comes to healing, our entire belief system is set on our modern medical system. Undoubtedly, the medical world has done wonders to extend the life span of individuals by treating the observable & measurable physical symptoms of a patient, but somewhere it is incomplete. This system does not consider healing the mind as a part of the treatment. A typical example would be a cancer survivor who gets treated and recovers on the physical plane but still deals with the after-effects and thoughts of survival for months and years ahead.

Modern techniques of health management such as exercises, weight training, diet management, etc., are all based on a physical approach. You go to the gym for a physical workout, and you go for meditation class for a mental workout. For us, exercises are a vehicle to gain physical strength and endurance, and mind is nowhere in question. However, when mind and body are so integrated, aiming both through workout must be the ultimate goal. The commercial set-ups lack this approach to health management. And so the importance of ancient exercising practices such as Yoga, Qi-Gong & Tai Chi has become all the more important in the modern world.

Often times we are not aware that our negligible feelings could be such a powerful sign of our disintegrated selves. We are unaware that our physical conditions, specifically the weakening of immune system could be due to our thought patterns. We often end up living life in a disconnected manner with a total focus on earning fortunes. Property, fame, money may be a mark of success in the material world but true success, health, happiness, and well-being are the true markers of our success in our health area.

Are you any of these?

- ❑ I have the best in life still I do not feel happy.
- ❑ I do not know what I what from life.
- ❑ I do not understand why I get angry.

- ❑ I often feel overwhelmed by my emotions.
- ❑ I often feel insecure and uncertain about myself.
- ❑ I don't like socializing, it makes me uncomfortable.
- ❑ I am looking for my purpose in life.
- ❑ I often feel insecure about losing my family and friends.
- ❑ I sometimes feel empty inside.
- ❑ I end up working through-out the day & do not have time for my passion areas.
- ❑ I often indulge in emotional eating.
- ❑ I often get so stressed that my head spins.
- ❑ I get an upset stomach when I am stressed, it feels weird.
- ❑ I end up serving others & I feel lost in the world.

If your answer to any of these questions is 'Yes, ' then consider yourself a victim of mind-body disconnect. Just introspect the following questions and look for answers from within:

- ❑ How often do you focus on your emotions, feelings & thoughts while undergoing medical treatment for any physical ailment?
- ❑ How many of you are aware of your body signals?
- ❑ How many of you take your minor health issues seriously?
- ❑ How many of you make conscious effort to release stress?
- ❑ How many of you think beyond body when getting into an exercising regime?
- ❑ How many of you think of food energy when eating your daily meals?

If you can find the answers to these questions, you will realize we just keep living lives on a fake plane and mind is never a priority except few acts of meditation. Remember, the first step to understanding the mind-body connection and its power is to become aware of your body. Start doing it now!

Facts:

Mind-body medicine is a science of interactions between the body & mind. For years the modern medicine believed and focused on treating the physical body while ignoring the psychological aspects of one's personality. However, now the medical world is shifting its focus towards mind-body medicine as an important part of healing. And the wave seems to be catching up with meditation and breathing exercises becoming an important part of doctor's recommendations. The science that our ancient texts have always focused upon, now it is being studied and experimented by modern science extensively. In past few years, there has been a paradigm shift in the focus on thephysical aspect to focus on emotional, mental, social, spiritual, experiential, and behavioral factors of a human being.

Today, we know how stress can affect our health. We often read in magazines and newspapers how high-stress hormone (cortisol) can lead to poor cardiovascular health. It is a research-based fact that managing stress for those who are aware of the mind-body connection is easier as they are in a better position to decide not to stress over situations. If we can control the mind and not let ourselves get stressed, the body automatically gets into a relaxed state. In such a case the symptoms related to stress such as fight & flight response, high blood pressure or rapid heartbeat begin to disappear. Research further suggests that the more positive emotions such as gratitude, love, thankfulness, etc. you maintain the better you learn to control negative emotions like fear and worry. However, it is the other way round if you choose to stick to negative emotions such as anger, resentment, anxiety, fear, etc. In a negative emotional state, our body becomes sensitive to infections, inflammation, heart disease, cancer, agingand even negatively impacted genes.

Few Facts to be Mindful of:

- ❑ A study published in Biological Psychiatry journal demonstrated that in stressed individuals, the mindfulness meditation promoted high-level thinking, focus, attention & better stress handling capability. Reduced inflammation was reported in the blood test of meditators. It could become a valuable tool in dealing with inflammatory diseases such as Alzheimer's disease, arthritis, heart disease, osteoporosis, and diabetes.

- ❑ A study by Ohio State University demonstrated that the blood of stressed and anxious women suffering from breast cancer had the lowest levels of white blood cells. They were in a weaker position to combat cancer and had weak body defenses.
- ❑ A study published on the issue of Social Science and Medicine demonstrated that people having a spiritual orientation had fewer cases of illness including cardiovascular conditions or cancer, as compared to non-believers of spirituality.
- ❑ A study done by the University of California at Los Angeles demonstrated that people recovering from melanoma surgery and seeking education and counselingon stress management had almost half the rate of cancer recurrence and third fewer death.
- ❑ As per Dr. John Sarno, the author of '*Healing Back Pain: The Mind-Body Connection*' mentions that suppressed emotions especially anger, can trigger back pain. Emotional pains are held in the body tissues to become physical in nature, and so he recommends being aware of one's emotions & understanding them is important when treating such pains.
- ❑ Study at Harvard has shown to lower high blood pressure and decrease the level of chronic pain after chemotherapy with the practice of meditation.
- ❑ Studies have shown a direct link between positive emotions and strong health benefits like reducing chronic inflammation and decreasing harmful levels of stress hormones.
- ❑ A study conducted at the University of Massachusetts Medical Center on a group of patients with psoriasis found

the skin of patients clearing more quickly who received relaxation training along with standard phototherapy.

- Studies suggest that stress may destroy the protective biological substances along the digestive tract and may lead to the development of inflammatory bowel syndrome.
- Research at Carnegie Mellon University demonstrated that the more stress or negative emotional state of mind a person has, the more likely they are to catch a cold and flu.

Mind-Body Connect at Biological Level:

It is important to be aware of how negative thoughts and emotions manifest into a physical problem?

We are often not aware or tend to ignore the effects that our thoughts have at the physical level. When it comes to handling stress, most of us display a weak composure and tend to get carried away by stress, tension, anxiety, depression, hate and other negative feelings, without even considering that it can affect us emotionally and physically, lowering our quality of life.

But, how do our negative thoughts becoming a physical problem at the biological level? Let's try to understand:

The mind-body connection is so strong that our thoughts and emotions trigger the production of certain chemicals within the body and create imbalances. From a biochemical perspective, each positive or negative thought triggers a series of chemical reactions in our nervous system and influence the molecules in our body. For example, serotonin and dopamine are two chemicals that our brain releases when we' re experiencing happiness or euphoria. Whereas, when angry, a biochemical reaction occurs in the body that raises the adrenaline level and causes us to relive the experience again and again. The chemical impact of positive or negative thought pattern gets set in the nervous system, muscular system, body chemistry and body tissues. When set-in into the tissues, we get locked into certain distinct patterns of thinking and behaving. The site where imbalances begin to happen due to negative emotions may get weakened overtime and potentially get broken down. The then weakened organ, gland or body part gets susceptible to other stresses such as inadequate nourishment, toxins, and fatigue, and overtime may become diseased or dysfunctional. Imagine with just a set negative thought process, how we may be driving ourselves towards disturbed energy flows in specific body parts.

When stress builds up in the brain, it has two outlets:

1. One, getting into the nervous system and changing body chemistry by changing the messenger molecules or neuropeptides that are bathing the nervous system, thus changing our moods. And, these altered chemicals not just impact the nervous system but create havoc all over the body.
2. Two, manifesting itself into distinct patterns of tension. Overtime, these specific patterns of tension become lodged permanently as chronic stress patterns, which mean we continue to be angry or sad without forgetting our anger or sadness over a long time. With these prolonged emotions, our brain keeps sending out the same messages to the same muscles, and thus it sets in our posture. There comes a time when our mind, muscles, energy distribution and posture permanently get fitted into that pattern, beginning to cause aches and pains initially and leading to a disabled state if continued.

Mind-Body medicine is such an interesting science that can decode the emotions that we are going through by focusing on the physical issues that we are facing. For example, fatigue, tiredness and lack of energy could be a sign of continuous internal sadness. Chronic neck pain could be a sign that we are not able to see different perspectives in life and keep taking stress over single thought. Pain in the hips could be a sign of fear and inability to make important decisions. Middle back pain could mean holding on to the past. Lower back pain could indicate stress specifically financial stress.

Placebo Effect – Psychosomatic Technique to Prove that Trust Heals

For years the concept of Placebo Effect has been used in clinical trials. It is a classic example to showcase how trust heals. During clinical trials, a set of identified people are prescribed a pill, procedure or a counseling session that does not have a direct physiological effect on the body. The concept of the placebo effect is primarily used for comparison purposes between the people who actually consume trial medications & who consume fake drugs. In placebo, the prescribed pill is a dummy pill with no active treatment ingredients. It is given to the sufferers based on their belief that they are on medication. The placebo effect has been seen to yield a favorable response in terms of bettering health condition of the participant sufferers. It is purely trust-based medicine, where the beliefs of sufferers create healing for them. A real-time example of the placebo effect is someone being injected with water, but being told that they have been injected with a drug for their cancer treatment. Sometimes, people's beliefs change their physiology & make them heal.

Holistic Perspective:

There exists a direct correlation between the emotional health and the physical health of a person. While western medicine recognizes emotions and physical issues as separate non-conflicting entities, TCM considers emotions as an integral and inseparable part our internal organs, and a potential primary cause of diseases. It is interesting to know how TCM classifies various emotions and associates them with each organ of the body. For example, a person who gets angry in the spur of the moment is considered to have a weak liver as the emotion of anger is associated with the liver. Similarly, a person who is too fearful is deemed to be having weak kidney as fear is the related emotion of the kidney. Though this may sound strange, in the real world this association seems correct when we see that a fearful child due to scolding may suffer from a state of uncontrolled bladder & pass urine in pants. It is a clear indication of fear affecting kidneys and the child not being able to hold! This science is so interdependent that it focusses that emotions and organs work mutually. So, if one has fear, the kidneys will automatically get weak despite right diet, exercise, and water intake. Similarly, if the kidneys are weak due to wrong diet and lifestyle, one may acquire the emotion of fearfulness automatically. See how closely our Mind & Body is interconnected! Further, as per this ancient mind-body theory, no feeling is good or bad, rather, it is indicative of the state of our physical & emotional health. Emotions are considered to be our survival instincts in TCM and hold true to different situations of life. For example, when the body senses danger, it is obvious to feel fearful and switch on our flight and flight response that gives rise to action and aggression to deal with danger. That's natural mechanism that nature has imparted us with to be able to survive in the danger state. However, without thinking too much about positive or negative emotions, if we let them flow freely, acknowledge them, respond to them appropriately in time and move on, we continue to enjoy optimal health. Patterns of disharmony and disease only arise when our emotions get stuck, or we try to ignore or suppress them.

Ancient sages divided human body into 4 separate entities existing at following planes:

Physical Body: The most focused plane responsible for movement and action in human beings.

Emotional Body: The most underestimated plane of human health that is responsible for feelings and connection with oneself, with others, our environment & surroundings.

Mental Body: The most overly used plane that is responsible for thinking, planning, deciding and direction.

Spiritual Body: The plane of human health that enjoyed much importance in ancient times and that has lost relevance in the material world. This plane is responsible for guiding and directing us right. Our intuition exists at this plane.

More than 2000 years ago, Ayurveda & TCM identified the close connect between these 4 planes of human's existence and developed holistic mind-body healing systems. Ayurveda, the traditional Vedic health care system introduced Yoga that is a science of physical postures, aligned breathing and techniques to cleanse the mind. TCM introduced Tai-Chi, Chi-Kung, Qi Gong & Martial Arts as vehicles to achieve mind-body connect. Each of these techniques caters to the needs of these 4 planes discussed above. For example, Yoga helps create flexibility, calm emotions, clear mind, help connect with ourselves, develop strength, endurance, vision, balance and energy through the practice of dynamic physical postures & breath awareness. Tai-chi is a science of slow, relaxed flowing movements derived by observing animal movements. It involves forming vivid images to discipline and focusing on mind while giving our body a slow-movement workout. It believes that by practicing slow movements, our emotions flow without a blockage and balance is recreated. Healing images and directing energy through movements cultivates our power and health. Martial Arts give physical benefits, instills a sense of self-confidence, determination and fortitude in the face of conflict or challenge. Chi-kung practice is more internally oriented that uses sustained postures, dynamic images, directed energy and focused breath to create physical health, emotional serenity, mental clarity and spiritual unity.

One common aspect of all these mind-body forms is that they are meditative in nature, and the focus is not about building body or losing weight, but growing awareness and achieving healing. So, whether it is Yoga, Tai Chi, Qi Gong or any other ancient mind-body technique, by practicing these meditative movements, dynamic postures, and conscious breathing techniques, one can achieve a deeper level of self-awareness and healing.

Take Away Thought:

It is important to question ourselves the following:

- ❑ Am I aware who I am?
- ❑ Do I know my path and purpose in life?
- ❑ Am I doing what I want to do?
- ❑ What is it that switches me on or off?
- ❑ Am I happy, content and joyous in life?
- ❑ Am I paying attention to what my body and mind communicate?

The clue to answering these questions begins with:

- ❑ Spending alone time with ourselves to understand our emotions and finding a way to vent our emotions in the right way.
- ❑ Thinking positive. Negativity never promises any better solutions. And luckily positive thinking can be developed as a habit with conscious mind training.
- ❑ Realizing that mind and body are united & the negative aspect of each impacts the other.
- ❑ Realizing that in today's times we all are disconnected with ourselves. The biggest challenge for us today is to know ourselves than knowing our work, projects, gadgets, cars and other material items. Work on knowing yourself.
- ❑ Preparing our body and mind for the new challenge of life each single day. We must develop an attitude of acceptance and change to deal with the changing world.
- ❑ Healing the diseased mind first & unhealthy body later. Use your positive thoughts to heal your physical body. Give your thoughts a healthy dose of positivity and to try to see the brighter side of things.
- ❑ Being aware of our thoughts & treating ourselves with ease and respect.
- ❑ Not getting stuck in the patterns of self-judgment, negative self-talk, and self-pity. Believe that you have the power to transform.

- ❑ Learning to communicate right. It solves half of the problems and is a great outlet for pent-up emotions.
- ❑ Taking a break & self-reflecting on the impact of negative thoughts and emotions on your lives and health.
- ❑ Transforming ourselves versus thinking and stressing over changing others.
- ❑ Surrounding ourselves with positivity. It has been scientifically proven that positivity releases hormones that are responsible for strengthening the immune system. It has also been seen to improve the quality of life drastically.
- ❑ Being aware of our thought patterns. It is the first step towards maintaining internal balance.
- ❑ Promoting alkalinity through the power of right thinking. Negative thoughts and feelings cause acidity in the body. Remain positive.
- ❑ Changing our lifestyles & habits if they can transform our life. Believe in change.
- ❑ Adopting a spiritual mindset as a supportive pillar for healing and health. And, it does not mean we become a saint! It just means that we must get to know ourselves, the functioning of our body & the universe so that we are aware of our limits.
- ❑ Respecting our body and treating it well through proper nutrition, exercise, and enough rest and sleep.
- ❑ Retrospecting ourselves & using sickness as an opportunity to realize where we stand physically, mentally, emotionally & spiritually.

CHAPTER 11 - LIVING UNNATURAL LIFE AND DRIFTED AWAY FROM NATURE

'Human life responds best amidst nature at all levels of existence. The more we delve into the man-made unnatural world of technology & the high-rise indoor environments, the more we drift our lives away from natural ways of living. This way we uknowingly create a niche for our health issues!'

Scenario

Diane, 42, lives in an overcrowded metropolitan city. She lives in a high-rise apartment situated in a noisy area. Her entire day is spent either in her office or at her apartment. Over weekends she likes to shop in a shopping mall, again deserting herself from the outside world. The landscaping in her apartment area is minimal, though there is a small nearby park for the residents. When at home, Diane likes to watch television or play games on her new Nintendo. She also likes chatting with her family and friends on her laptop or on cell-phone. Diane has equipped her home with all modern luxuries including latest electric gadgets. She has a cook at home who prepares dinner for Diane. Breakfast is a quick meal which generally is either a sandwich or quick oats along with a cup of tea and cookies. Diane uses microwave quite extensively for cooking and heating purposes. To be precise, Diane's routine life is all about indoor air conditioned environment, her regular foods quite a lot consists of processed foods, she is highly exposed to air and noise pollution being in a metropolitan city, her daily exposure to chemicals in the form of self-care products, room fresheners, and home care products is high and her life majorly revolves around technology. Though Diane is okay at the physical level, at the emotional level, she tends to be irritated, moody and fatigued. Despite of living a life that Diane always wanted, she is unable to understand why her emotional health is always on the edge!

Food For Thought:

Do you think Diane's artificial life could be a cause of her emotional distress? Why is it important to be connected with nature? Why is it that the meditative sounds are all natural sounds of animals, flowing rivers, oceans versus sounds of honking cars or any other unnatural sounds? How much time do you spend outdoors each week?How often do you take advantage of nature for your mental, physical, and spiritual balance? Is being away from nature impacting our lives in any way?

Case Analysis:

Diane's disconnect with nature reflects in the way she eats, lives, self-cares works or entertains herself. Whether it is her home, car or office, Diane spends most of her day indoors. Her urban set-up is surrounded with motorized transport system including rattling sound of buses, motor cars, and other vehicles. Diane is highly exposed to noise pollution, air pollution, food pollution and water pollution. Additionally, her extreme exposure to gadgets including microwave, television, laptop, iPad, cellular phones, the internet, fax, and technology is taking her more into the unnatural virtual world. It looks exciting though, but at the core foundation level, the disconnect with nature has a deep impact on our psyche. Diane's exposure to other kinds of pollutants include polluting gasses, metal dust particles in the air, smoke, carbon-di-oxide, carbon-mono-oxide, nitrous-oxide, toxic & polluted air, water and unnatural environment. Further, Diane is not exposed to the oxygenated environment. Research suggests that people in the cities are always under tremendous pressure and stress due to the unclean and unnatural environment. Diane's disconnect with nature may be holding the key to her stress, mood swings and general fatigue!

Our Beliefs:

Today, the world primarily belongs to the carriers of technology – 'The Gadgets'. The entire world is connected through cell phones or internet, be it family, friends, neighbors, colleagues or a person sitting next door! The whole world has access to nature through technology just with the click of a button. A lot of people relate to the nature within their home or office premises on their computers! The sense of touch, smell, sight, feeling and experience has just got limited to sight! And this is the hard fact of our lives. We see nature on the screen! We are slowly becoming dissatisfied, anxious, depressed, hurried, frustrated race emotionally and a sicker race physically. More and more people are becoming prone to diseases like asthma, bronchitis, cancer, heart ailment, diabetes and others. We have less recreational spaces outdoors. Our air, food and water quality is worsening, stress hovers over us all the time, relaxation has become an occasional retreat, noisy heavy traffics have replaced the calm of peaceful and natural sounds. Our calm zones have got limited to our washrooms, and fresh air is being sold in bottles or has been hijacked by air purifiers. We consume more alcohol and colas than water, and our entire focus remains to equip our homes with luxuries and latest gadgets. Walks in open green environment have been replaced by machine based gymming environment. Though the quality of life is getting better in terms of affordability of comfortable life, it is massively deteriorating in terms of personal health and well-being.

Amidst the unnatural environment that we thrive in today, we are truly missing on the magic of fresh breezy air, the refreshing aura of flora and fauna, sense of vastness achieved by looking at blue skies, charm of a beautiful scenery, mystic wilderness, soothing sight & sounds of beautiful birds, sense of flow developed from enchanting streams, sense of freshness achieved from plants and trees, brightness received from the sun, sense of calm felt under moonlight, knitting hopes and dreams under the shining stars and the magic of the rain. Our sense to be in nature and appreciate it has gone with the past generations who worshiped nature for its importance of being giving & nurturing for the human race.

Facts:

It is no surprise that nature is being destroyed by the advancement of mankind. The balance of nature started getting disrupted with industrial technology a few decades back, and now the technology & gadgets are taking a toll on nature.

Research Findings on Nature:

- ❑ Dr. Richardson mentions that research evidence shows a direct correlation between exposure to nature and reduction in hypertension, cardiovascular illnesses, and respiratory tract diseases. He further suggests a direct link between nature and improved vitality and mood, improvement in mental well-being, lowered anxiety levels, restoration of attention capacity and elimination of mental fatigue. Most importantly, natural surroundings have been closely associated with a sense of life satisfaction, happiness, vitality, mindfulness, and purpose in life.
- ❑ According to the University of Washington, mental illnesses and mood disorders are more a trait of urban areas, also partly due to reduced access to nature.
- ❑ Professor Frances Kuo, a professor of the landscape and human health mentions that people residing in places surrounded by greenery are more generous, sociable, calm and trusting. It has been found that in less green environments, there are higher rates of aggression, violence, and crime.

- In a study by theUniversity of Essex, it was mentioned that walking outside in nature daily can be effective in treating mild to moderate depression.
- Studies suggest that natural beauty can boost the feelings of awe and can be a sure shot way to experience a mental boost.
- A study on students sent to the forest for two nights reported lowered levels of stress hormone cortisol and heart rate as compared to those who spent that time in the city.
- A study on office workers concluded that even the view of nature from a window is associated with lower stress levels and higher job satisfaction.
- As per an Australian study, increased time spent outdoors is directly associated with lower prevalence of myopia among 12-year-olds.
- Research suggests that being outside in the park for just 20 minutes might serve as a safe, inexpensive, widely accessible tool for managing attention-deficit symptoms.
- A research concluded that students performed 50 percent better on a problem-solving test after performing immersive stretches in nature while being disconnected with any sort of digital technology. It offered significant benefits for their creativity and problem-solving skills.
- Researchers in Sweden have found joggers who exercise in a natural green environment feel more restored and less anxious, angry, or depressed than people who burn the same amount of calories jogging in an urban setting.
- In his most well-known study, Ulrich investigated the effect that views from windows had on patients recovering from abdominal surgery. He discovered that patients whose hospital rooms overlooked trees had an easier time recovering than those whose rooms overlooked brick walls. Patients able to see nature got out of the hospital faster, had fewer complications and required less pain medication than those forced to stare at a wall.

Special Bond between Nature and Children

In earlier times, 'Go out and play' used to be one of the most repeatedly used simple, yet so powerful directive for the children. In today's times, we need to realize the power of this directive when it comes to children's health.

Have you seen an infant having the time of her life when left on the green ground? She wants to run, grab, observe, listen, react, eat, play and does every possible thing on that piece of land amidst trees and surrounding plants and greenery. Children are inquisitive by nature and have an innate desire to explore and learn through observation. It hardly makes any difference to them if they play with a dog or a butterfly or a cat or around the trees. They are so connected to the nature naturally. One can see a clear connect between nature and children in the way they interact with it and the way they feel rejoiced, happy and content amidst nature even without any company. With their own silent language of communication, children in earlier times learned a lot all by themselves by being out in nature.

The bygone era was the golden time for children. They could go out and explore fearlessly. Outdoors was the only playground that they ever knew. They had all the energies to play from morning till night. They used to automatically learn companionship, conflict handling, strength and other qualities during the play. By the end of the day they had so many stories to discuss, unlike children of today who just know the stories that they get to read in story books. The kind of unstructured play that they were involved in taught them the unpredictability of everything in life making them more fearless and experimental.

However, today the scenario is very different. Author Richard Louv in 2005 came up with a term, 'Nature-Deficit Disorder, ' to define the increasing separation of children with nature. Based on research for a decade and after interviews with the children, teachers, and parents, he concluded that as children started to get away from nature, more incidences of physical, emotional & behavioral issues began to emerge. Today's children go out on a scheduled play date, they play games that are structured and instruction based, they remain indoors in the plastic replicas of the nature, they play organized rule-based sports on manicured grounds, they are loners engaged with their computer games or iPads during most times of the day. The phrase 'Go out and play' has gotten replaced by 'Sit quietly and watch TV.' As mundane adult life, a child's life has also got restricted to school, school activities, gadgets and technology. In cities, we hardly see children cycling or playing in groups together after school. Additionally, today's parents have specialized focus on children. They spend massive amounts on their education and structured activities and less time in getting involved in their stories and creativity. Parents want to protect their children from the hazards of the natural world such as getting drenched in the rains or catching infections from a muddy play. Parents are rather more comfortable letting their children play with electronic devices to keep them clean, infection-free & engaged! Consequently, children have become irritable, seek undivided attention, have grown weak internally and remain sick with weather and other triggers. Their behaviors reflect their innate desire to be able to grow-up naturally! Research has substantial evidence demonstrating that with the diminishing connection with nature, the social, psychological and spiritual implications become apparent. The saddest part is when a child's behavior is discussed with experts, 'Go out and Play' power is never taken into consideration. However, with younger generations getting trapped in adult-type health issues, there has been a considerable focus by various groups on the importance of 'Go out and play.'

Studies provide evidence that nature buffers children against the stresses of life and makes them mentally strong as compared to children who predominantly live in man-made sheltered environments. Research also suggests that nature could be the answer to a child's all-round development, emotional issues, obesity, Attention Deficit Hyperactivity Disorder (ADHD), behavioral problems, irregular sleep, violent tendencies, poor academic performance and lost creativity. It is important to realize that humans are hard wired to nature. Close experiences amidst nature can help better our concentration levels, boost our creativity, develop problem-solving skills & critical thinking, impact decision making while also developing soft skills such as empathy, forgiveness, sense of appreciation, etc. Unstructured play activities such as climbing a tree or fishing, boating, playing in parks, building a sand castle can fuel a child's imagination, creativity, sense of peace, satisfaction, relaxation and focus. From personality development perspective, nature offers children an opportunity to observe, interact, know, understand, realize, play and be friendly. From physical and emotional health perspective, children spending time in oxygenated outdoor green environments have been found to have a lower rate of childhood obesity, lifestyle disorders including cardiovascular diseases and lower mortality. From the perspective of developing a community, nature equips children with a sense of neighborhood, social ties, sense of unity, mutual trust and willingness to help others. Whether it is science, sports, relationships, art, discoveries, and innovation have always evolved from the unknown and nature is a direct route into the world of unknown. Children form their own language of communication with animals, they are comfortable in the water, and they want to experience nature the way it is. There is no better way to understand the world, than sharing a bond with animals, parenting plants, cultivating the land, relaxing in green parks, developing a sense of vastness near oceans and rejoicing in open spaces. So, tell your children to 'Get out and play, ' but choose outdoors wisely!

Holistic Perspective:

In all ancient cultures, we observe an inseparable mention of nature. Hindu mythology considers natural world as divine. In fact, in Hindu culture the animal idols, rivers and other elements of nature are worshiped along with the idols of deities. Flowers, rivers, oceans, animals, seasons and all other nature's elements have always been combined with spirituality in Hindu, Greek, Japanese, Chinese and Buddhist cultures. In Christianity, there is a mention of an earthly paradise in the form of a flower garden. Buddhism considers all forms of life as holy and worthy of compassion, and hence, their philosophy of spirituality is centered on compassion. In many villages in India, natural phenomenon's such as rain is worshiped, and land is addressed as mother earth. Fire is considered holy and constitutes a part of important ceremonies as it is believed that fire purifies. However, we need not be religious to understand the importance of nature.

The ancient world was much closer to nature in all aspects including food, sound, and body movements in the form of exercises or dance or music. For example, Tai Chi, Indian classical music & Indian classical dance are inspired by the movements and rhythms of nature. The 7 Indian classical sounds addressed as 'sur' which include 'sa' , 're' , 'ga' , 'ma' , 'pa' , 'dha' , 'ni' have inherited their sound from the sounds of animals. Today, with a lot of focus on sound therapy, such classical sounds are gaining importance due to their meditative effect. Tai Chi, a slow movement based exercise inherits its movements from animal postures.

In ancient times nature played a full-fledged role in all areas of healing. Centuries back the only known medical system was plant-based medication, and the approach to health was more focused on preventive medicine. Where plants and trees served as the pharmacy to heal people of anything that they acquired, yoga, tai chi, breathwork and other techniques ensured that the body maintained its balance through preventive measures. The ancient sages developed ways of breathing, living, eating, fasting as preventive measures for health management.

Further, nature works in a particular fashion. Like there are seasons in the nature, there exist seasons within our body too. Ever thought why is it that we experience hair fall during the fall season? Internally, our body works exactly the same way as the seasons and nature. This means that nature operates internally, exactly the way it operates externally. We have a fire inside our body that helps in metabolism, digesting food and keeping us warm. We have the wind inside our body in the form of oxygen and other gasses. When these gasses go into a state of imbalance, we experience issues related to gastric trouble. Considering that we are so closely united to nature, it is important to observe and behave as per the rules and changes of nature for optimum health and well-being. The more harmonized we get with nature, the more we can enjoy good health and longevity.

Take Away Thought:

Nature was never different from all of its elements including human beings, rivers, oceans, flowers, trees, animals, etc. Varying degrees of nature's elements including earth, fire, wind, water and metal form all life forms. Our ancient wisdom always believed in our oneness with nature. Our everyday routine life, advancements in technology and more focus on the material world has deviated our attention from the importance of nature. We are spending more time indoors and online, but we are continually getting affected by our environment in ways that we are not aware of! If we analyze our needs for maintaining optimal health, everything boils to the basics of life. However, these basics have become a threat to our survival, check below how:

Our Basic Requirements	Replaced With
Air precisely Oxygen	Smoking, polluted environments, artificial fragrances
Natural Food	Artificial foods and flavors, chemical-laden foods, processed foods
Water	Colas, alcohol, caffeinated drinks
Exercise precisely mind-body uniting activities	Dissipated forms of exercises, sedentary lives

(Continued)

Right Breathing	Stressful environments, incorrect breathing patterns
Sleep	Late night culture, work commitments, entertainment slots
Elimination	Overeating, Disturbed body chemistry due to wrong lifestyles and foods, emotional pressures

Though your doctor may tell you that you suffer from diabetes due to blood sugar high or insulin resistance, from holistic health perspective each single factor mentioned above has a positive role to play to make us reach a stage where we are declared as a diabetic or a cancer patient.

Some of the immediate and noticeable benefits that can be noticed by just being in nature include better focus, stress release, mental stamina, cognitive performance, happy state of mind, igniting creativity, better moods, rejuvenation effect, peace, learning opportunity, balance, harmony and much more. If we can benefit so much just by spending time in the nature, imagine how much more we can benefit if we start getting involved with the nature, starting to eat and drink what nature has to offer, starting to breathe what nature created as life-force, starting to play in nature, observing and understanding it for our as well as nature's wellness! The bottom line is to nurture & and go back to nature!

CHAPTER 12 - NOT OWNING THE RESPONSIBILITY OF OUR OWN HEALTH

'Until we are one with our mothers, she nurtures us naturally through her internal resources, & so we are born absolutely healthy & well. However, our life is our own journey & our health is no doctor's or anyone else's responsibility! Taking care of our health is our foremost responsibility, earning a living comes later! Thankfully, our ancient practices provide us with all resources, means & techniques to achieve physical, emotional, mental & spiritual health. Industrial revolution & technology have conditioned us to believe that the medical system is the way to perfect health! It is because we have shifted the responsibility of our health in the hands of an external system that knows nothing about us except the forms that we submit as patients. It is high time that we begin taking the control back in our own hands!'

Scenario

James, 50, takes at least 8 pills in a day. Few for high blood pressure, others for heart disease, high cholesterol and some for diabetes. His doctors have advised him to control his diet and perform mild exercises to maintain his health. James is aware that he must not be consuming animal fat and high proteins, but these being his favorite foods, he simply confronts that he cannot stop living life. He further justifies his point by stressing that he is already on medication for his physical issues and so it is ok for him to consume what he likes. When it comes to exercising, James mentions that he walks through the day to the convenience store. He picks his grandchildren from school & goes for his evening walks regularly. James is proud that he follows at least 80% of doctor's recommendations. Though, he goofs up a little on dietary aspect. James is confident that physicians are treating him right despite of the fact that his blood pressure has shown same high numbers for years and his cholesterol and diabetes have been with him since ages. James stomach often remains upset & he visits washroom to clear bowels once in 2 or 3 days. However, the most worrisome part is that James is convinced that his health state is stable and his health-defining numbers are stable. He has been able to maintain the same blood pressure & diabetes numbers in the last few years.

Food For Thought:

Is James' attitude towards his health condition correct? Should James only be following the medical advice and get away with his responsibility towards his health and illness? Do you think it is justified to lay off the responsibility of our health on a system that just knows us through a few tests and mechanical diagnosis? If yes, just think why is it that like James, all people who are on medications keep taking drugs forever without getting better? Does medication treat us or heal us? Who is responsible for our health and well-being? Does having a medical system in place mean that we stop all self-efforts to heal ourselves? Does our body accept the pills internally, the way our mind is convinced? Has the pill culture made us so lazy & unconcerned about our health?

Case Analysis:

From the disease management perspective, James is following medications and medical recommendations the same way as the entire world would do. Considering his already deteriorated health state, medications are much required. However, the other way to look at his health is that by keeping body on medications and by not changing himself, James is continuing to feed his illness. It acts something like cleaning a room from the front and keeping spreading the garbage on the back, hoping that the chamber will get clear someday! Unless James directs his personal efforts to stop spreading the garbage and makes efforts to clean the room, he may never be able to emerge clean and get disease-free. He has a pre-set notion that his health is his doctors' responsibility, which his doctor is well taking care of. He believes that whatever is being recommended to him medically must be followed wholeheartedly to get well. So, when a physician says it is ok if his bowels get cleaned once in two days, he is ok with the thought and does not make any effort to improve his condition by himself. If a doctor prescribes him to eat highly fibrous foods such as wheat or oat bran, these are the only changes that he will make to his diet. James is 100% hard wired to the instructions of his specialist. He simply does not possess the sense to think beyond disease management and begin thinking of health management and the healing aspect of his illness. When asked about his opinion, he simply mentions that he is doing all that has been prescribed to him. With that statement, he easily tends to escape the onus of his own responsibility towards his health. He is not interested in educating himself about the roots of his conditions. Neither is he interested in listening to what his body communicates & to act on healing himself from within.

To summarize, James' external symptoms of the disease may seem to get better with medications, yet, internally the following mind-body factors keep him devoid of enjoying a disease-free body:

- ❑ Feeding roots of his illness which could range from wrong dietary habits, lifestyle habits, sleeping patterns, stress or lack of body movement.
- ❑ Toxicity of medication safely termed as 'side-effects' including gastric issues, constipation, nausea, low moods, skin rashes or depression.
- ❑ Lack of attitude towards self-change.

- ❑ The belief that by investing all his faith in his treatment & by following doctor's recommendations, his job is done.

Our Beliefs:

Traditionally, all ancient healing therapies have always focussed on holistic internal healing including mind, body, and soul. However, modern developments in the area of health and medicine have largely separated all holistic aspects of human existence in the name of localized treatments. The 'magic-pill' culture rules the world because it is convenient, provides quick-fix, does not disturb one's existing lifestyle & keeps one rest assured that the problem is being taken care by an expert. Further, the following top most authorities have managed to convince the world that health & well-being responsibility of each individual is a medical and government affair.

FDA: Food and Drug Authority is the highest authority for defining nutritional and dietary standards. What FDA approves, the world follows. And so we are so glued to the calorie system of nutrition, than considering our own distinct uniqueness while seeking our health solutions.

Western Medicine: The mother of 'pill culture, ' western medicine has made life convenient and added years to one's life by treating the body with a pill! However, the great invention of the pill, if not combined with the right holistic efforts, fails to produce the desired results. Sadly, western medicine majorly vouches for only a 'pill,' versus focusing on a holistic aspect of healing along with the pill treatment.

Medical Insurance Companies: It is ironical that insurance companies are nothing to do with the actual treatments of an individual but manage to bag the biggest slice of cake when it comes to individual health. So, firstly the world was convinced that the responsibility of their health lies in the hands of medical and government authorities, and then health insurance sector emerged to further support the laziness of an irresponsible man by facilitating all funds and resources to get oneself treated. Though it is a much-required support in current times, it mainly cushions an individual with all the conveniences to get them treated without owning the responsibility for their health through other lifestyle factors. It is a prevailing thought process amongst people today that they need not worry about their health because western medicine has answers to their maladies and medical insurance covers them well to go for treatments of any highest degree.

Government: Government directives on health have gone westernized too. The existing policies are more about treating than healing, and the world moves accordingly! Governments do have a duty to provide their citizens with the affordable healthcare. However, it is individual's efforts and responsibility that produces the desired health results.

Having mentioned this, it is an undeniable fact that medical intervention is a must for people with illnesses that they couldn't prevent or they find hard to treat. The problem occurs when people blindly consider medications as total healing. For example, we quite often see that someone having diagnosed with a lung cancer after years of smoking considers taking a medical treatment only, in case they decide to quit. However, if this person takes the responsibility of his health and combines his own efforts with the treatment in terms of eliminating what caused him lung cancer, focussing on bettering his lung health, beginning to live life in a smoke-free environment, concentrating on breathing patterns and detoxifying himself, focussing on bringing down high levels of body acidity, there is a brighter chance that he regains his health holistically and much quickly.

Research suggests that modern lifestyle and conveniences in all walks of life have made it harder for the people to live a healthy, active lifestyle. The primary causes reported include:

- ❑ People think that self-health maintenance demands time and they do not have much time for themselves.

- ☐ People are too lazy and comfortable in modern conveniences to think beyond a pleasant day.
- ☐ People think that diet, exercise or lifestyle is a personal choice.
- ☐ People are ignorant about how adversely their actions can affect them.
- ☐ People run away from facts and truth and keep continuing their current lifestyle in false hopes.
- ☐ People do not care and believe that we have only one life, merry and rejoice.
- ☐ People think they lack funds, means or resources to care of themselves.

Facts:

In past few years, the modern health system has projected its quick health solutions in such a way that we believe our health is an external affair to be taken care by the specialists. However, if one thinks logically, when we suffer health problems it is we who feel the pinch and pain. When our body suffers from pain, it communicates to us in the form of uneasy feelings and symptoms, and yet we ignore and distrust our own body feelings and symptoms to find our solutions in a mechanical world. The body is highly intelligent and gives us clues as and when it feels uneasy. We must be the first ones to listen and act on it rightly than a machine detecting major issues within our body years later!

Destructive Facts:

- ☐ The majority of us get ourselves treated today than being healed.
- ☐ We have become the masters in managing technology, and misers in utilizing our ancient wisdom about managing our own health.

- ❑ We invest millions in gaining higher education. However, we have no knowledge about our own body functioning. Ultimately, after accumulating fortunes through our experience, we spend multi-millions in trying to gain back our health!
- ❑ Preventive health has just got limited to nutrition, exercise, and diet. There is much more to it!
- ❑ The 'pill-culture' is the most destructive culture ever, more hazardous than a nuclear war! Here, we are losing the war against self-created diseases, & sadly each individual is fighting his own war.
- ❑ We seek external solutions to our problems than internal analysis and investigation.

Owning the responsibility of our health begins with:

- ❑ Listening to our body and taking measures to heal health issues from their roots.
- ❑ Adopting a preventive diet and lifestyle pattern versus a treatment mindset.
- ❑ Maintaining balance in all aspects of life.
- ❑ Understanding how the human body operates and the unity of our existence at mind, body and soul level.
- ❑ Learning to breathe right.
- ❑ Taking measures towards proper elimination techniques to get rid of body wastes.
- ❑ Consuming natural foods.
- ❑ Steering away from destructive habits such as smoking, drinking, overeating, overworking and stressing.

Taking responsibility of your health will empower you to:

- ❑ Help connect with yourself.
- ❑ Understand yourself, your body and mind's needs in a better way.

- ❑ Listen to your body and take timely action before the body communicates its miseries in a harder way.
- ❑ Change yourself for better no matter what state of health you are in.
- ❑ Experience health and life in altogether a new way.
- ❑ Have a lifelong purpose to self-care & self-heal.
- ❑ Make right choices and decisions.
- ❑ Save yourself from unexpected health surprises.

Though this is easier said than done, knowing the important aspects of our own functioning will empower you to make right choices and decisions when it comes to health and well-being. The hard fact is, we do not get bothered until a disease strikes. However, we must understand that we can avoid disease situations altogether than living a tough, helpless, confused, painful and diseased life later, by owning the responsibility of our health and taking right measures to incorporate healthier lifestyles.

Holistic Perspective:

The ancient healing practices promote the concept of self-healing and self-care. These philosophies believe that nature had imparted humans and other life forms with all mechanisms and resources to be healthy and well. It is upto us to realize this fact and be responsible for ourselves.

Just think, in otherwise normal circumstances, have you ever come across any newborn baby entering the world either sick, with a fever, with a sore throat, cough or an allergy?

Why is it so?

Because nature intended us to be happy on earth and gave us life in a healthy form only.

Do you know of any life species that does not find what they need for survival on earth?

No, because nature provided us with all means and resources that were essential for the survival of all life forms. And so, nature also intended us to take care of ourselves with all the provided means in the right way. It is only because we have drifted away from this intent of nature that we are suffering the perils in the form of diseases.

Ayurveda takes health into the realm of personal responsibility. Once we 'Choose' to be a part of this realm, we stop looking ourselves as victims and our perception towards our health and diseases changes. We work towards healing ourselves versus treating ourselves. We become empowered to participate in our own healing process. Nature has imparted us with a healthy body and a sound mind naturally. It has blessed us with all resources to live healthily. It has imparted us wisdom to understand ourselves and act in accordance with nature. This is because nature never wanted us to be sick. This also means that we have invited our problems. We need not lead an unhealthy life under the shadow of pill culture. Through healthy living practices and by making ourselves aware of natural ancient healing systems we can survive at our full potential. However, this approach does not negate the value of western medicine in case of acute diseases, but simply gives us a holistic perspective to healing.

Take Away Thought:

Self-reflection is the key to being aware. Some important questions to self-reflect include:

- ❑ Thinking how we get sick, diseased or obese?
- ❑ Thinking whether we were born sick?

When you begin to think on these lines, you realize that most of it is what we have created for ourselves. It is the choices and decisions that we have made & the passive and convenience mode that we have switched to that is creating our diseases. Additionally, our blind faith on whatever the modern world offers, without using our sensibilities of right and wrong is deciding the course of our health & well-being.

Tips to be Self-Responsible About Our Health &Well-being:

- ❑ Do no ignore minor or routine health issues, as these are paving the route for bigger deficiencies.
- ❑ Be aware that both the creation and the healing of a disease is under your control.
- ❑ Be aware change begins with the mind and the body follows.
- ❑ Be mindful of the fact that the way we participate fully in the creation of our disease, similarly, we can also participate in the healing.
- ❑ Be aware of the side-effects of Western medicine. The side-effect is a disease in itself.
- ❑ Be aware that handing over our health's full responsibility in the hands of an outside system may cost us physically, emotionally, physiologically and financially.
- ❑ Be mindful of the fact that healing does not begin externally but internally.
- ❑ Do not focus on treating symptoms but cure the roots.
- ❑ Be conscious of what you eat, live, exercise routinely.
- ❑ Be aware that your body responds to the impact of positivity equally the way it responds to the impact of negativity.
- ❑ Ignite the will to change, you will never repent.
- ❑ Our original nature is to be happy and healthy naturally.
- ❑ Help yourself with right sources and the right environment for healing.
- ❑ If possible, get in touch with a holistic health practitioner who can mentor and guide you about the true roots of health and wellness.

CHAPTER 13 - LACK OF FOCUS ON THE RIGHT FOUNDATIONS OF EXCELLENT HEALTH

'In traditional times, the art of maintaining health & well-being had been the most cherished legacy being passed from generations to generations globally. This art has gotten lost in the midst of lifestyle pressures, financial management, convenience foods, industrialization & modernization!'

Scenario

Shally, 25, is a little heavy & holds a negative image about herself. She is quite inspired by the glamor world and seeks to be perfect physically. She plans to go under the knife for quick slimming results. She followed a diet plan for quite some time that made her lose some weight, but at the same time left her weaker, frail and irritable. She likes fried, junk and heavy foods. She exercises 2 hours each day to get into perfect shape. She admits getting obsessive about her self-image. Her grandma did her best to counsel her about the holistic foundations of health, but Shally is more influenced and convinced by the modern methods of weight loss. Her irritability over her self-image is a direct clue of the self-created pressure that she is feeling.

Food For Thought:

Does Shally bank a lot on modern ways versus right foundations of achieving her health goals? Has the modern world made us believe that health and wellness is sold in clinics? According to you what must be the first transformational step for Shally to achieve her goals? Do you think with a negative self-image she will ever be able to enjoy herself even if she achieves her goal?

Case Analysis:

Shally's is unaligned with the right foundations of health and well-being. Her negativity makes her desperate and keeps her away from looking at her goals from a holistic perspective. Shally is exploring modern ways to achieve weight and inch loss without considering or trying out her grandma's thoughtful suggestions and living life in accordance with nature. She is not ready to examine her eating habits, her waking and sleeping patterns, her digestive health, her food choices as an important measure to achieve weight loss. Shally is exercising in excess without realizing that too much exercise may give her other problems. To summarize, Shally is directionless about her goals & carries a negative mindset about herself. She is ready to try the modern unnatural ways of weight-loss rather than working on transforming the foundations that gave her pounds.

Our Beliefs:

Our way of dealing with our problems has lost a natural touch. We do not think the root cause of our problems anymore. For example, for some of the below-mentioned problem areas, realize the quick fixes that we seek and the foundations that must be considered:

Problem Areas	Our Immediate Responses to our problems	Holistic Foundations – The Way to go
Weight Loss	Fad diets like protein diet, medications, surgery, any and every exercise	Holistic diet and lifestyle approach considering mind and body healing together, proper rest and relaxation, sleep, controlling overeating and unnatural food habits and consuming the right foods

(Continued)

Sleep Issues	Medication, over exercising	Waking and sleeping early, realizing and reducing the stress factors, moving and relaxing the body and mind, staying away from stimulating activities later at night, limiting the television time, creating right sleeping environment, reducing toxic burden, consuming foods meant for relaxation
Disturbed Thoughts/ Emotional Issues/Stress	Living with the emotional issues majority of the time, consulting a phycologist or a physiatrist, consuming medications	Finding the cause of disturbed thoughts, strategizing, getting involved in peaceful activities like meditation, pursuing a passion or anything that cuts one off, including relaxation therapies in one's routine, addressing shallow breathing patterns, spending time with family and friends
Fatigue/ Headache	Medications, living with the problem, consulting doctors after doctors	Stress control, finding techniques to relax, nourishing oneself with nutritious foods, toxicity control, being away from polluted environment as much as possible, spending limited time with gadgets, spending time outside in nature and amidst greenery
Digestive/ Gastric Issues	Anti-acids, living with the issues while not controlling the causes	Changing our dietary and lifestyle habits, consuming more digestive system strengthening foods, consuming more alkaline foods, taking measures to get rid of body acidity

(Continued)

Allergies	Anti-allergic medications	Eliminating allergy causing foods including dairy, consuming foods to strengthen the immune system, exercising to better lung functioning, equipping oneself nutritionally, avoiding allergy-inducing triggers, incorporating self-care techniques in daily routine

We see above that our responses to our problems today are limited to fixing them quickly. We lack the understanding that these issues are bound to bounce back with greater intensity if not taken care from their roots. And so we see how the entire world continues to get diseased with numerous quick fixes.

Facts:

Consider what constitutes a human being? What are the needs of human body and mind? If you begin exploring the answers for these, you come down to the parameters that define the foundations of good health and well-being. And so, we conclude that our life primarily sustains on the following aspects:

- ❑ 'Air' inhaled in the form of freely available oxygen rather than polluted smoky environment or paid scents.
- ❑ 'Water' consumed in the form of mineralized water rather than in the form of aerated drinks and alcohol.
- ❑ 'Food' from nature's resources rather than fancy foods wrapped in impressive packaging.
- ❑ 'The Sunshine' taken freely rather than being in artificially heated or air-conditioned environments.
- ❑ 'Rest and Relaxation' to be consciously focused routinely rather than making time for it as and when convenient.
- ❑ 'Sleep' to be taken seriously for optimal body functioning rather than compromising on it in the name of work or

entertainment.

- ❑ 'Family and Few Friends' to spend a good time with rather than having hundreds of friends while all are unavailable.
- ❑ 'Positive Thoughts and Emotions' to be chosen rather than living with the negativities.
- ❑ 'Pleasure and Happiness' derived from our area of interest rather than living fake under work pressures and stress.
- ❑ 'Livable Environment' to be consciously created rather than blaming authorities.

Any other attribute in life builds upon these foundations. If these foundations are weak, we cannot enjoy other pleasures.

Holistic Perspective:

'When the foundation of good health has been laid, by making the most of the sunshine, fresh air, sleep, water, and food, it will be time to turn to the little details about the care of one's complexion, hair, teeth, and nails.' – Vatyayana

Though the phrase above is more inclined towards the beauty to be laid on right foundations, it is important to be aware that anything in life is laid upon these foundational factors. Compromising on the quantity or quality of these factors affects us slowly and steadily each single day.

The foundations of health and well-being are laid upon harmony between the body, mind, and soul. When one is free from physical disabilities and mental distractions, one experiences real bliss far different from the definition of pleasure and happiness at the superficial level. Health and well-being is not just about diet and exercise. It is the unity of various areas of life and so we as human beings are holistic in nature.

When it comes to the internal functioning of our body, the ancient healing practitioners focused on the following as important signals of one's health and wellness state:

- ❑ Proper chewing
- ❑ Healthy Digestion
- ❑ Proper absorption and assimilation
- ❑ Balance between consumption and elimination
- ❑ Sweating
- ❑ Breathing
- ❑ Body movement
- ❑ Nutritionally equipped body
- ❑ Positive & calm mind
- ❑ Mind free of disturbances
- ❑ Sleep, Rest, and Relaxation
- ❑ Self-caring
- ❑ Enough resources to lead pleasurable & happy life
- ❑ Doing work that gives one pleasure & not working out of bondage
- ❑ Sense of inquisitiveness and exploration towards the mysteries of life

Take Away Thought:

Health and well-being is more than being free from a disease. Achieving and maintaining health is more of a holistic approach to be focused upon in all important areas of life. Diet, exercise, work, relationships, passions and stability of mind all come under the vast umbrella of true foundations of health & well-being.

The journey to healing the foundation of our health may begin with:

- ❑ Consuming the right foundational, strengthening, body building and nourishing foods.
- ❑ Practicing & maintaining peace and calm through breathing and meditative techniques.

- [ ] Understanding your instincts.
- [ ] Achieving beauty goals naturally through natural self-care techniques & nature's own beauty secrets.
- [ ] Stretching to open up the body.
- [ ] Living life as per the biological rhythms, which means eating meals at the right time, sleeping and waking up at the right time.

CHAPTER 14 - FOCUS ON EXTERNAL TREATMENTS THAN INTERNAL HEALING

'You come out of your kitchen either healthy & radiant or diseased. There is no third aspect to it. So, if your system seems out of balance, first look into your kitchen & practice healing, & later look at a medical centre for getting treated!'

Scenario

Garima, 38, is an enthusiastic women entrepreneur who suffered from eczema for a decade until 2 years ago. When she first met me her skin was in bad shape. Her skin had been peeling throughout the body & she was too sensitive to tolerate the sun. She was itching all day and had developed a social stigma because of which she gave up her career. She figured it as an allergic reaction to something that her body was not accepting, and it manifested into eczema. She had consulted the best dermatologists. She had tried everything including topical solutions, steroid-based treatments, and therapies. However, her skin condition was getting worse. From the mind-body connect perspective, Garima got a big hit on her self-confidence due to her physical state. After multiple failures in her treatment efforts, Garima decided to transform her foundation after she heard me talking about these concepts in a workshop. Soon after she consulted and began her transformation. Surprisingly enough, a decade old problem was 80% better in just 21 days. It was when Garima set her focus on internal healing, Garima reaped much more benefits than just gaining back her skin health.

Food For Thought:

What do you do when you face health problems? Do you seek solutions in the outside world? Does Garima's remarkable transformation make you believe in inner healing? Why is it that despite of having best treatments available, the diseases that must decline are increasing?

Case Analysis:

Garima has gone through a remarkable transformation by primarily believing in herself & by focussing on the roots of her problem. Her eczema was a manifestation of her allergic reactions to various foods & her lifestyle. These factors had weakened her immune system & eczema was the symptom. Garima adopted right ways to eat and live, making conscious decision to transform, choosing to look for internal solutions and sticking to her decision to change. As a result, she could get rid of her decade-old skin problem that no medication could cure. She got completely ok in a few days through all natural dietary and lifestyle recommendations. She realized that holistic health and well-being is not just about diet and exercise, but about adopting a balanced & holistic approach in all areas of life. She also realized that as per her body type she must live a particular lifestyle only to be healthy & well. Today, Garima continues to live and follow the transformational dietary and lifestyle recommendations. She enjoys a much more smooth, soft and supple skin. She is too happy as her skin now has an even tone, glows, and is more radiant. As a bonus, her family is eating much healthier food. She acknowledges that her problem was gone in a couple of months but what remains with her forever now is the knowledge and understanding about herself. She learned a valuable lesson through this consultation that our solutions lie within & we just keep finding them outside!

Our Beliefs:

External treatments are what we bank upon today. Our faith in quick solutions is making us sicker, and we still do not accept the fact! External treatment or inner healing is a matter of individual choice, but it is important to know how the two aspects work.

When faced with a health disaster our first and only reaction is to get ourselves treated. Consider the case of cancer. The entire world knows that chemotherapy is the way to go to treat cancer. But just think, does it fade away the probability of you acquiring cancer again? No, because what caused your cancer still exists. Treatments do treat & give a person a false sense of confidence that all is well internally when it is not really so. Cancer & Tumors can be burned away, but if you do not put a stop on what caused cancer, the probability of recurrence becomes high. It is high time to correct our belief system about our health.

Facts:

Treatments are much more than common side-effects. If the trends are to be followed, it is quite obvious that people despite of seeking best treatments continue to suffer more and more from allergies, cold, flu, cough, hormonal issues, menopausal problems, cancer, heart disease, lupus, multiple sclerosis, muscular dystrophy, diabetes, asthma, joint, neck, back pain, migraine headaches, acid reflux, ulcers, stomach problems, chronic fatigue, insomnia, Irritable Bowel Syndrome (IBS), sexual dysfunction, infertility, arthritis, constipation, fibromyalgia, prostate problems, yeast infections depression, stress, anxiety, bad skin, acne, dandruff and other health issues. More and more children are being diagnosed with attention deficit disorder and hyperactivity. More and more people are getting diagnostic testing done such as blood tests and X-rays. More and more people are on non-prescription drugs like never before. And doctors are seeing more patients than ever before, despite of tremendous medical advancements.

External Treatments Versus Internal Healing

External Treatments	Internal Healing
Includes simpler applicability	Includes balancing methods such as nutritional balancing, tai chi, yoga, massage therapy demand equal involvement from the individual
Follows one-size-fits-all approach	Considers each individual unique based on specific gene traits, body constitution & condition
Camouflages deeper problems by providing relief from warning symptoms. For example, simple fatigue can be a signal of underlying disease, but this approach suppresses the symptom to make one feel ok at the outer superficial level	Approach includes eliminating the deeply rooted toxicity, which means a person initially may feel worse because of a lot of suppressed toxicity being broken and mixed into the body and blood for removal
Patients never really get well because the philosophy is not about making you well internally but making you feel relieved externally	Patients heal from within and experience a new realm of energy and approach to a new life
Creates more imbalances within the body in the name of treating the health issue	Works on the foundation to balance body imbalances
Quite expensive	Quite affordable or may even be free
Works on body or mind individually	Works on body, mind, and soul collectively

(Continued)

Causes 'adverse effects' or side effects. Side effects happen due to the interconnectedness of the body. As this approach heals only the main problem area, it doesn't consider other areas that might get impacted due to the original treatment. Remember, It is impossible to just change one part of the body without affecting the rest of it.	Since it works on body, mind, and soul all together in a natural way, it heals all together and does reverse your health conditions at all levels
Provides symptomatic relief	Heals as well as provides symptomatic solutions
Sets problems deeper inside	Brings issues to the surface to eliminate
Does not consider patients history or background while recommending. The patient may choose or not choose to change their habits and ways.	Considers a person's complete history and background and requires one to change their dietary and lifestyle habits for healing
Disease keeps progressing at slower rate	Disease keeps diminishing at slower rate
Looks at minor nagging health issues as one-time episodes to be treated through medication for quick relief	Looks at minor nagging health concerns as the greatest clues of something else manifesting inside
Health overtime gets worse even if one gets relieved of their general health concerns. Overtime episodes of these health problems become stronger	Health overtime gets better, one becomes cleaner and energetic form within and may turn back the roots of one's disease

(Continued)

The process of external treatment makes one lazy, too dependent upon convenience. It unintentionally makes people lose wisdom to think of one's health as one's responsibility	The process of inner healing transforms a person at mind, body and soul level. It teaches self-contentment, discipline, patience, persistence, honesty, happiness. It provides one a purpose for life and builds mental skills, emotional skills and attributes that tend to create health and well-being on a longer-term basis. It is more of a lifestyle than atemporary fix. It works on unraveling the layers of physical, emotional, mental and spiritual imbalances gently, and so you come out as a transformed being.

Holistic Perspective:

For centuries, people have turned to natural ways of healing based on their understanding of their relationship with the nature. Another aspect of healing in ancient times was not to prolong or keep living with minor illnesses and to root them off before any minor health issue becomes a major one in no time! Our ancestors did not used to linger on with ailments and were quite particular about applying natural healing remedies to ward off their issues from its root as soon as the body showed signs of disturbances. For example, in ancient times honey-ginger juice was considered to be an excellent remedy to ward off a cough and cold even if it aggravated the problem initially. Similarly, fermented foods were considered as a natural remedy to balance the intestinal flora to get rid of digestive disorders. Sleep and rest were considered as important aspects of holistic healing. The healing principles worked on the fact that either our system suffers from deficiencies or is in an imbalanced state that it begins to show the signs of imbalances in the form of physical issues. However, today honey-ginger juice has been replaced by cold and cough medications that wrap a cough with a superficial quick fix that dries up the phlegm and blocks the surrounding areas including sinuses. This provides immediate relief but creates other imbalances. Fermented foods have been replaced by anti-acids that do nothing to improve the underlying cause but work something like putting water on the fire at a superficial level. Similarly, the theory of creating balance has been replaced by getting quick relief, even though the diseases keep resting in a volcanic state deep within.

The literature of Ayurveda and Traditional Chinese Medicine emphasize that every human being is a creation of the elements of nature including earth, fire, water, metal, space, and air. These elements actually form us physically and show up in the form of blood, bones, muscles and other body parts. The advanced theory of such concepts explains how body organs, feelings, emotions, behaviors and external forces are so closely associated with each other that any disturbance in one single area can entirely change a person's physical, emotional and mental state of being. Nature's elements that form us include:

Elements of Nature	**Association With Human Body**
Earth	Earth element signifies the dense, heavy and hard matter. It is known to bind other elements including fire, water, and air in various proportions. All solid structures and tissues within our body such as bones, nails, teeth, muscles, cartilage, tendons, skin and hair are considered to be the manifestations of the earth element. After death when burnt, earth elements become earth (its original eternal form) back again by burying or burning the body. The dominant Earth element in an individual is visible in the following traits:

(Continued)

	Positive Qualities: Reliable, Ambitious, Sober, Respectful, Consistent, Perseverance, Punctual, Cautious, Responsible, Careful, Firm, Stable, Strength, Comfort, Grounded, etc. Negative Qualities: Sensitive, Irregular, Timid, Superficial, Lazy, Indifferent, etc. Physical and emotional imbalances of Earth element arise in the solid structures of the body, for example, bone disorders, obesity, weight loss and weight gain, etc.
Water	Water element signifies the body liquids and the soft matter of the body. It contains magnetic properties. All fluids within our body such as blood, tissues liquid, saliva, nasal secretions, digestive juices, eye secretions and fluids within the cell are considered to be the manifestations of thewater element. The dominant Earth element in an individual is visible in the following traits: Positive Qualities: Intuitive, Understanding, Mild, Trustworthy, Devoted, Forgiving, Modest, Compassionate and Internally Focused. Negative Qualities: Rigid, Lack of Risk Taking Capability, Heartless, Unstable, etc. Physical and emotional imbalances of Water element are associated with the liquid body states such as phlegm issues including cold, sinus, asthma; blood disorders including clotting and blood thinning, kidney issues, etc.
Fire	Fire element signifies the hot and light aspects of the body. It consists of electrical and creative properties. Within our body, it is associated with the heat generating or heat requiring activities including enzyme functioning, regulating body temperature, digesting, absorbing and assimilating foods, regulating metabolism. It is further considered that all body fluids such as blood, tissues liquid, saliva, nasal secretions, digestive juices, eye secretions and fluids within the cell are the manifestations of the water element. The dominant Earth element in an individual is visible in the following traits:

(Continued)

	Positive Qualities: Will, Desire, Lust, Power of Creativity, Decisiveness, Zeal, Enthusiasm, Power, Passion, Courage, Recognition, Appreciation, etc. Negative Qualities: Irritability, Quarrelsomeness, Jealousy, Hatred, Anger, etc. Physical and emotional imbalances of Fire element are associated with skin diseases, coldness or fever, loss of energy, mental disorders, mental illness, diabetes, and acidity, etc.
Air	Air element signifies the moving, cold and rough aspects of the body. It is a detaching or temporary element and enables co-existence of fire and water elements. Physically and emotionally it is associated with every body movement including intestinal movement, lungs contraction, muscular movement, movement in each cell, thought, desire and will. The air element can be felt consciously through the breath activity, however, at atomic level air remains around us eternally. The dominant Earth element in an individual is visible in the following traits: Positive Qualities: Knowledgeable, Free, Joyous, Smiling, Trusted, Clear, Thoughtful, Intellectual, Aware, Independent, Optimistic, etc. Negative Qualities: Dishonest, Cunning, Lack of Perseverance, Gossip, Inconsistent, etc. Physical and emotional imbalances of Air element are associated with blood problems such as hypertension, lung disorders, nervous disorders, depression, etc.
Space	Space element signifies the clear, subtle and space aspects of the body. Physically it is associated with the spaces in the body including the mouth, abdomen, respiratory problems, nostrils, thorax, and cells.

(Continued)

	Vibrations travel in space as well as within our body. The dominant Earth element in an individual is visible in the following traits: Positive Qualities: Centered, Transcendence, Transformative, Timeless, etc. Physical and emotional imbalances of Space element are associated with throat problems, speech disorders, epilepsy, thyroid disorders, ear diseases, etc.

The existence of entire universe including humans comprises of these 5 elements. With varying composition and balance of these elements, all nature's resources & life-forms are formed. Universe or any life form cannot exist if any element is eliminated. The law of nature states that nature strives to maintain this balance internally in all life forms and externally in the universe. Additionally, to make these elements come live in all life forms through the 'Life-Force. 'Diseases are considered to be nothing but manifestations of the impact of imbalances in these 5 elements in our body. The healing mechanism of ancient practices is based on creating balance at this foundational level. When the balance of energy and these 5 elements is restored, an individual begins to get better physically, emotionally and spiritually. This happens automatically because health, wellness & spiritual inclination is the original nature of human beings.

To understand the manifestation of these 5 elements in nature, let's see its applicability in real life.

- ❑ Roots of a plant that absorb water and minerals from the Earth for growth – Elements of Earth and Water come into being here.
- ❑ Tree breathes through its leaves – Element of Air comes into being here.
- ❑ Tree receives warmth and light from the sun–Element of Fire comes into being here.

- ❑ Like the original nature of fire to burn and release, wood from trees when set on fire, releases other elements. Water evaporates, ash becomes back Earth that that further becomes minerals for other life forms. Oxygen is released from trees & enables the burning process to make wood ash.

And throughout the lifecycle of any life form, these 5 elements keep interplaying and shifting roles at varying degrees to sustain life.

Take Away Thought:

The concept of internal healing is an age-old concept and has been used by our ancestors for ages. Modern medicine operates on treatments, for example, bones, tissues, muscles, blood, and other parts and organs of the body. Where the ancient wisdom suggests restoring the balance of body and mind, modern medicine focusses on the issues created in body parts and organs due to the imbalances in underlying forces. Internal healing is a deeper science, whereas modern medicine is an on-the-surface science.

Though inner healing or external treatments is a matter of personal choice, at all levels of being this choice decides whether one experiences a happy and healthy state of being or a sick and disturbed state of being.

CHAPTER 15 - RADIATION FROM GADGETS – LIMIT GADGET TIME

'Diseases thrive on triggers & have their starting points. In the disease world, the latest trigger is electromagnetic radiation. If It does not make you die, certainly it is dragging you towards it!'

Scenario

Jim, 35, is an investment banker who had been diagnosed with a brain tumor five years ago. For a case study on the potential dangers of cell-phone radiation, one of the researchers got in touch with him. Jim had been quite open and vocal about his health issue and explained to the researcher that his tumor was located just behind his right ear. Talking about his profile as an investment banker, he further mentioned that in investment banking they had been using cell phones since 1990's. He admits that on being diagnosed with atumor, he immediately suspected it could be a result of his excessive cell-phone usage. Trying to self-reflect on the causes that may have caused him a tumor, he tried talking to his neurosurgeon about the probable causes. To his surprise, the neurosurgeon mentioned that he is seeing more and more cases of cell-phone-induced tumors, specifically in young, healthy businessmen who had been using their cell phones obsessively. To another surprise, some official acquaintances of Jim had already died from brain cancer, and the more such young tumor cases he encountered, the more certain he felt that it wasn't a coincidence!

Food For Thought:

Do you think radiation from cell phones or microwaves may cause health hazards? Are you using cell phones, microwaves and other radiation emitting gadgets obsessively? Do you take detox measures to strengthen yourself so that the radiation impacts you less? Do you take any protective measures to limit radiation exposure? Are you even aware what these gadgets may do to you or to your child? Do you ever consider radiation in your work environment to be a cause of your health issues such as nausea, dizziness, headaches or other? Do you think high radiation exposure is anything to do with high incidences of emotional and behavioral problems in children?

Case Analysis:

Though the research on the potentially harmful effects of radiation has not picked serious wave and is still happening discretely, cases like Jims' make one believe that excess of everything including gadget and technology is unhealthy. Though there are no research studies that directly correlate Jim's tumor state with his excessive usage of cellphones, time and again there have been numerous pointers that indicate that after viruses, bacteria and lifestyle disorders, radiation may be the next-generation carrier of diseases. Jim could sense and relate his condition could be due to overuse of cellphones, considering knowing few other official acquaintances who faced the same health state & who shared the same profile as his – 'High cell-phone usage profile!' Further, his doctor confirming of seeing many young technology-oriented patients walking in with similar health conditions, makes his trust grow stronger! Quite probable, you may not die of radiation; the fact that it may take you closer to a weakened health state cannot be denied. Probably you may not die of radiation, but symptoms like nausea, headache, diarrhea, malaise, and fever at your workplace or car or home in a radiation-full environment, may be good indicators of your future health state.

Our Beliefs:

Gadgets and technology are integral elements of our world today. It is a matter of pride for anyone to own the latest iPhone model, or even knowing about its latest feature list even before the phone gets launched. Women undoubtedly are hooked to gadgets much more than their families and children. Men own more devices than the number of friends. Children seem to chill out with gadgets in their peer group and owning devices is considered is to be a mark of status-symbol among youngsters. When talked about the type of devices in vogue, mobile phones, iPads, cameras and laptop all top the list! Everyone aims to own all and get addicted to the virtual world. We see the technology addiction seeping into the most basics of our daily life. Two neighbors talk over cell-phone, children's books are replaced by iPads, and people carry laptops instead of handbags today.

Our beliefs and close association with gadgets and technology is slowly becoming a grave concern.

- ❑ We know cellphones, microwaves, iPads and other wireless tablet systems emit harmful radiation.
- ❑ We do not bother to practice precautions. For example, iPad recommends users to hold the iPad eight inches from an adult body, which is a distance far greater than most toddlers' arms. Hardly have we seen anyone following the security instructions.
- ❑ Our babies play with gadgets versus toys and toddlers are growing and learning amidst the gadget world.
- ❑ Babies sleep listening to music being played under their pillows. We are actually sleeping with our murderers – the radiation emitting gadgets!
- ❑ Our children look for gadgets all the time for all their activities including study, entertainment, time-pass, travel or just sitting among friends chatting with each other than talking directly.
- ❑ Headaches, dizziness, sleep disorders and tumors have become a regular part of our life, quite probably due to the impact of radiation.

Sadly, with such visible signs and impact on health, we are still waiting for some more proofs and disasters to be exposed by the researchers before we begin to take steps to limit our radiation exposure!

Facts:

'There is no question EMFs (Electromagnetic Fields) have a major effect on neurological functioning. They slow our brain waves and affect our long-term mental clarity. We should minimize exposures as much as possible to optimize neurotransmitter levels and prevent deterioration of health' - Eric Braverman, MD, Brain researcher and Director of Path Medical in New York City and The PATH Foundation.

Thinking of life without technology and gadgets is tough today. Communication, organization, employment and social engagements, each single group activity is dependent upon technology and gadgets. Whether it is a cellphone, a laptop, an MP3 music player or an iPad, all aspects of life do not seem to function unless we are technologically connected.

However, when it comes to our health, we hardly know the facts about the dark side of technology.

Hard-to-Believe but Important-to-Know Facts About Technology & Gadgets:

- ❑ A study on mobile phones conducted by Dr. Ewa Gustafsson, a researcher, and ergonomist at the University of Gothenburg, Sweden, stated that out of 56 young adults who habitually send text messages every day, half of them suffered from the arm, wrist, neck, and back pain.
- ❑ A study conducted by a Swedish team in 2004, indicated that regular use of a cell phone for over a decade was directly associated with an increased risk of brain tumor. Another publication titled 'Public Health Implications of Wireless Technologies' reported that the use of cell phones before the age of 20 increased the risk of brain tumors by five

times. A study done by French national case-control in 2014 indicated a possible connection between heavy cell phone use and brain tumors and increased risk of gliomas by 8 times.

- ❑ The headlines in a few highly reputable international newspapers and journals over the past few years mention the following:
  - ❍ Hamburg Morgenpost in 2006: 'Are we telephoning ourselves to death?'
  - ❍ Danish journal Dagens Medicine: 'Mobile phones affect the brain's metabolism. '
  - ❍ Agence France-Presse in December 2007: 'Israeli study says regular mobile use increases tumorrisk. '
  - ❍ London's Independent in January 2008: 'Mobile phone radiation wrecks your sleep. '
  - ❍ Australia's The Age in September 2008, : 'Scientists warn of cell phone cancer risk. '
- ❑ Studies suggest a relationship between cell phone usage and reduced sperm count and quality.
- ❑ In newborn babies, infants, toddlers and young children the exposure to cell phone radiation penetrates far deeper than midbrain as their skulls are thinner.

A. Host of Radiation Hazards the World is Suffering From:

Technology and the gadget world is going to cause havoc in future, and the effects have already begun to show in people associated with technology since a decade or more. Some emerging and visible signs of destruction from radiation include:

Cancer: Most commonly linked cancers include brain, skin, leukemia, breast, thyroid and stomach.

Back Pain: Multiple back pains are a direct consequence of the excessive use of gadgets and humped postures.

Sleep Disorders: There is a scientific reason behind developing sleep disorders due to excessive use of gadgets. The artificial light from a cellphone or a laptop interferes in the production of melatonin that is a hormone that stabilizes the human body's natural time cycle or body clock. As light is associated with activity and wakefulness, our brain confuses this artificial light with wakefulness and signals you to be awake. This light simply interferes with our natural body clock in the form of disturbed hormones. High exposure to gadgets at the night time has become a major concern as it has been reported to manifest into stress, sleep disorders, depression, behavioral & performance issues in children and adults.

Dry Eyes: Eyes are the most directly affected part of the body due to excessive usage of gadgets. Research suggests that the people in Information, Communication, and Technology (ICT) field report a maximum number of itchy, dry eye or multiple infections cases.

Stress: Your easy accessibility through a cell-phone means that any important and unimportant matter can be communicated instantly. While trivial matters still can be put to rest, all of us tend to tense over important calls. Reaching out anyone anywhere just does not let your mind switch off and be at rest anytime of the day. This indirect stress does build up in mind and manifests into shoulder pains, back pain or any other unexplained pains.

Infertility: With many people in urban set-ups seeking fertility consultations, this aspect of gadgets and technology is one of the most talked about topics in the world. Though we may hesitate to admit technology as a probable cause of infertility, research suggests that using a cellphone for more than 18 hours in the day can decrease the production of sperms in a man. However, we know infertility is becoming a reality as technology and gadgets are becoming a craze!

Tennis Elbow: Often referred to as Tennis Elbow, it is the soreness of the elbow caused due to excessive use of gadgets. It hampers the blood circulation in the elbow area.

Physical Strains: For the ones working in Information Communication & Technology (ICT), it is no secret that they tend to suffer from inflamed tendons, thumb joints, and index fingers. Continuous pressing, tapping and swiping leads to overuse of thumbs and index fingers. There have been real life instances where the index fingers of people have been operated due to damage from excessive tapping and pressing keys all the time.

Poor Posture: Poor posture among children is becoming more and more prominent. Forward head, hunched back, rounded shoulders, frozen wrists have started to show up as health issues in younger children. And we know childhood habits die hard. Additionally, the curvature of bones and cartilages forms in childhood. Since child's bones are soft and flexible, what is formed in the childhood becomes really tough to correct in adulthood because thebody takes that form. Specifically in children, limiting gadget time and pointing them on poor posture must be each parent's due responsibility! A proper posture makes all the difference between a confident child with agreat personality and a shy child struggling to better their personality later in life.

Riskful Pregnancy: What is outside gets penetrated deeper inside. So, a pregnant woman in front of light and radiation of gadgets may have a direct impact on the fetus. It may slow down the rate of brain development of the fetus and may make it a hyperactivity baby with behavioral issues. The number of hyperactive children outgrow normal children today. Could exposure to technology be a probable cause behind it!!!

Obesity: One of the most noticeable impacts of being hooked to technology is obesity. It makes you lazy, a couch potato, sedentary, disconnected from the actual world and making you to just eat, eat and eat!!! The ultimate effect manifests as obesity.

Aggression: Children & adults today are quite aggressive. It could be exposure to aggressive content or will to own and be with gadgets all the time or some innate feelings of loneliness or just an innate desire to show-off in the peer group. Whatever it is, the result is aggression which is quite visible in people's behaviors today.

Hypersensitivity: Symptoms such as burning sensations, fatigue, sleep disturbances, dizziness, headaches, feeling sick, heart palpitations, and even issues with the digestive system are quite on the rise in people due to electromagnetic rays. It is termed as sensitivity to electromagnetic rays!

Cognitive Effects: A study done in 2009 confirmed that overuse of mobile phones leads to slower response times and impacts working memory. It further confirmed that performance also gets affected with high radiation exposure.

B. Blake Levitt, the Former New York Times journalist and author of 'Electromagnetic Fields' mentions:

'Ambient man-made electromagnetic fields (EMFs), across a range of frequencies, are a serious environmental issue. Yet most environmentalists know little about it, perhaps because the subject has been the purview of physicists and engineers for so long that biologists have lost touch with electromagnetism's fundamental inclusion in the biological paradigm. All living cells and indeed whole living beings, no matter what genus or species, are dynamic coherent electrical systems utterly reliant on bioelectricity for life's most basic metabolic processes. It turns out that most living things are fantastically sensitive to vanishingly small EMF exposures. Living cells interpret such exposures as part of our normal cellular activities (think heartbeats, brainwaves, cell division itself, etc.) The problem is, man-made electromagnetic exposures aren't "normal. " They are artificial artifacts, with unusual intensities, signaling characteristics, pulsing patterns, and wave forms, that don't exist in nature. And they can misdirect cells in myriad ways. Every aspect of the ecosystem may be affected, including all living species from animals, humans, plants and even microorganisms in water and soil. We are already seeing problems in sentinel species like birds, bats, and bees. Wildlife is known to abandon areas when cell towers are placed. Radiofrequency radiation

(RF)—the part of the electromagnetic spectrum used in all-things-wireless today—is a known immune system suppressor, among other things. RF is a form of energetic air pollution and we need to understand it as such. Humans are not the only species being affected. The health of our planet may be in jeopardy from this newest environmental concern—added to all the others. Citizens need to call upon the government to fund appropriate research and to get industry influence out of the dialogue. We ignore this at our own peril now.'

Holistic Perspective:

GURUKULS

The ancient Vedic education culture of India consisted of 'Gurukuls, 'where children were supposed to learn and become knowledgeable amidst nature. Gurukul was the schooling system that was residential in nature & was generally situated in quiet, calm, serene and green environments preferably near forests, lakes or rivers, far away from ornate architectures of ancient times. It was a place where children learned amidst green and friendly environment with no distractions around them. On bright days and in favorable weather conditions the classes used to be held under the shelter of the trees. In the rainy season, the Gurukul operated under thatched roof.

Now, why do you think that was the case? Why is it that the kings of great kingdoms would want to send their children to a simple, plain nature-based Gurukul when they could have afforded to build ornate learning centers for their children? Why is it that the Gurukuls were not ornate structures with high-end décor? What could have been the reason behind constructing Gurukuls amidst dense nature like forests and lakes? Why would the teachers conduct classes and learning sessions in an open environment versus closed rooms?

So, this probably answers our questions that humans are direct beings of nature and the old generations reaffirmed the thought that children must be exposed to nature in their formative years. Learning and growing amidst nature makes them respectful and empathetic towards other people and animals. It makes them positive and imparts them cosmic energy to live happy and healthy through their lifetime.

Connect with nature is how humans have been designed to function and operate. This fact is highly being taken for granted in modern times. We become alive with the energy of the cosmos and our connect with nature is a much-required need of our body and mind.

Taking of gadgets and radiation from a holistic perspective, the worst negative aspect of this trend has been that it has made us lose track of our surroundings and nature and intoxicated us with technology.

To steer away from the adverse effects of radiation and gadgets, there is nothing like limiting exposure and living by the rules of nature. However, with all areas of life so deeply connected to technology, we cannot manage to disown technology. So, the key here is to go holistic by strengthening our health foundation & practicing precautions. We must begin creating basic health and strong immune system. One must focus on alkalinity, well-functioning body, focus on organ strength and aiding the movement of the lymphatic system. We must reduce the consumption of acidic, chemical-cased processed foods to strengthen our defense mechanisms. Cutting dairy is also a significant step towards creating radiant health!

Take Away Thoughts:

Electronic devices such as cell phones, cellular antennas, network towers, microwaves and cordless phones emit aninvisible fog of electromagnetic waves that exposes us to serious health risks. Researchers term it as a next generation destructive power for the human race.

It is important to move along with the changing times, yet sensibility is about being rooted to the right ways of living life and not over indulging in anything. Maintaining equilibrium in all areas of life is the key to living through radiation and its side effects.

Few Take Aways Include:

- ❑ Limit cell-phone usage per day.
- ❑ Interact with people face to face versus on cell-phones.
- ❑ Follow the usage instruction provided along with the gadgets.
- ❑ Work on the habit of engaging yourself in the constructive body and mind-building activities.
- ❑ Avoid high radiation exposure in case of children as much as possible.
- ❑ Educate yourself about the hazards of technology, gadgets, and radiation.
- ❑ Sleep gadget free. Gadgets must not even be near to the vicinity of the sleeping area.
- ❑ Talk to children about technology and its effects. Unless they are aware, they are not in a position to make right choices for themselves.

Lastly and most importantly, remember that the side-effects of radiation are very much real and have been seen to have a strong relation with attention and hearing deficits, Alzheimer's, autism, behavioral changes, ringing in the ears or tinnitus, insomnia, Parkinson's, and a broad array of other disturbances of nervous system. Awareness and precaution is the keys here!

CHAPTER 16 - LIVING AGAINST THE PRINCIPLES OF NATURE

'Nature operates in a certain way & so does our body. Seasons change when the right time arrives, a baby is born when it is the time to enter the world & the sun rises & sets at the designated time. No one ever created these nature's patterns & no one can ever change these patterns, they just exist! Learn to observe the nature, and it holds amazing clues to reflect how nature works & how we function in a specific pattern according to nature's principles. Going against these principles are bound to create sufferings in some form or the other!'

Scenario

Tara, 32, lives ideal routine as per modern benchmarks. She follows a diet plan with a strict focus on healthy and home-made foods. She avoids eating out. She is settled in her career & her work profile demands to be awake till late night for management calls. She needs to munch something during calls and is very particular about eating right at such times. She likes curd-based salads or any fruit shake such as banana or a mango shake as a quick respite for hunger. Her morning begins at 9 a. m. due to late night calls, and breakfast is cereals eaten by 11 a. m. in the office. Tara goes gymming in the evening 5 times a week. Life seems perfect for Tara, she eats well, sleeps 8 hours a day, exercises and is in a satisfying career. Health-wise Tara faces some negligible health issues. She experiences body bloating and digestive issues. She feels constipated often but is ok as long as the elimination gap does not go beyond 2 days. She feels life is much more than keeping track of her bowel activity that can be trackedthrough few dietary changes. Tara is planning a family for past few years but is not able to conceive and is undergoing treatment. She feels fatigued and tired often and relies on common stimulators such as coffee several times a day. Sometimes, she comes back home with a stressed body and a heavy head. Precisely, Tara is doing everything right for her health. Still, she does not feel fully fit.

Food For Thought:

What seems wrong with Tara when every effort that she is making is right from the health perspective and absolutely matches the modern benchmarks of health maintenance? Why despite of eating well, living well, taking precautions about diet, Tara is not able to feel her best?

Case Analysis:

Tara believes and continues to meet the modern benchmarks of health and well-being. With changing times, Tara is conditioned to believe that if she is eating right and exercising regularly, her health will be maintained. Tara keeps up till late at night, she eats at odd timings, her food combinations are incorrect & she does not mind popping pills for her manageable health issues. Most importantly, toxins are continuously moving within her body due to constipation and other external factors.

Tara is unaware that the body rejuvenation happens at night 'In the State of Rest. ' She continuously deprives her body of rest and sleep at night, and the rejuvenation work gets impacted. This impacts her resistancc to illnesses and weakens her immune system. Tara is also not aware that certain important biological activities such as few chemical and hormone secretions happen at night only that carry out the cleansing and rejuvenation task of our body. If she misses timely sleep, she is disturbing the important biological activities of her body. Probably, Tara's inability to conceive is related to her hormonal imbalances due to her late night calls routine.

Tara eats healthy but eats at odd hours that may be disturbing her fundamental biology. She does not realize that human body is not a machine that can be switched on or off whenever one feels like. There is a specific order of our biological functioning and violating this order begins to disturb inner chemistry, thus creating imbalances. Over time these imbalances manifest into diseases. Further, Tara is missing balance in life, which means she is violating the following rules of nature:

- ❑ The day is meant to work and night is meant to sleep. Tara must consider revising her schedule specifically the late night calls.
- ❑ Human body & mind is not designed to handle extreme stress. Beyond a certain point, it begins to show up as headaches, weakened immunity, allergies, etc. Tara works overtime and is accumulating stress at a sub-conscious level. She must consider ways to ward off her stress & adopt some relaxation techniques in her daily routine. This may include meditation, slowing down or take up an activity that helps her relax.
- ❑ Even a super-healthy diet consumed at odd hours will make us sick. Tara must avoid eating at odd hours.

As a transformational action item, I suggest Tara to try sleeping early and wake up at 5 a. m. in the morning, consume her healthy meals in time and perform her physical activity to feel the difference in her physical & emotional state.

Our Beliefs:

Our perception of health and wellness has drastically narrowed down over time. Today our total focus is on building physical health, which is an entirely opposite perspective compared to what our ancient wisdom suggested. Health & well-being in ancient times was considered to be a total amalgamation of body, mind, and soul. However, our psychological health only comes into picture when it begins to show up adversely in behaviors, attitudes, and actions. We often perceive our health and wellness as:

- The absence of a disease. As long as we continue to carry out our daily activities despite of minor health issues, such as sinuses, cold, flu and allergies, we think we are healthy.
- State of physical health. We keep living under the impression that physical health is wellness.
- Longer life span despite of poor quality of life. Just try recalling the number of people in their progressive years who do not suffer from any health issues. Hardly any! People are living longer with slowly progressing diseases, medications, medical support, where some of them are even incapable of taking care of their routine activities.
- Acceptance of health issues & looking forward to treatments there after. Rather than transforming ourselves for inner healing, we accept our illnesses as our fate & go ahead with convenient treatments for recovery.
- Living life in a disintegrated state of body and mind. Even though fatigued & stressed, we keep pushing ourselves hard to achieve our goals. Stress, mood swings, and behavioral issues are not taken seriously until professional help seems to be an absolute must. However, even after the diagnosis of a psychological issue, our primary focus remains medications. Hardly do we think of changing the way we think, live & eat.
- Lastly, our perception of health and well-being is a secured health insurance policy!

Facts:

Our body rises with the sun & sets with the sunset. That is the reason we feel active and fresh in the day and sleepy at night. The fact is, we do not have any control on our internal body processing. It functions as per the Sun cycle. Accordingly, our internal biological processes have designated tasks to be done through the day in a particular nature-defined order. Further, health & well-being does not mean the absence of a disease but also includes a happy and sound mind, energy, vitality, contentment, and an absolutely great feeling throughout the day. When you live by the principles of nature you become truly healthy, you do not feel stressed, anxious, or depressed regularly. You are able to cope up with daily stresses with positivity. You do not suffer from headaches or unexplained pains in your body. You are not overweight, and you do not suffer from allergies, cold, fluor frequent sicknesses. You do not acquire diseases, your digestion is healthy, your appetite is good, you don't deprive yourself of the foods you enjoy, and you live a balanced life. You have a sound sleep and a clean and clear working body system. Your persona reflects a beautiful you including a graceful and flexible body, happy mind, radiant skin, lustrous hair and strong nails.

Today, we are eating healthy and gymming regularly, yet, the research figures indicate that in the coming years the incidences of chronic conditions such as arthritis, cancer, and type 2 diabetes are going to rise drastically. It is estimated that by the year 2030, the increase in the number of diabetic patients is going to rise to 4. 6 million. The professional and corporate people are already experiencing a rapid increase in obesity, blood pressure & gastrointestinal diseases. Chronic liver diseases are yet another risk for the modern world due to the free flow of alcohol in the professional circles. Further, sedentary lifestyles, low levels of physical activity, compromised rest and sleep, poor eating habits and indoor lives are bound to create diseased generations in future. A new league of unrecognized diseases such as laziness, stress, dullness, fatigue, low energy, aggression and mechanical activities have slowly created a space for themselves in our lives, along with the growth in technology. With our work profiles becoming 24/7, we work like machines. We do not respect the importance of time, keep taking the stress and do not listen to our body's silent signals. The most worrying trends are showing up in younger generations who are getting affected by disorders that once affected the older people only.

We continuously ignore and disrespect the way nature works and end our quest for health by exercising and eating healthy as per our understanding of health. However, despite of our best efforts we still have chemical imbalances, nutritional deficiencies, fatigue, frequent minor illnesses and disturbed moods. We fail to realize that our choices, moods, being in an unsatisfactory job, exercise at wrong timings, eating at odd hours, sleeping late nights, pressures and stresses of life, are taking us a step closer towards diseases each single day. However, this journey of a disease is so subtle that as a whole we do not realize it until a substantial damage is done. It is important to be aware that the only route to health, wellness, happiness, contentment and beauty is by knowing, respecting and living by how nature intended us to live!

Holistic Perspective:

Ancient texts of Ayurveda and TCM focus on ourclose connect with nature. So much as that our body internally behaves as per the outside happenings of nature. For example, when it gets hot outside, we begin to feel the heat inside. The life principles laid down by these ancient texts are timeless and have been applicable to each individual till date. These principles are the same for nature & for all life-forms including trees, animals, forests, oceans, seasons, human beings, etc. Both Ayurveda & TCM are based on the premise that human body is made up of the same elements that exist in nature, including fire, water, earth, air, and metal. Each person contains these constitutional elements in a particular ratio. Equally interesting fact is that these constitutional elements may vary in degree in each individual, and yet each person is considered healthy irrespective of such variations. The body of most people have a predominance of one element which results in a particular physical build, appetite and set of personality qualities that constitute one's nature or 'Dosha' , as Ayurveda defines it. The three primary dosha types include:

- Vata Type pre-dominated mostly by air element.
- Pitta Type pre-dominated mostly by fire element.
- Kapha Type pre-dominated mostly by earth element.

Each of these doshas has a set of specific characteristics associated with them. And so you can categorize an aggressive angry man predominately as a Pitta type – the fiery element. If a pitta type person lives by the rules defined for pitta type personalities, he or she may experience optimum health and well-being, if not, the imbalances will surface leading to diseases. And that explains why some foods or way of life suits someone while may not suit others. Similarly, these ancient texts suggest that certain principles of life have been devised by the observers of nature years ago. These principles are based on the patterns of nature and provide us a direction to how we must live. Few of these principles include:

- We are all born with unique inborn physical and mental traits. Acting within the boundaries of our traits is important.
- We must maintain a balance between consumption and elimination. Whatever we consume in the form of food, or experience in the form of emotions, must be either be eliminated or channelized through proper elimination channels. Our physical and mental state must be like a hollow pipe, whatever goes in must be consumed right & the rest must be eliminated.
- Lack of elimination of physical & emotional excesses such as constipation or pent up emotions respectively will lead to toxic body state and is bound to create imbalances that manifest into real diseases.
- We must take up tasks that we are born to do. We must pursue our passions that will create a harmonious relationship between nature and ourselves.
- We are directly impacted by the variations in nature. To support our inner healing, we must act as per nature's changes. For example, during winters it is our body's need to

be warm, and we must support this requirement by wearing and consuming hot items.

- ❑ Holistic health is built upon right nutrition, right lifestyle, smooth and slow breathing pattern, physical activity, regular self-care and living stress-free in harmony with nature. Any other way to achieve health is unnatural and short-lived, and this is the most underestimated truth of modern times!"

Take Away Thought:

There is a particular order to life. Elderly people used to say, 'The more you laugh, the more you will have to cry!' The more we deviate from the fundamental rules of nature, the more imbalances we create within ourselves, themore we pave the path for diseases. We are such an integrated species of nature, that if our mind and thoughts are disturbed, our body gets diseases automatically. Further, we lack balance in life. Our body and mind thrive on balance. Our body gives constant clues of imbalances being created in the form of minor health issues that manifest into bigger problems as time passes by.

PART 2

This section is all about understanding ourselves. It explains how each individual is unique, how the human body is designed to function, how our perception of health & well-being has transformed negatively over the years, how we create our diseases, how we are ourselves responsible for our health issues & how only we can help ourselves. This is a one-of-its-kind section that does not talk about your body & its functioning from biology or chemistry perspective, but from a very logical perspective in relation to nature's functioning. If you are seeking control of your health, information in this section is a must-know!

INTRODUCTION - INTRODUCING YOU TO YOU

'Behind every successful man is his self-awareness, self-consciousness, health & well-being . . .
. . . Any woman owes any credits much later!'

Consider the following facts of life:

- ❑ India is 13 hours ahead of California, but that does not mean California is slow, or that India is fast. Both countries are in time as per their own time-zones!
- ❑ Someone graduates at 22 to wait for a good job till 5 years, while someone may graduate at 28 to bag the best job even before completing graduation!
- ❑ Someone struggles and stretches too hard to become a CEO at 35 and becomes diseased or dies at 50, while someone follows his own pace to become a CEO at 50 and lives for 90 years!
- ❑ Someone fails an engineering exam just to realize that it was nature's way of communicating that they are good at something else, some other path of excellence awaits them!

'Individuality' of body constitution, mental makeup, genes, thoughts, beliefs, feelings, reactions, choices, and perceptions is what differentiates one human being from another. At the physical level, we all are born with individual traits such as long or short fingers; small, big, round or doe eyes; flat, pointed or broad nose; short, medium or long height. At the emotional and mental level, we are different in terms of thoughts, reactions, feelings and perceptions. So, we all are unique individuals in our own ways. Our own thoughts guide us, drive us, hold us and make us happy or sad. Our own choices make us healthy, diseased, obese or slim.

It is important to realize our uniqueness at all levels of existence. We all are different, someone good at something and someone good at something else. Someone is born with a mindset to create an airplane, and someone else is born with a mindset to just sit and enjoy calm amidst nature. And this justifies the fact why a failed engineer may become a renowned singer by realizing his specific traits or purpose in life. Similarly, the best performer in a corporate might just end up working hours and hours and still be unhappy at the end of the day because he did not realize their true identity yet.

Ancient texts of Ayurveda understood the uniqueness of each individual about 5000 years ago. Ayurveda clearly mentions that when we work against our uniqueness and will, we build up a negative energy that impacts all aspects of our life negatively. Our purpose must be to live life in sync with our own uniqueness and nurture it right. Our thoughts, passions, diets, exercises or lifestyles must be a reflection of our thought-process, our beliefs & our value system. We must tailor our health choices as per our own body requirements, personality and spiritual path. For example, following a diet plan that is created based upon our body constitution and condition will deliver more precise results than beginning to follow any generic diet plan meant for any friend or a relative. When it comes to health specifically, there must be no comparisons. Remember, there is no quick-fix pill that will fix your health in a day. You took years to create body imbalances & diseases, you must work on it right and participate in your healing the way your body wants you to. Irrespective of our situations and circumstances, we all are a product of our own uniqueness, individuality, wisdom, choices, thoughts, feelings, emotions, diets and lifestyles. Nature's plans for everyone are unique, and we must recognize who we are, understand our unique traits, our purpose in life and follow our own unique path. And this may very much mean failing engineering and not getting upset, but realizing that nature intends you to be excellent in something else than scoring average in those areas of life that are not meant for you.

We often see people shifting careers at certain points in their lives, specifically when they are at their peak. Ever thought what makes people opt for this shift?

It begins with living in civilized societies where children are taught to look at education from a perspective of bagging the best job someday. The individuality and creativity of a child is crushed under the societal pressures to excel. Ultimately, the child learns to disconnect with the self and grows up to become an engineer and earning the best compensation, yet, ends up feeling stressed and unhappy. The manifestations of this deepset thought and pressure to, 'Become an engineer or a doctor someday, 'makes a child become an unhappy and diseased engineer someday!

Ancient wisdom clearly mentions that if we forcefully put our energies into something that we do not want to do, or do something that we are not, the outcome for that individual would be sufferings either in the form of physical issues or mental and emotional upsets. Generally, people realize this after reaching the peak of their life or career. It happens when the fame, power, fortune and their enormous pay cheques are unable to fetch them the happiness and sense of achievement that defines their real footprints in the world. Many people at some point realize their intuitive power and decide to follow a new path based on their inherent traits gifted to them by nature. This is the point where people get connected with themselves, listen to their inner voice and follow what their intuition directs. Research studies suggest that the happiest people are the ones who listen to their intuition, follow their heart and invest their energies in something that they realize they were born to do. So, for a happy and healthy you, be in your time-zone, do not compare, keep your pace and just be yourself!

CHAPTER 17 - AYURVEDA'S SAY ON INDIVIDUAL UNIQUENESS

'Individual uniqueness is real. All individuals on earth are born & live by some specific traits that make them different from others. However, in today's process-oriented automated world, our uniqueness has been sieged by a defined set of protocols in the areas of health, disease, exercise, work or any other area of life. Today individuals are not healed based on their uniqueness, but are treated based on a set of generic diseases. Somewhere, we have stopped respecting the individuality of humans. Probably, that is the reason that despite of best generic world-class treatments, the health hazards are severely on a rise!'

Ayurveda helps us understand the uniqueness of each person precisely. It makes us figure out why one sibling from the same set of parents talks non-stop, while the other prefers to be quiet. Why some bosses are cool despite of high-pressure environment, while some find their solace in their disturbed state. Why some children are busy doing their own activities, and some need attention all the time. Interestingly, as per Ayurveda, there is nothing right or wrong with any personality. We all behave as per our inherited traits that we are born with. Each one of us is just the manifestations of the underlying traits that have formed us. Life, health, and happiness is all about understanding ourselves, realizing our own individual traits, and living a life based on our individual existence. That also explains why everyone cannot be an engineer or a doctor, why passionate people are more creative and live in their own world and why we must know and understand ourselves truly and follow our path of passion as intended by nature.

To understand the working model that explains the uniqueness of individuals, Ayurveda takes into consideration the 5 primary forces that exist in nature. These 5 forces are earth, water, fire, metal, and air. Ayurveda explains that the foundational composition of everything in the universe including earth, human beings, animals, oceans, rivers, birds and everything else consists of these 5 prime forces. What characterizes each individual differently is the combination and manifestation of these 5 primary forces in each life form. From different combinations of these 5 forces originate the unique inborn traits of human beings which are broadly categorized in Ayurveda as 3 'Doshas' namely 'Vata' , 'Pitta' and 'Kapha'. It is the applicability of the specific traits of these 3 doshas that make each person unique. Now, since these 3 doshas exist in each life form, it does happen that someone may be a combination of two or more doshas reflecting traits of their ruling doshas in their behavior, body build and mental makeup. Hence, in total there may exist 10 different personality types. As per Ayurveda, each particular mind body personality type possesses some common characteristics. These traits govern our original nature, behavior, thought process, physical make-up, choices, reactions, decisions and everything that makes a human being. Our choices, strengths, talents, likes and dislikes may be very similar to a person of similar dosha type.

Let's explore the three dosha's:

VATA

Vata means 'air' element that governs the underlying characteristics of a person. It signifies subtle movement in its balanced state, which is the actual nature of air. Air is associated with traits such as lightness, dryness, quickness, coolness and airy.

Recognizing Vata Personality Physically

Very tall or very short people often turn out to be Vata types. They may also seem fragile and underweight. They may have protruding joints and irregular features. Facial skin may seem like dry, dark, cold and rough, like the typical character of the air. They may have small, dull, itchy and narrow eyes. Hair may seem scanty, dry, wiry and dull. As air dries out liquids, Vata type personalities may have hard time sweating. Vata types may display insufficient stamina and must not be stretching themselves too much. A short period of rest keeps them in balance.

Recognizing Vata Personality Mentally & Emotionally

As is the nature of the air that flows, restless and scattered, vata personalities demonstrate similar traits mentally and emotionally. As their nature flows like air, inconsistency automatically forms their character. This inconsistency may put them at a risk of imbalance in various areas of life, and to strike a balance they must work on having a consistent routine, with ample time for short and restful breaks and time for self-nurturing on a daily basis.

Recognizing Vata Personality's Lifestyle Habits

As the underlying nature of air is to flow & it cannot hold, vata type personalities resist holding on to anything, be it cultural rules or societal norms or anything that does not appeal them. Though they are considered inconsistent, it is because their underlying dosha makes them inconsistent. Young children are deemed to be excessive in vata dosha as they are restless, want to be at places and you cannot hold on. The other trait of vata types is flexibility. They can fit anywhere to fill the gaps! That defines the air or vata that is at its best when moving slowly and in rhythm. And so, vata type people respond to slow fluid movements the best, when it comes to exercising. Some favorable forms include mindful movements like gentle yoga, walking, tai chi, or swimming.

Recognizing Vata Personality's Food Habits

Food habits of vata type people are based on an inconsistent pattern. They may have an irregular appetite. Light foods with gaseous tendency may not suit them and keep them gastric or constipated. To balance their flowing and light tendency, foods that are heavy, settling, moist and hot are best for them to settle down their flowing and dry nature within.

Recognizing Vata Personality's Sleeping Habits

Sleep haunts the vatas. Vata type people find it hard to sleep consistently, specifically when the weather is dry or cold.

Recognizing Balanced Vata Personalities

Balanced vata personalities showcase the traits of enthusiasm, spiritual inclination, vibrancy, maturity, quick learning, creativity, flexibility, and adaptability, like fitting in anywhere! Imbalanced vata manifests emotionally as fear and anxiety. Flowing or mobile processes within the body are majorly ruled by vata element of nature. Such processes include the pulse of the heart, flow of the breath, flexibility of the muscles, blood tissue and other tissue movement, cellular movement and most importantly the signaling between mind and nervous system.

Recognizing Imbalanced Vata Personalities

Broadly, a person with gaseous tendency best describes a Vata type personality, though there are various other traits to be considered. Such personalities are prone to nervous disorders, disturbed blood circulation, issues with the elimination of wastes such as sweat, urine. Someone suffering from a Parkinson's disease is a typical case of vata type personality. When Vata is out of balance in mind, it often manifests as increased anxiety, fear, indecisiveness, restlessness, insomnia, panic attacks, paranoia, hallucinations or mental instability. Excess vata dries out the body tissues & shows on the outside as dry mouth, dry lips, constipated colon, dry skin, dandruff, arthritis, gas and bloating.

Way to Healing for Vata Types

For the imbalanced state of vatas that shows up as nervousness, anxiety, nervous disorders, bloating, constipation, dry skin, etc. the opposite characteristics help vatas get back in balance. They must have a disciplined routine and must try to maintain a serene, warm environment. Warm, nourishing foods that are naturally sweet, salty and sour in taste may help vatas calm down and balance their vata element. Cooked warm foods and warming herbs like black pepper, cinnamon and ginger can further help such dosha types attain their balance. Such people must try to avoid raw, cooling, bitter, dry, astringent and pungent foods.

PITTA

Pitta refers to 'fire' and 'water' elements that govern the basic existence of a person. It signifies warmth in its balanced state, which is the actual nature of fire. 'Fire' and 'Water' is also associated with traits such as sharpness, hotness, lightness, oily and liquid. By its defined nature fire spreads and is associated with warmth. Water flows and spreads in the laid out direction.

Recognizing Pitta Personality Physically

People with Pitta personality are mostly recognized by their toned and athletic bodies. They are medium in height and have a medium constitution. Their weight gain happens evenly throughout the body. Pitta's personality shows on their skin as hues of yellow and red skin tone. Due to the heat factor prominent in their personality, such people have sensitive skin prone to sunburns, freckles, and rashes. They generally have golden copper red tinge in their hair that is usually straight. Such people are also prone to early graying of hair or balding. In terms of internal body functioning, the pitta feature governs nutrition, metabolism and body temperature. Pitta individuals are physically active people and make good athletes, though they need to keep a check on their aggression that in its imbalance form may turn into unresolved anger.

Recognizing a Pitta Personality Mentally & Emotionally

Emotionally and mentally the pitta type personality displays fiery traits such as competitiveness, motivated, driven and focussed on achieving success. Pitta types are usually courageous, energetic and persistent. They exhibit the traits of a profound sense of vision, intelligence, precision, and a natural ability to organize and lead. On spiritual front, pitta types possess a great capacity to achieve and maintain balance in all walks of life. They have an innate desire to live in harmony with the nature. Such people are great appreciators of beauty. All creative careers such as architecting, designing, teaching, art, etc. perfectly suit the people of this mentality type. In their imbalanced state Pitta shows aggressiveness and hot-headedness, similarly like fire shows aggression when out of control!

Recognizing Pitta Personality's Lifestyle Habits

As pitta personalities are fiery personalities, overheat in taste, feelings, experiences may irritate them. Such people like cold environments to balance their fiery elements inside. In their daily routines and habits, such people are highly focussed, leaders, ambitious and innovators. It is important for pitta types to slow down and not rush to balance their fast pace.

Recognizing Pitta Personality's Food Habits

As Pitta types have speeded metabolism, whatever they eat, it burns at speed. Due to their good food burning capacity, such people can eat large and filling meals. Hot and spicy foods fascinate them, and alternatively, they also crave for cooling foods and cold drinks. They have a sweet tooth. Such people must avoid overly oily, spicy, or fried foods to keep their body balance on!

Recognizing Pitta Personality's Eating Habits

It is no surprise that Pitta type people may often get disturbing or violent dreams. If they skip sleeping in time, say before 10 p. m., they might be awake until 2 p. m. then or may experience disturbed sleep. They must retire to bed before 10 p. m. to get adequate rest.

Recognizing Balanced Pitta Personalities

An aggressive personality, highly ambitious, creative and mostly in shape, is what describes a pitta personality. Their nature shows the traits of hotness and sourness. Balance in such body types shows in the form of positive and focused aggressiveness in their areas of interest, intelligence, and sharpness.

Recognizing Imbalanced Pitta Personalities

Imbalanced Pitta personalities can be recognized as irritable, raging, angry, criticizing, discontented and arrogant personalities. Physically, Pitta type people may feel hot and thirsty and may be prone to heartburn, ulcers, acidic body state. Skin rashes, itching, hives, eye irritations may also be a typical pitta trait.

Way to Healing for Pitta Types

For the imbalanced state of pittas that shows up as inflammation in the body and joints, acid reflux, nausea, heartburn, etc. the opposite characteristics help pittas get back in balance. They must practice moderation in all areas of life and must try to maintain cooling, pacifying environment for themselves. Cooling sweet, bitter and astringent foods help pittas strike a balance. Cooling herbs such as cilantro, fennel, and coriander can further help pittas to pacify their fiery element. Such people must try to avoid pungent, sour, salty, hot foods.

KAPHA

Kapha refers to 'earth' and 'water' elements that govern the basic existence of a Kapha person's elements and signifies binding, structure, and solidification in its balanced form, which is the actual nature of earth. 'Earth' is also associated with traits such as oily, dense, heavy, slow, cool, cloudy, soft and smooth. By nature, earth solidifies and lends cohesiveness required to maintain a particular form. Balanced Kapha within the body supports

a gift for you
MACROBIOTIC WELLNESS

TERMS & CONDITIONS

WWW.MACROBIOTICWELLNESS.COM

This voucher is not redeemable for cash.

There will be no replacements provided if this voucher is lost, stolen, destroyed or used without permission.

This voucher cannot be combined with other vouchers and is not valid with other promos and offers.

For registration mail at deeptimacrobioticpractice@gmail.com.

Offer valid till 31st September 2017.

immunity, protects the tissues and moisturizes the skin. They are full of love and compassion and signify flesh or mucus elements when associated with our body.

Recognizing Kapha Personality Physically

People with Kapha personality are identified by their strong and compact build. Physically, such people may display various traits of beauty with large attractive eyes, fair complexion and thick, abundant, black, or wavy hair. Such personalities are also abundant with mucus secretions and hence, may suffer from sinus, cold, cough and respiratory issues often. They have softness in their voice. The typical trait of Kapha dosha is to bind and hydrate all body cells and systems and lubricates the joints. Within our body Kapha element exists as bones, teeth, muscles and everything with a dense structure. Kapha is typically the largest of the body types. Physically, they have wide hips/shoulders, thick wavy hair, & good physical stamina. Mentally, Kapha types tend to be slow to learn, but they have great memories. Emotionally, they tend to be very loyal, stable, and reliable – they are often referred to as the "rocks" in a relationship.

Recognizing Kapha Personality Mentally & Emotionally

Kapha's charm, even-temperateness, and reliable nature make them stand out in the crowd. They are great appreciators and followers of beauty, music, and poetry. They like living life at a slow and methodical pace in an organized manner. Concern for others makes them care for others genuinely. Such people are family-oriented people and have a tendency of creating a comforting environment in their surroundings. Like the typical traits of Kapha dosha, Kapha people showcase the characteristics of steadiness, slowness, coldness and heaviness. When out of balance, Kapha people become lazy, needy and heavy in body and mind. Emotionally, Kapha people possess a solid charm and radiate balance to the extent that vata and pitta types may feel rejuvenated just by being in the presence of a Kapha personality.

Recognizing Kapha Personality's Lifestyle Habits

Kapha people live best in summers and tend to suffer in cold and moist weather. As Kapha lends the laziness trait, such people have a lazy and lethargic tendency, and they may end up living a sedentary lifestyle. They must follow a strictly disciplined schedule to keep their Kapha element in balance. Contrary to their lazy nature, Kapha people are very hard working. As a solution to their laziness, such people can benefit immensely from the most intense forms of exercise. For a Kapha person, an ideal routine must be to wake up early, have a shower and perform solid exercise before breakfast.

Recognizing Kapha Personality's Food Habits

Kapha's are food lovers and love to eat rich, indulgent foods. They may often end up overeating. Their sense of smell and taste is just outstanding. Just by their sense of smell and taste, they can make out the ingredients used in any cooked food. Such people typically have a tendency of consuming light breakfast or missing it altogether, consuming a bigger lunch and preferring a light dinner by evening. If you fall into this category, you may benefit by limiting carbohydrates and starchy foods and consuming more of light, warm, little spicy foods along with lots of vegetables.

Recognizing Kapha Personality's Sleeping Habits

Sleeping for kapha's can be never-ending. They can sleep endlessly for 'n' number of hours. Such people may try to be out of bed by 6 a. m., after which the Kapha time in the environment starts which can make their waking up all the more difficult. They might also end up with a lethargic and heavy feeling throughout the day if they wake up after 6 a. m.

Recognizing Balanced Kapha Personalities

A balanced Kapha personality will come across as a calm, radiant, attractive, nurturing, family-oriented, loving, grounded and a reliable person. Kapha types are very graceful, have a natural, erotic sensuality about them, and are usually very fertile.

Recognizing Imbalances in Kapha Personalities

A typically imbalanced Kapha personality comes across as a lazy person who sleeps for hours, wakes up late and is prone to mucus related health disorders. When in an emotionally imbalanced state, such people tend to show the traits of possessiveness, stubbornness, lethargy, anger, low moods, and melancholy. The imbalanced behavior of kaphas may show up in their overeating and oversleeping habits. Physically in their imbalanced state, they may suffer from sluggish metabolism, a heavy feeling in the body and mind, respiratory disorders, quick weight gain and excess mucus.

Way to Healing for Kapha Types

For the imbalanced state of kaphas that shows up as excess mucous, thick white tongue, slowness and dullness in their nature, opposite characteristics help kaphas get back in balance. They must consume foods that are pungent, astringent and bitter in taste such as black pepper, cumin, ginger, and cinnamon. They must consume light, dry and warm foods to regain balance. Warm foods, warm environment, and warm natured people gel perfectly with kaphas. Lively music, good company, invigorating fragrances and real experiences bring kaphas back to balance. They must avoid heavy, oily, sweet, sour and salty, cooling foods, overeating, and heavy meals.

CONSTITUTION - DOSHAS THAT WE ARE BORN WITH

Ayurveda Philosophy emphasizes that each one of us is born with certain inborn traits passed to us in our genes. These specific characteristics fall under the category of Vata, Pitta and Kapha doshas. We all contain some element of each dosha type, but the prominent ones make us a particular dosha type personality. This means that depending upon the predominant traits that we are born with, we are either a particular dosha type or a combination of doshas. By birth, each one of us falls under any of the 10 constitution types based on our physical, mental and emotional traits. This also means if we are any particular dosha type by birth, our balance lies in maintaining the traits that we are born with. So, balance in each individual varies and is dependent upon the dosha type blessed by birth. And this forms our constitution or 'Prakriti' -what we are born with.

Dosha that we are born with, impact all areas of our existence including physical body and health, our physiology, our habits, our likes and dislikes, our emotional and mental states, our choices and what switches us on or switches us off. Our body naturally tries to maintain this balance that we are born with. It self-regulates its internal processes to maintain a state of internal equilibrium. When body gives up its efforts of maintaining stability due to our personal choices and actions such as poor diets, lack of exercise and other health disasters, we lose balance and begin to become sick and diseased. When, as per our 'Prakriti, ' we are able to maintain balance, we enjoy health and integrity. For example, for a pitta personality, too much aggression can be harmful, and they must balance their aggressiveness by performing activities that give their aggression an outlet. However, for a Kapha type personality, a little positive aggression is much required as laziness is their very nature. And so, the definition of balance for each individual varies as per the dosha type they lie in. Modern science does not consider this aspect of one's personality and treats all individuals equal considering all humans are made up of organs, blood, and internal functional systems.

The bottom line is that whatever one's basic 'Prakriti' is, one must strive to maintain their own balance based on understanding who they are. Trying to follow a generic healing pattern may create more problems than healing them, even if the mechanics of healing are correct such as right diet, proper exercise, and right lifestyle. Going out of balance causes illness and diseases.

CONDITION – INTERNAL STATE OF DOSHAS CAUSED BY OUR FOOD & LIFE-STYLE CHOICES

'Vikriti' defines our condition or the current state of health and well-being. It also refers to the manifestation of our state owing to what we create within ourselves depending upon how and where we live, what we eat and drink, how we feel and what kind of thoughts we live with. 'Vikriti' is easily relatable to our ways of living and eating and the combination of 'Prakriti' and 'Vikriti' makes us unique physically, mentally and emotionally. Based on these two aspects, nature decides whether we are healthy or diseased.

Unlike 'Prakriti, "Vikriti' is very much under our control. We can become the masters of our health by altering our 'Vikriti' by making right choices, eating right foods, living life right, exercising, thinking right and by living a balanced life.

Doshas can be an incredible personal tool for understanding the natural strengths and vulnerabilities determined by our constitution. It is also a great tool to correct any imbalances that might be affecting our health. As you are reading through the descriptions of Vata, Pitta, and Kapha below, keep in mind that your constitution undoubtedly includes all three doshas. This being the case, you may see elements of each dosha within you, some more prominent & some less prominent.

Dosha theory in Ayurveda helps one understand exactly who they are, what suits them, what does not suit them, what environment is ideal for them, what works for them & what does not work for them. It is a real science of realizing one's individuality, and living life according to our true potential. Balancing doshas is an important aspect of Ayurveda's healing system.

CHAPTER 18 - OUR NOTIONS ABOUT HEALTH AND WELL-BEING

'Drifting away from our ancient wisdom has narrowed down our notion of health & well-being. Today, our notion about our health & well-being ends at following a diet plan, visiting a gymming centre regularly or getting a medical insurance done!'

Living in a modernistic society, what is the first thing that comes to your mind to insure your health?

Is it buying a life insurance!

Do you ever consider changing your ways of eating, living and thinking as your biggest insurance against a disease?

Ironically, it is not just our health that has deteriorated with time. Our understanding of health and well-being has equally degraded with time & modernization. For educated modern women, health means slim body & ideal weight. For an educated parent, health and well-being of a child is limited to the suggestions from a doctor, whether it makes sense or not! For an elderly wise couple, the definition of health means regular health check-ups. And, for a successful professional male, health & well-being is all about buying a medical insurance!

The two most important terms associated with health today are 'Health-Care' & 'Health Insurance.' 'Self-Care' and 'Self-Discipline' is nowhere in the picture. Health for us today is more about the absence of a disease, nothing more nothing less! Our understanding of health and well-being has got limited to be able to perform our daily tasks comfortably. This is the most real and worrisome mindset prevailing in our modern societies today. We have become blind to minor physical issues. Discomfort feeling a little run down, tired, sad, having a cold or a headache, and holding on to the call of nature, mental stress and emotionally suppressing issues are an ignorant part of our daily lives. I often see elderly groups and young women groups happily discussing severe health concerns trending in the world today over a cup of tea and processed snacks! I wonder why don't people realize sitting and discussing these issues over wrong foods at wrong timings will make them be a part of this diseased group someday! The cushion that western medicine has provided in the form of 'pill-culture, ' has truly devastated the thought process & our perception of our health & well-being. We are suffering today because we have over-relied on medical support, & have started to misuse what we have been provided as a last resort solution. Believe it or not, we take 10 years to feed cancer within us before it surprises us. So precisely, we have at least 10 long years to take the responsibility of our health & transform ourselves before chemotherapy is prescribed to us!

We believe we are aware and have a good understanding of what is right or wrong for our health. Yet, the world is living under the threat of lifestyle disorders. It is our narrow approach to our health and well-being that is making us sicker by the day. Our ignorance towards our body signals is making our diseases become bigger right infront of us. No one else but we ourselves are feeding our diseases due to wrong notions of health and well-being, and the lost wisdom to live well. It is high time that we turn back ancient, at least where our health and wellness is concerned!

CHAPTER 19 - WHY DO WE GET SICK?

'We are not born to ultimately get diseased, & this is the universal truth of all times. We are neither born with any sickness or a disease, nor does the nature intends us to be diseased ever in our lifetime. Health, wellness & well-being is our natural state of being. Sickness & diseases are nothing more than our choices & what we do to ourselves over time. Our state of health is a result of many factors beginning with our lack of awareness, faulty diet, sedentary lifestyle, negative thoughts and non-willingness to change!'

Shaira, 35, often suffers from severe headaches. Her quick and regular solution is ingesting a medicine for immediate relief. And, she has now been doing the same for as long as her headache issue exists.

Do you think Shaira must stop and ask herself what is causing her a headache so frequently? Whether it is her job stress, fatigued body, too much of travel, lack of sleep or toxic internal state, or any other reason?

More than half of the world is diseased and on medication today. So, while we consider medication as our last resort to get better, do we ever think why so many people including children are dealing with health issues? Is it our weak immunity that is making us sick? Is it our diet, lifestyle or lack of exercise that is at fault? Are we not taking good care of ourselves that we are getting sick? Is it the polluting environment that is making our body weak from within? It is bacteria, virus, genetics, or any other force that is evading the human race slowly and steadily?

An interesting study on the origin of Vitamin D deficiency goes like this. There was a time when sunscreens did not exist & people used to work under the sun the whole day. Back then, people were perfectly ok with rare or unheard cases of skin cancers and Vitamin D deficiencies. Research suggests the incidences of Vitamin D deficiency came into limelight initially in Europe when people adopted the flats based housing culture and began living in tall buildings devoid of sunlight. Soon after, the concept of Vitamin D fortification was introduced where Vitamin D started to be added to our foods, while it was still freely available through direct sunlight. Today we have all means available to counter Vitamin D deficiency, yet the incidences of Vitamin D deficiency are rising by the day! We are indeed getting sicker…

Consider decades-old human activities & their health states below:

Activities	Consequences
People lived in natural environment	People were happier & totally in sync with the nature
People did a lot of physical activity	Their body was active & mind was focused. The physical stress used to be good as it used to induce relaxation and better sleep
People ate what nature had to offer	Body used to be in its best functional state internally with lesser incidences of chronic diseases
People breathed pure air that was well regulated with physical hard work	Respiration and usage of lung capacity used to be at its fullest
People enjoyed working under the sun	The most dominant energy source ensured no Vitamin D deficiencies
People slept with the setting of the sun and used to wake up early to begin the day before sunrise	No mental fatigue, fogginess, and insomnia used to occur

(Continued)

...Back then the incidences of extreme body aging like Alzheimer's, cancer, diabetes, nutritional deficiencies, low immunity, muscles weaknesses, etc. were unheard. Above all visits to doctors used to be limited to a few times in one's lifetime. The people then were happy, healthy and peaceful and their narration of experiences in life was way different than our experiences in modern times. They lived life being actually 'alive, ' and their work and relationships were their sources of earning, enjoyment and happiness.

As the human species developed & modernization happened...

Activities	Consequences
Mental activity replaced the physical activity	Body is in one place, and mind is unfocused running in various directions leading to chronic stress
Real food replaced processed, refined & junk food	Deteriorating health conditions such as bad digestive health, weakened immunity, etc. started rising leading to huge rise in chronic health conditions
Breathing toxic air indoors and outdoors became a norm and acceptable	Frequent lung and respiratory issues are on a rise & less usage of lung capacity is the trait of every other individual
Being off-sun became a fashion and sunscreens became a must beauty product	Frequent mood swings and Vitamin D issues started to emerge
Sleeping time became the core entertainment time & working time	League of sleep-deprived insomniacs roam on Earth when the world is fast asleep. Fatigued people with restless minds and lousy mindset are troubling the world

(Continued)

Aging fast-forwarded its grip on human race	Cases of mind & body diseases are on the rise. It seems like the fate of every adult will ultimately be Alzheimer's, Dementia, Parkinson's, Diabetes, Osteoporosis, High Blood Pressure or Cancer in their progressive years

... Today, everything is split, nutrition, work, entertainment, thoughts, and relationships!

Compare the two scenarios, and you realize that the universal truth is our diet, lifestyle & perception towards the world is making us sick and diseased each single day. The comparison gives a clear clue that if human beings work in accordance with nature, they are bound to live happy, healthy & peaceful life. The more we drift away from nature & create artificial cocoons for ourselves, the more problems we invite for ourselves.

Does that mean we should reconsider the old ways of living that were in harmony with the nature...Think about it!

MODERN VIEW OF SICKNESS

'Our holistic environment makes us what we are. One single factor does not make us sick or healthy. If you are obese, it is not just because of your diet, neither is it only the lack of exercise & , nor it is stress alone! The biggest myth that modern view of sickness carries is considering the root cause of any sickness as one single factor and blindly focussing on the probable target cause only, which in most cases is just limited to 'Diet' & 'Exercise. 'It is important to realize that we are healthy or unhealthy because of our entire ecosystem that consists of our choices, thoughts, diet, lifestyle, actions & reactions. '

Ironically, till the time the healthiest cultures in the world including Indian, Chinese, Japanese cultures continued to live life as per their ancient wisdom, the cases of cancer, diabetes, heart diseases, acid reflux, obesity, Parkinson's or Alzheimer's diseases were unknown to them. When these cultures started to adopt the western culture leaving behind their ancient healing cultures, they began to see a rise in diseases in their communities. People who were never fatty began to become obese, people who knew how to live happy till their end began to suffer from emotional and mental upsets and individuals who sweated and were active through the day began to live lazy, dull and unhappy lives amidst modern luxuries.

Though the western medicine was a revolutionizing concept, still it is struggling to heal people of their maladies from the root. This is partly because the idea of modern view of sickness is just limited to the part of the body that is diseased and partly because time and again western medicine has been seeking external answers to internal human diseases. For example, during the evolvement of modern medicine system, initially, viruses and bacteria were considered to be the sole creators of diseases for the human race. One of the most deadly diseases of ancient times 'tuberculosis' was caused by bacteria. However, by the time modern medicine took control on virus and bacteria-based diseases, there started to emerge another league of diseases purely created by humans and termed as 'lifestyle disorders. 'Though the term' lifestyle disorders' literally implies that this league of diseases is getting a quick entry in the human world by direct invite from humans itself, modern science developed a different understanding of the reasons behind these diseases. Today, about 80% of common sicknesses are 'lifestyle disorders' , which means created by humans themselves due to wrong ways of eating, living, and thinking. Modern viewpoint started to look at these diseases as issues with the affected parts of the body while disintegrating them with their real causes of occurrence. Hence, when cancer occurs, our lifestyle, dietary patterns, high sugar consumption, lack of sunlight, acid pH base, sedentary lifestyle and other related factors are not considered and cancer is looked upon as a disease of the blood or organs or tissue or any other related part where it occurs. Over the years now, we have been conditioned to believe that diseases just occur and we have no control over them. Sadly, today we are losing touch with our ancient wisdom to live well, eat well and think well. Specifically, the cultures that have a deep connect with the nature and have ancient sacred texts that guide them towards right ways of life, are leaving back their wisdom and adopting disintegrated ways of living life, and hence are suffering the consequences. We think when we get diseased western medication is the way to go, and that is all we know about our health and sickness! Isn't it?

PROBLEMS WITH MODERN VIEW OF SICKNESS

Lacks Holistic Approach to Health & Well-being: Modern view of health & disease is based upon a disintegrated view of body, mind, and soul. Western culture does not consider human body, mind, and soul as the holistic force behind our total health & wellness. In modern medicine, the health relation with the mind is only considered in the context of internal chemical functioning. Aspects like how one thinks, behaves, or feels is not a part of modern medicine's diagnosis.

Focus on External Treatment: Modern view of health & sickness is limited to external treatment versus inner healing. The only focus in modern medicine is on the physically visible or diagnosable aspects of a disease. Modern medicine considers that the causes of any disease are external and popping pills will relieve one of their health issues at physical, mental or emotional levels. This method heavily relies on machines and instruments to detect diseases versus considering the subtle signs of disturbances that body communicates such as allergies, cold, flu, weakening immunity, etc. For example, a cancer patient is just treated for the cancer lump, what they feel or go through emotionally is not under the scope of modern medical treatment. The modern view of sickness is limited to individualistic factors, whereas human body is a combination of body, mind, and soul, which means we exist at different planes and our health at all these levels is essential for our well-being. Treating just one aspect does not lead to true healing at the core level of the health issue.

Minor Issues Dismissed to be the Messengers of Progressing Diseases: Can you imagine that frequent cold and allergies may someday surprise you with cancer? The simple logic is that both cold and cancer are caused due to weak immunity, and due to high toxic and acidic state of the body. However, modern medicine does not consider the idea of weakening immunity to manifest into cancer someday unless it actually happens!

Creating Secondary Disease While Treating the Primary Disease: Side-effects is a safe term used in modern medicine to dismiss the development of another disease while treating the prime illness. The modern view of sickness is just limited to the treatment of localized part of the body where the disease occurs. While treating the diseased part, if something else manifests as a side-effect of the treatment in some other part of the body, we have already been prepared to believe that it is ok to acquire another disease in the bargain of one.

Root of Disease Not Considered: The foundational causes of a disease do not score anything on the cards of modern medicine. Think of cancer logically. Do we develop cancer or catch it? Do we develop diabetes or catch it? Do we develop obesity or catch it? It is evident that we do not catch cancer, diabetes, or obesity. Neither do we catch a headache or arthritis, not even PMS! We birth all these diseased health states within our bodies, which means that all disastrous diseases of current times are neither spread nor caught by a bacteria or a virus, but are self-created within our own body. Now, if we would have caught these diseases, we would have been in a much better position because our body is well-equipped internally to fight off anything that is caused by external factors. That's why we have been blessed with an immune system. Since modern diseases are not caught but are developed internally due to internal imbalances, toxins, nutritional deficiencies, load of modern unhealthy foods, sedentary lifestyles, polluted environments, unless we correct the foundations that caused the diseases, we keep feeding our diseases and creating them more and more of them each single day, despite of best treatments available! This is the real truth, and this is the reason why all of us must be empowered enough to find answers for our diseases and illnesses, the reasons for our sickness and self-reflecting what can truly heal us.

Focus on Common Treatment for All: If you get a headache for any underlying reason, say due to stress, or hunger, or upset stomach or anything else, what must be your healing action? A medicine or correcting the root? The modern view of sickness is based on the understanding that when some disease strikes and impacts say an organ, we must treat that organ. What caused that organ to become diseased and accordingly adopting an approach that also corrects the root cause is not considered in modern view of sickness. Our body is made up of a trillion cells (a trillion = 1,000,000,000,000,000,000). Each cell is an intelligent functional unit in itself and has a role to play. Each cell dies after its lifetime and new cell births automatically. The individual behavior of this smallest functional unit within our body impacts us at physical, emotional and mental level. Which means, there could be 'n' number of permutations and combinations of cell functions that cause a diseased organ or any other diseased body part. The modern view of sickness is limited to this understanding of a disease as a whole. It does not consider different patterns that caused the same problems in various individuals. Further, modern medicine offers a common solution for a diseased state of an organ irrespective of its 'n' number of underlying patterns that caused it. This also means that though the modern medicine is capable enough to treat the diseased organ, it lacks focus on the underlying causes of diseases & the impact of treatment on other body parts. This leads to different side-effects in different individuals.

Emphasis on Dependency on Health Practitioners Versus Incorporating Acts of Self-Change: Modern view of sickness projects your high dependability on medical practitioners. It does not focus on the first and most crucial line of healing that begins with self-change in various areas of life that caused the disease.

ANCIENT VIEW OF SICKNESS

'It is ironical that our understanding of health & well-being is deteriorating with time. The science of life is an art to be understood rather than dissected into parts & analysed individually. Our ancient ancestors realized this fact 5000 years ago & adopted an integrated approach to health & healing. Are we going years ahead or years behind in the name of modernization! Today, we are just waving off the idea of ancient as old and adopting the modern. However, the consequences or modern are quite visible in their worst form globally!'

The ancient view of sickness as defined in Ayurveda, TCM & Macrobiotics is entirely opposite from the modern view of illness. These ancient texts believed that the sickness is body's own way of communicating that internally things are not right. And when things go wrong, the approach to healing must begin with realizing the factors that disturbed the body's chemistry. Then, take an integrative approach to reverse the causes that created a disease & side-by-side treat the body part that got impacted due to internal disturbances. The healthiest cultures of the world including ancient Japanese culture, Indian culture, Greek culture or Chinese culture have their own ancient wisdom to trust upon for healthy living. Where the Indian culture is backed by Ayurveda, the far-Eastern cultures like Japan and China have the concepts of TCM to guide them through life in the right light. Whether it is Ayurveda, TCM or Macrobiotics, the cultures practicing these ancient texts till-date know the importance of routine, whole & natural foods, right timings, toxin elimination, positive thinking, exercising & mediation. During ancient times people always lived by the rules of nature. They were aware of right food combinations, right cooking styles, right foods to heal, the right time to eat, fasting when required, moving body regularly and maintaining a positive approach to life. And needless to say, for a long period of time in the past, people belonging to these cultures enjoyed health, happiness, peace, and joy.

The ancient understanding of sickness is very unlike the modern view. Where the modern view considers the onset of a disease as an external influence, ancient view believes that majority of modern diseases are caused as a result of internal imbalances caused due to our wrong ways to living and eating. The modern view does not consider the role of nature in one's sickness, while the ancient view closely associates happenings in the nature with the changing chemistry within our body. The way modern science diagnoses sickness is by performing diagnostic lab tests, whereas ancient science understands and forecasts ill health by understanding how sedentary we are, to what extent do we consume processed & modern foods, how much time we spend indoors, how much we remain in front of gadgets, how much high-calorie/low nutrition beverages we consume, how we look, what health impressions show up on our face or how much convenient fast foods we consume. In the ancient Indian culture, our body was considered as Temple. However, the symbolic relevance of treating the body as a temple was to treat our body sacred, keep it neat and clean & well taken care of & being conscious of what and how much we eat, drink and what do we apply on our body.

Ayurveda, TCM & Macrobiotics are by and large the sciences of life which believe that the healthy state of a person is a cumulative outcome of the following factors in their life:

- ❑ Co-coordinating our activities with internal physiological functioning by following a right time for doing activities such as waking up before sunrise, sleeping early, consuming dinner at least 2 hours before sleep etc.
- ❑ Keeping our lifestyle, habits, behavior and dietary patterns as clean and health-supporting as possible.
- ❑ Not suppressing natural urges and listening to our body.
- ❑ Investing substantial time in physical and emotional self-care.

- ❑ Maintaining a balance between consumption and elimination by closely focusing on waste product removal in the form of feces, urine, sweat, tears and carbon-di-oxide.

AYURVEDA's VIEW OF SICKNESS

'Ayurveda strongly emphasizes on the role of minor sicknesses in creating the major illnesses. It mentions that way before a disease is diagnosed in its worst form through machines & instruments by modern science, our body begins preparing for a disease which is communicated in the form of minor illnesses. In Ayurveda, minor digestive issues are also a big disease and occasional allergic issues are also a big disease, not because they are big in themselves, but because they are the subtle progressive signs of body getting deteriorated & which overtime may transform into a disastrous disease!'

Ayurveda emphasizes that the health deterioration begins to happen years before a disease is diagnosed. It also focusses that the groundwork of disease making happens in our food processing factory – The Digestive System. Our metabolism is dependent upon digestive fire called 'Agni'. Any impairment of this digestive fire is the beginning of health deterioration. This is because if Agni is weak the food will be metabolized partially. So, even if you end up eating healthiest foods on earth, and if your digestive fire is weak, the goodness of consumed healthy foods is of no use to your body. Rather, these healthiest foods within the body will get putrid and toxic in a partial-digested state. This putrid and toxic matter in the digestive tract is called 'Ama'. Ama, is believed to be the mother of diseases. Ama is created when partially-digested food remains in our digestive tract and begins to interfere with the functioning of other digestive processes including the processing of food by good bacteria, enzymes, hormones, catalysts etc. With this disturbed internal balance, the body functioning gets impacted & over time results in sickness.

Ancient texts of Ayurveda mention that Ama is caused due to the following reasons:

- Overeating, eating less than required, gulping food, partial chewing or improper digestion.
- Eating at inappropriate timings, for example, late in the evening.
- Eating wrong foods & poor diet.
- Eating during times of stress.
- Wrong food combinations, for example, eating fruit immediately after meals.
- Eating when digestion process of previous meals is still not complete.
- Not eating local & seasonal foods.
- Preparing foods using artificial ingredients.
- Cooking with a negative emotion.

The accumulation of ama leads to toxic accumulations & stagnation of impartially digested foods in the digestive tract. Physically this shows up as minor sickness, nausea, digestive issues, bloating, feeling of heaviness, weakness, fatigue, body aches, headaches, bloating, foul breath, mental confusion, fogginess, constipation, low appetite, thick white coating on the tongue, cravings for wrong foods, eczema, psoriasis, cysts, painful or swollen joints, blocked arteries, feelings of internal uncleanliness and a stagnant feeling.

Another view of sickness in Ayurveda is attributed to our disharmony with our environment. We do not live in harmony with nature when we adopt unnatural & unhealthy food habits, sedentary lifestyle & negative & irrational thought patterns. This disharmony with the nature leads to weakened body state and makes it easy for bacteria, viruses and other pathogens to thrive within is. The flexibility of our muscles gets impaired and our nervous system gets a strong hit that further disturbs the smooth energy flow in the body.

For mental and emotional illnesses, stress is considered to be the biggest contributory factor. Even medical science suggests that any kind of known or unknown stress alters the chemical balance of our body and creates toxins that weaken body's defense mechanism. It makes you more prone to frequent sickness. And this trend is clearly visible in stressed people. People today are highly stressed and fall sick often.

TRADITIONAL CHINESE MEDICINE'S VIEW OF SICKNESS

'Diseases enter through the mouth' , is a famous Chinese proverb. If thought logically, you realize that all ancient cultures of the world developed similar understanding of health & sickness. It is worth thinking, is that a co-incidence!'

A very famous Chinese proverb mentions, 'When you are thirsty, it's too late to dig a well!' It simply means that when you develop an illness, it means the damage is already done & it is too late to go back to your original state of health. If you want to avoid illnesses, your priority must be to incorporate right ways of eating & living, or else it will be too late.

The Chinese culture holds a viewpoint that as long as body energy or 'Qi' , flows in a harmonious pattern within the body, a positive state of health is maintained. Sickness roots when this smooth flow of energy gets disturbed. All ancient Chinese and far Eastern healing modalities work on balancing the energy flow to heal a person.

CHAPTER 20 - LIFE CYCLE OF A DISEASE – THE MODERN & ANCIENT VIEW

'The roots of health & well-being begin to get disturbed years before you realize you are diseased. Nature never wanted humans to be in pain & gifted us a body that is intelligent enough to communicate its concerns in subtle signs of discomfort frequently. Nature also has a unique way of making us learn if we keep ignoring these subtle communications, simply by sending louder & stronger signals & hence a disease knocks our door many times before finally taking an entry! Whether it is modern view or the ancient view, all healing modalities understand that each disease progresses in a defined life cycle. Amazingly, the roots of this life cycle are mostly the same – wrong diet & wrong lifestyles that lead to imbalances & chemical disturbances. At a point where the imbalances have already occurred, what makes a difference is whether you decide to treat yourself externally or heal yourself internally!'

MODERN VIEW OF DISEASE PROGRESSION

Modernization does not mean disconnecting with our ancient roots. If modernization means progression, the positive progression should also have been in the physical & emotional states of human beings & no one should have been falling sick. Ironically, the more modern we are becoming, the sicker we seem to be getting. Now, we must connect back to our roots & analyze whether or not progressing right, or along with progression we are also paving a path for human deterioration!'

The modern view of disease progression begins where the ancient view of disease progression ends. So, as per the ancient view, when at the root level the imbalances and disharmony in the body begins to occur and the chemistry of the body changes, the second stage of disease begins to appear. This second visible stage may vary in different individuals depending upon where in the body the imbalances have occurred. So for some, it may show up as weak immunity or frequent tendency to get sick or allergies or simply cold, cough and flu. At this point where the physical signs of imbalances begin to show up, the modern view of disease progression comes into being. The reasons for disease progression in modern science are based on these 2 theories:

Catching a Disease

This view of disease progression is external, where modern science believes that we catch diseases such as cold and flu, from our external environment through virus and bacteria. When a disease is 'Caught' , it starts from the outside and sets in deeper inside if not healed properly. And so, a cold may become bronchitis or pneumonia or asthma by beginning outside & setting in deeper inside. When we are not able to fight off 'germs' , external factors make us sick. Modern science does not delve any deeper into the thought that what makes our immune system weak!

Developing a Disease

This view of disease progression is internal, where something develops in the body on its own. The major causes of this imbalance are:

- ❑ Toxic body state leading to weakened immune system.
- ❑ Nutritional deficiencies where our body strives for right elements that make it work optimally.
- ❑ High exposure to artificial and processed foods.
- ❑ The imbalance between consumption and elimination.
- ❑ High exposure to electromagnetic chaos exposing us to the dangers of radiation.
- ❑ Physical, emotional and mental stress.
- ❑ Sedentary body making internal functioning dull.
- ❑ Negative environment.

Modern science does not delve any deeper into the thought that what makes us toxic, nutritionally deficient, imbalanced, stressed or a negative thinking personality.

To conclude, any disease at the foundational level is the combination of one or more factors. Common diseases including cancer, diabetes, arthritis, heart disease, acid reflux, etc. are not originating in a day. These diseases are just the manifestations of our wrong choices and wrong habits.

ANCIENT VIEW OF DISEASE PROGRESSION

'What begins to happen in our body years before a disease is diagnosed, do we ever give it a thought? Most of us just accept what we create! Knowing the life cycle of a disease can change our entire perspective to look at our disease & this knowledge must be imparted to all human beings since childhood. With that knowledge & empowerment only we can create a disease free world!'

A disease passes through various phases of development and maturity before it lets us know that it has finally arrived. Ironically, first, we ourselves create our diseases & then are forced to welcome the invited guest!

AYURVEDA'S VIEW OF DISEASE PROGRESSION

Ayurveda mentions that a disease passes through various developmental phases before being diagnosed as a life-threatening disorder. The life cycle of a disease from Ayurveda's perspective goes as follows:

Creation of Imbalance: The first stage of disease progression begins with imbalances inside the body created due to wrong dietary, lifestyle and thought patterns. For example, consuming junk foods such as pizzas and burgers regularly will create nutritional imbalances. Such imbalances show up as tiredness and fatigue initially & deep inside they impact the functioning of our body and create further imbalances. If we continue living the same lifestyle for years, the imbalances set in deeper and over time our body gives up & makes a disease.

Weak Digestive Fire: Our digestive fire that is responsible for burning and metabolizing foods gets weakened due to our wrong dietary & lifestyle practices. This leads to partial digestion of consumed foods. These partially digested foods convert into toxins and accumulate and reside in the digestive tract, before progressing our disease forward.

Accumulation: Due to imbalanced body state & weak digestive fire, the accumulation of toxins begins to surface. It physically shows up as lethargy, heaviness of the limbs, bloating, weakened digestion, burning sensations, increased body heat, bitter taste in the mouth, stomach acidity, pale skin, acne, breaking skin, gastric issues, eczema, increased anger, body dryness, stiffness, flatulence, constipation, disturbed emotions, emotional upsets, mood swings, disturbed sleep, allergies, cold, flu, cough etc. At the initial state of accumulation & when our diseases show up in the form of these signs, it is relatively easy to handle our health state. If not healed (and not treated!) at this stage, accumulation of toxins leads to internal blockage. For example, for a sinus issue if we keep taking medications without strengthening our immune system, without correcting nutritional deficiencies and without putting a stop to allergic foods, over time sinus will surely become asthma!

Aggravation: When the accumulation of anything increases, it begins to aggravate and exert pressure. Aggravation can happen at physical as well as emotional level. At this stage, the accumulated internal blockages begin to aggravate and get deeper. They continue to increase and exert pressure in their areas of blockages. At this stage, the initial symptoms begin to become impactful & show up in the form of frequently occurring health issues such as frequent headaches or frequent allergies etc. This stage is even a stronger indicator that our disease is setting in deeper. However, it is still easy to roll back the symptoms and regain health at this stage, as till now the organ damage or any other serious damage is not done. However, if you go ahead with any treatment to suppress the showing symptoms, you are setting your problem still deeper! Healing will require changing your ways of diet and lifestyle while treatment will not demand anything from you except popping a pill to suppress the issue. You will definitely feel temporary relief with a pill but the issue will surely resurface again!

Overflow: Like a bucket full of water spills if the water supply is not stopped. Similarly, i: aggravation of toxins is left uncontrolled, the toxins begin to spill over in the neighborhood and look for new places to settle down. Needless to say the symptoms at aggravation stage begin to get worse and may show us as feelings of vomiting, pain in the colon and painful elimination, burning sensations followed by diarrhea, gastritis, excessive sleepiness, talkativeness, activity or strong emotions of joy or sadness. Until this stage also the damage is reversible as still, it has not damaged any functional body unit.

Localization: Due to the overflow of toxins to their neighborhood, the localization of toxins begins to occur. This means that the toxins move within the body and localize in some area and begin to deteriorate those areas. The deterioration may lead to malfunctioning of the localized area or structural damage at the place of toxin localization. This is the stage from where the beginning of specific degenerating diseases and susceptibilities to serious infections begin. However, healing is still possible until this stage.

Symptom Manifestation: After settling at various localized sites, the toxicity manifests as the initially recognizable signs of a chronic disease. It is at this point that the western medicine is able to detect, classify or diagnose the signs of chronic diseases such as arthritis, PMS, cancer, diabetes or any other modern disease. At this stage, the disease begins to erupt physically on the outside as obvious clues such as inflammation, skin eruptions, enlarged glands, abscesses etc. This is a cleansing act by the body to get rid of toxicity that is already upto the brim by now. It erupts as swelling, skin eruptions or tumors under the skin. Though it becomes tougher, by this stage, our body still privileges us with healing scope if we turn back to the right ways of living and provide our body with right healing environment. However, healing at this stage requires a lot of dedication & may take much longer.

Differentiation: This is the final chronic stage where the manifestation of symptoms get deeper to the extent that it damages the functional units of our body such as heart, kidneys, lungs etc. This is the stage where you complete the life cycle of birthing your own disease after years of abuse on your body. However, it is important to know that this stage arrives only after giving us ample clues at different stages in last few years. It is only when we keep ignoring the clues that this stage arrives. This stage requires serious efforts & healing & treatment go hand-in-hand at this stage.

TRADITIONAL CHINESE MEDICINE'S VIEW OF DISEASE PROGRESSION

As per Traditional Chinese Medicine the progression of a disease is dependent upon the following elements of nature:

Heat: Heat disorders are related to the burning sensation inside the body. The feeling is somewhat similar to how we feel under the strong sun, like, tired, burning, lethargic, weary, thirsty and dull. When we are under the influence of heat, we seek coolness and only cold things get us back to life. Physical manifestations of heat show up as body heat, red face, hyperactivity, talkativeness, weak heart, fever, boils inflammation, constipation, dry skin, dry mouth or high pulse. Heated body condition is energy depleting & rapidly dries out the body fluids causing dehydration and exhaustion.

Cold: Cold disorders are related to cold sensations. This feeling shows up in the form of chills, fever, body ache, pale face, lethargy, grogginess, headache, craving for heat and sleepiness.

Wind: Wind disorders are related to the nature of moving air causing some bodily issue of the other rotationally. This feeling shows up in the form of broken skin, lung issues, twitches, fear, headaches, seizures, dizziness, ringing in the ears and a stuffed-up nose. Windy body condition is also related to changing thoughts and instability.

Dampness: Dampness disorders are somewhat like a damp backyard that becomes a breeding ground for viruses, fungi, and bacteria. This feeling shows up in the form of heaviness, body expansion, stuffy chest and abdomen, heavy limbs, stiff joints, nausea, lack of appetite, upset stomach, swollen abdomen, sluggishness, lethargy, sticky body discharges and diarrhea.

Dryness: Dryness disorders are related to the cracked dry earth. This feeling shows up in the form of dehydration, dryness, respiratory problems, asthma, dry cough, acute pain, drying body fluids and fever.

Ancient Chinese culture believes that diseases are a manifestation of these natural forces settingin deeper into our body system and becoming more serious. For example, a minor cold is an external condition caused by cold and may set in deeper to become pneumonia. Other miscellaneous causes of diseases in TCM include stress, thoughts, trauma, feelings, environmental pollutants, parasites, poor posture, drug and alcohol use, poor dietary, lifestyle habits and disharmony with nature.

EMOTIONS AS A CAUSE OF PHYSICAL DISEASES

When you feel stressed why do you get a headache? `

When you feel hungry why do you begin to get angry or irritated?

Traditional Chinese Medicine considers a strong connect between thoughts, emotions & physical diseases. As a matter of fact, the ancient Chinese texts associate different emotions with imbalances in different organs of the body. Specifically, if a person carries negative emotions for long, it may be an indication of weakness in the associated body part. For example, frequent anger and short-temperateness is associated with liver & may impact its functioning over the years. The following emotions are considered to be the prime causes and crucial indicators of major internal illnesses in specific parts of the body:

Grief and Sadness: Grief is a normal response to loss. However, if it lingers on, it begins to damage the lung functioning. Like all other emotions, the grief cycle must cross its stages of denial, anger, bargaining, depression and acceptance. If you get stuck in the grief cycle, it blocks the energies in the lungs and may emotionally manifest into an inability to let go off, sadness, low self-esteem, rigid belief systems and being judgmental.

Worry: Worry in its normal state affects you from time to time but rationalizing thoughts balance worry. Worry may turn into obsessiveness and may give rise to irrational behavior. Too much of worry affects the spleen functioning and vice versa.

Fear, Fright, and Anxiety: Fear and anxiety are closely associated with our negative thought process. Fright is more of a reaction to a shock. Though fear and anxiety are not considered as disease causing emotions in modern medicine, in Chinese medicine it is believed that your kidney function is directly impacted by feelings of fear. Rather, weak kidney function may give rise to anxiety, panic attacks and lack of willpower.

Joy: The expression of joy is symbolic of happiness and is directly associated with the heart health. The heart is considered to be the house of emotions. Positive feelings of joy, love and happiness birth from a healthy heart.

CHAPTER 21 - KNOW YOUR GUT – YOUR MOST POTENTIAL DEFENCE SYSTEM

'Digestive system holds the supreme seat in human health. Ayurveda recommends healing the gut first, irrespective of any serious illness. However, in case of no disease, prevent diseases by healing the gut!'

First Level of Digestion – The Mouth: Digestion begins in the mouth. Chewing is of prime importance and the most underestimated digestive activity. On chewing, the salivary glands begin digesting the foods and make it alkalizing. Chewing well is also the beginning of your detox process. Going wrong at this stage may cause gastro-intestinal troubles including gas, acidity, bloating and digestive issues.

Second Level of Digestion – The Stomach: Stomach is the second chamber of digestion where the food breaks down into nutritional elements. If you chew your food well, consume fiber-rich foods, consume fermented & enzyme based foods, reduce sugar consumption, your stomach acid that is hydrochloric acid strengthens and leads to good digestion. If you consume high sugary foods or alcohol, they mix with the blood instantly at this stage, causing blood sugar disturbances, hyperactivity, a sudden rush of energy, bloating and negative impact on immunity.

Third Level of Digestion – Digestive Juices & Liver Act Upon Food For Further Processing: After nutrition is extracted from foods, it is further acted upon by the digestive juices. If you consume high sugars, it will get converted into fat and will be stored in the liver. If you consume a lot of chemical-based stuff and toxins in other forms, the liver will be burdened to detoxify all. If you consume a lot of foods containing saturated fats, trans-fats or hydrogenated fats, it may all be converted into fat and may cause fatty liver and body toxicity.

Fourth Level of Digestion – Extracted Nutrition Reaches Small Intestine For Nutrient Absorption:

At this stage when the core nutrition from previous activity reaches the small intestine, the nutrition is absorbed and mixed with the blood. If the quality of this core nutrition is not good because of our unhealthy dietary habits, the blood will be toxic & will contain low-quality nutritional extract. This toxic blood circulates and reaches the entire body and spreads toxicity to all cells, tissues, and organs. If the quality of your food is highly nutritious, the blood carries good extract and nourishes the whole body.

CHAPTER 22 - BLOOD – MEET THE TRANSPORTER

'You only receive what a transporter supplies, irrespective of what all the world has to offer! In case of our body, blood is the transporter & nutritional extracts from our food commute through this medium to reach & nourish all parts of the body. There is no other transporter of nutrition to nourish the body, & hence, the quality of nutritional extracts really matter!'

What's in the blood?

EVERYTHING! And, the phrase 'You Are What You Eat' comes true when you understand how your food forms blood and how blood becomes you.

What you eat → Breaks Down Into Nutrition →Nutrition gets absorbed in the small intestine →Mixes With the Blood → Blood Stream Flows Through Arteries → Nutrition Reaches Cells, Tissues & Organs.

Our blood plays an important role in keeping us healthy or making us diseased. If we eat clean and nutritious foods, our blood quality becomes pure & it is able to supply the good quality nutrition, hormones, water, chemical messages and even information, to each nook and corner of our body. However, if our food quality is poor and contains toxic elements, the same toxicity mixes with the blood to be passed on to the entire body. So, it is important to maintain the quality of blood through right dietary and lifestyle ways.

To transform yourself physically and emotionally including your skin health, digestive health, immune health and overall well-being, you must work on improving your blood quality. Improving blood quality requires a minimum of 3-4 months. This is because our red blood cells keep dying and new cells keep forming every 3-4 months. So, ideally, the way you look and feel today, is all that you carry in your blood for last 3-4 months. What you eat today and for next 3-4 months will decide the state of your health 4 months later. Most importantly, what you eat, drink and absorb over this time creates your blood. For example, if you ate too much junk food in last 4 months, the blood cells that your body creates will contain the toxic elements manufactured from junk food. Same toxicity will be passed to the whole body. Good blood quality is the small little secret to protect ourselves from deadly cancer. Rather, your moods, mental function, and moodiness also highly depend upon how clean or toxic your blood quality is. Good blood quality keeps away aging, makes you feel and become youthful, energized and active at all levels of existence.

CHAPTER 23 - ART OF LISTENING TO YOURSELF

'Somebody rightly said, 'Listening is an art to be developed!'. Our body communicates with us often & shares its inconveniences. We must develop the art of decoding what our body tries to communicate...body never lies!'

Next time when you ignore your body's signal to defecate because you are watching your favorite TV serial, think again. The exponential effect of a momentary pleasure may be impacting your entire body!

Learn the art of listening to your body. If your body signals tiredness, give it rest. If it signals hunger, feed it right. If it signals thirst, quench its thirst with water. Listening to ourselves is about respecting our body and its needs. Our body only bothers us to indicate that something inside needs our immediate attention. Our body's call is always genuine & it only troubles us when it is in trouble...trust it for your own good!

Ayurveda has laid special emphasis on few body signals that must be attended to immediately for a healthful state for years. For example, your breathing difficulty may signal dehydration initially. If ignored, it may come back again as a more serious call with something else wrong within. Cancer calls you out to communicate the body lacks nutrition, oxygen and that lessen your sugar & dairy intake. It keeps communicating that the cells inside the body are behaving notorious. Bear in mind that your body never ditches you unless you stop listening to it. Rather, it does not ditch you in the state of disease too. If you fail to listen to it, it keeps trying to self-heal till the end. As its own effort to self-heal, our body is left with no choice to disturb some other internal parameters. This happens only if we continue with our inappropriate ways of eating & living.

Seemingly minor body signals may be communicating something important, even if your doctors do not believe or interpret it. It is only you who can listen to yourself, master the art! Specifically, the natural urges must not be ignored at any cost.

Hunger Call: You get this call when your body is in dire need of right nutrition to perform its internal functioning. Ignoring, controlling or suppressing the signs of hunger continuously, or feeding your body the wrong foods will lead to weakness, dull lifeless skin, anorexia, body aches, depression, dizziness, unstable moods, weight loss, and exhaustion. It is also important to differentiate between fake and actual hunger calls.

Thirst Call: You get this call when your body is in dire need of hydration. Ignoring, controlling or suppressing the signs of thirst continuously, or quenching your body with wrong drinks such as cola's, artificially sweetened beverages or alcohol will lead to internal imbalances. Some symptoms of chronic dehydration include emaciation, dry mouth, exhaustion, deafness, weakness, generalized debility, deafening and heart disease.

Cry Call: You get this call when your body is full of uncontrollable emotions and is in dire need of an emotional outlet. Controlling or suppressing this call may cause rhinitis, eye issues, heart disease, running nose, headache, dizziness, mental issues and depression due to emotional blockage.

Sleep Call: You get this call when your body needs rest and is in dire need to rejuvenate. Controlling or suppressing this call may cause drowsiness, constipation, body ache, headache and heaviness in the eyes, delusion lethargy, indecisiveness, confusion, mental fogginess, lack of enthusiasm, habitual insomnia, and digestive issues.

DefecationCall: You get this call when your body has done its job of extracting nutrients from the food and is in dire need to eliminate the leftover waste matter. Controlling or suppressing this call may cause toxicity, headaches, flatulence, abdominal issues, colonic issues like hemorrhoids and even heart block up in emergency cases.

Flatulence Call: You get this call when your body is producing excess wind for various reasons and is in dire need to get rid of the wind. Controlling or suppressing this call may cause abdominal pain, ulcer, tumor, indigestion, constipation, digestive issues & chest pain.

Urination Call: You get this call when your body purifies the blood & fills the bladder with waste liquids that need to be eliminated urgently. Controlling or suppressing this call may cause weak kidneys, pain in the bladder and groin area, headache, bloated lower abdomen, urinary tract infections and body aches.

Sneezing Call: You get this call when your body is in dire need to get rid of irritants such as germs, dust, pollen and other pollutants. Controlling or suppressing this call may cause a headache, dizziness, impact on vision, neck stiffness & even facial paralysis.

Vomit Call: You get this call when your body is in dire need of eliminating high body toxicity. Controlling or suppressing this call may cause skin issues such as itching, nausea, blemishes and anorexia.

Yawning Call: You get this call when your body is in dire need of more oxygen. Controlling or suppressing this call may cause stiff neck muscles, headaches, dizziness, convulsion, tremors, and numbness.

Hard Breathing: You get this call when your body is in dire need of more oxygen by force such as after exercise. Controlling or suppressing this call may cause heart disease, abdominal tumor, and fainting.

Cough Call: You get this call when your body is in dire need of clearing the breathing passage of mucus, irritants, viruses, bacteria & mucus. Controlling or suppressing this call may cause loss of appetite, respiratory issues such as asthma, tuberculosis, loss of appetite, heart disease & hiccups.

Burp Call: You get this call when your body is in dire need of eliminating stomach gas caused by certain stomach intolerances.

Controlling or suppressing this call may cause tremors, chest pain and loss of appetite.

Allergy: You get this condition when your immune activity is weak. Ignoring allergies can make them set in deeper, for example, over time minor sneezes, cold and cough can reach the respiratory tract to become bronchitis or asthma. They may also manifest into eczema, wheezing or itching.

Cravings: You get this condition when your body is craving for certain nutritional elements. Consuming wrong foods may lead to further deficiencies, weight gain, blood sugar imbalances & immune and digestive issues. Cravings for the body may mean the following:

Craving	Body's Need	Foods That Satisfy Craving
Chocolate	Magnesium	Raw Nuts & Seeds, Legumes, Fruits
Cool Drinks	Manganese	Walnuts, Almonds, Pecans, Pineapple, Blueberries
Menstrual Cravings	Zinc	Seafood, Leafy Vegetables, Root Vegetables
Overeating	Silicon	Nuts, Seeds, Avoid Refined Starches
	Tryptophan	Cheese, Raisins, Sweet Potato, Spinach
	Tyrosine	Vitamin C Supplements, or Orange, Green, Red Fruits & Veggies
Craving Liquids Than Solid Foods	Water	Flavored Water With Lemon & Limes

(Continued)

Sweets	Chromium	Broccoli, Grapes, Cheese, Dried Beans
	Carbon	Fresh Fruits
	Phosphorous	Fish, Eggs, Dairy, Nuts, Legumes
	Sulphur	Cranberries, Horseradish, Cruciferous Vegetables, Kale, Cabbage
	Tryptophan	Raisins, Sweet Potato, Spinach
Oily/Fatty Foods	Calcium	Mustard & Turnip Greens, Broccoli, Kale, Legumes, cheese, Sesame
Bread/Toast/Refined Carbohydrates	Nitrogen	High Protein Foods
Alcohol/Drugs	Protein	Meat, Poultry, Seafood, Nuts
	Avenin	Steel Cut Oats
	Calcium	Mustard & Turnip Greens, Broccoli, Kale, Legumes, Cheese, Sesame
	Glutamine	Supplement Glutamine Powder, Raw Cabbage Juice
	Potassium	Sun-Dried Black Olives, Potato Peel Broth, Seaweed, Bitter Greens

(Continued)

Coffee/Tea	Phosphorous	Poultry, Fish, Eggs, Dairy, Nuts, Legumes
	Sulphur	Egg Yolks, Red Peppers, Muscle Protein, Garlic, Onion, Cruciferous Vegetables
	NcAI (Salt)	Sea Salt, Apple Cider Vinegar
	Iron	Meat, Fish & Poultry, Seaweed, Greens, Black Cherries
Chewing Ice	Iron	Meat, Fish & Poultry, Seaweed, Greens, Black Cherries
Soda & Carbonated Drinks	Calcium	Mustard & Turnip Greens, Kale, Legumes, Cheese, Sesame
Burned Food	Carbon	Fresh Fruits
Acid Food	Magnesium	Raw Nuts & Seeds, Legumes, Fruits
Salty Food	Chloride or silicon	Raw Goat Milk, Fish, Unrefined Sea Salt

CHAPTER 24 - DRUGS SIDE EFFECTS – THE UNTOLD STORY

'Treatments cost you money, effort, time, pain & side-effects! Side-effects is a safe-term to define a readily accepted disease in return of another one!'

The easy availability of over-the-counter drugs has increased their consumption multi-folds. Where a lot of people consume these drugs for quick relief from their illnesses, subtly and with acceptance, they are ingesting another disease in the bargain of the previous one!

The 'Side-Effect' epidemic has risen over the years, specifically for the people who are continuously on medications for their chronic conditions. Though we willingly accept a drug with its side effects, for our body a side-effect is still a sickness even if it is acquired as a bargain to treat another disease. For example, overuse of antibiotics destroy the intestinal flora causing digestive issues to crop up. Medications for chronic diseases such as Parkinson's play havoc not just on the digestive health but moods and emotional health as well.

In many cases of sickness, the medications can be totally avoided, specifically the minor health issues. Ironically, we take medications for minor issues such as sinus, allergies, headaches, stomach issues etc. without even giving it a second thought. However, we never give a thought to what we can change in our diet or lifestyle that these issues do not cropup at all. Simple dietary and lifestyle changes can work wonders to strengthen your own defense system against the sickness battle. Due to your lack of health & awareness or due to unwillingness to change, you may be playing with your own health.

All drugs during their trial periods must go under stringent testing phase. Drugs that are being developed to cure a disease end up giving back a disease. This is even after the trials are declared successful & happen in an unbiased environment & under stringent rules & regulations.

However, our body is not a testing lab where only one chemical operates under controlled environments. Numerous processes operate within us simultaneously. When a tested drug enters our body, how it reacts inside depends upon person to person. If you are simultaneously on several medications, you don't know what side-effects other medications may be causing & what is the cumulative effect of various side-effects manifests into!

The reasons for a medication to go wrong inside our body may be plenty even after clinical trials. This is because the labs in which medications are tested may test just a small fraction of possibilities of the medication going wrong. For some drugs, the side effects actually appear after their usage and it has happened in so many cases. So, many drugs have been banned in the past by the regulatory authorities after their continuous use reported severe side-effects. Some drugs are known to have an addictive effect, specifically the cough syrups. However, what side-effects an individual experiences totally depend upon an individual, medication dosage, disease, gender, age and how chronic the health state is.

The regulatory law says that if a drug is reported to be causing severe and dangerous side-effects, the Food & Drugs Association (FDA) holds the authority to ban the drug and recall it from the market. Now, why do you think that will be the case? Because somewhere FDA is aware of the fact that no medication is totally safe and this law keeps them in a safe zone. Further, the numbers in case of drugs are highly profitable and the users get relief quickly. We see how much we pay for our treatments! It works as a win-win situation for both the drug manufacturers and the patients, as long as they get treated!

Some known and reported serious medication side-effects include:

Dizziness: The most commonly known side effect, it can give vertigo like feeling. It may make anyone lose balance and get hurt.

Nausea & Vomiting: Again a commonly known side-effect, it does not even count as a side effect, we are so used to it! Apart from disturbing the routine, it may cause various other internal problems such as dehydration. Chemotherapy drugs, pregnancy medications are known to cause this side-effect.

Heart Conditions & Stroke: Research suggests that heart conditions & strokes may happen as a side-effect of many drugs. Rather, in somecases, doctors are quite aware of dangerous side-effects of prescription drugs and prescribe refraining from their long-term use. Strokes may happen as a result of blood clots which is a known side-effect of many drugs. Some painkillers have been associated with strokes.

PART 3

This section empowers you to understand yourself & the way human beings operate as per set patterns of nature. It discusses the universal laws of nature that help us set our beliefs in self-healing. It tries to explain why we are so intricately connected with the nature & how our body responds to positive thoughts and creates a healing environment inside. Alternatively, how our body responds to the negative thoughts & creates a diseased environment inside. Why we are inseparable beings of the nature & how nature's activities & patterns impact our body machinery. This is an empowerment section that helps you to understand how the human body is designed to function in a particular fashion & why it is so important to live a disciplined life that begins with the rising of the day & slows down with the setting of the day.

INTRODUCTION - THE HOLISTIC CONNECT OF BODY, MIND & SOUL

'The essence of our holistic connect is visible in the intricate, inseparable & interdependent connect between our body, mind & soul. When on a healing journey, these three aspects are considered equally important. It is because each of these is a real aspect of ours that exist at different planes. Over the years, our understanding about health has just got limited to our physical being because of its visible & tangible aspect! Rest two planes, 'mind' & 'soul' form us at feelings, thoughts and beliefs level. This invisible & intangible self of our body often gets ignored as an important part of our treatment the modern way. However, true healing is a culmination of these three real planes. So, repairing the mind to heal the body and recovering the soul is a one-liner crux of holistic healing!

Do you feel dull and irritated if you are continuously constipated?

Do you feel stomach or digestive issues when you feel low and depressed?

Do you feel an overwhelming rush of thoughts when you are physically fatigued?

When you feel depressed does your body slow down or ache?

And, do you see the connect?

With each of your physical miseries, a complimentary emotional misery is connected! Our holistic connect is very much a reality & it shows in our day to day life functions. Let's explore this connect in further sections.

CHAPTER 25 - UNIVERSAL LAWS OF NATURE – ANCIENT GUIDELINES FOR MODERN HEALTH

'Universe & nature seem to be working within the scope of their own inherent intelligence. No one created the day & night by coding something somewhere. No one ever taught anyone how to eat or eliminate. No one grows a fetus in a mother's womb, nor does anyone makes the weather's change. There exists some inherent intelligence in the patterns of nature that rule the functioning of all life-forms on earth!'

Our universe is inherently intelligent including all its elements and life-forms. The universe operates on unchangeable universal laws that apply equally to everything. Knowingly or unknowingly we all abide by these universal rules. For example, nobody initiates a weather change, it happens all by itself. Rather, the intelligence of nature is quite visible in its ability to cool the weather as soon as it gets too hot. No one makes a fetus grow in a mother's womb. Nature has its own intelligence to phase-out this growth and initiates the birth when a baby matures. No one makes any machinery run to flow the flowing rivers. No one creates hunger inside our body, our body is inherently intelligent to figure out its depleting resources and communicate its needs to our senses. No one created the rule to sleep at night and work through the day, it all works automatically based on nature's inherent intelligence.

Ancient sciences had been quite aware of the universal laws of nature that apply to the entire universe as a whole. Interestingly, the laws that govern the nature also govern our body systems and its internal functioning. Whether it is our digestion, hormonal activity, immune system, sleeping or waking cycle, elimination cycle, our

Healing Foods Cookery Classes

COOKING ALKALINITY

HEALTH & LIFESTYLE

TRANSFORMATION THROUGH EMPOWEREMENT

Macrobiotic Dietary & Lifestyle Consultations

Health Empowerment Workshops

MACROBIOTIC WELLNESS

thoughts and brain functioning, everything operates in a specific pattern based on this intelligence and universal laws.

In modern times, we continuously violate these laws of nature and the impact shows in our continuously deteriorating physical and emotional health. When we understand these laws and begin to live as nature intended us to live, the positive signs of transformation in our body and mind begin to show up. The knowledge of these laws also empowers us to take right decisions with respect to diet, lifestyle, relationships, choices and other areas of life. That's how ultimately we get transformed by knowing who we are, how we operate, how our body operates and how we are so closely connected with the universe and its happenings.

The dominant laws of nature that apply to our everyday life include:

- ❑ Humans are intricately connected tonature. Any changes in the nature outside impacts the human body from inside.
- ❑ The human body is highly intelligent & functions in accordance with the cycles and rhythms of nature. The fundamental rule to maintaining good health and well-being is to abide by these cycles such as sleeping early and waking up early.
- ❑ Nature has designed the day to work & night to sleep. During the day, nature has designated times to perform particular activities. For example, morning 9 a. m. – 11 a. m. is considered to be the best time for taking important decisions & doing crucial work for best results.
- ❑ Health is a natural state of the body. We were born to be active, happy & healthy, & that's how we are designed to departure.
- ❑ Nature reverses its negative course on humans if humans begin supporting the nature intended ways of eating & living.
- ❑ Human beings create their diseases themselves by making faulty decisions & choices about diet, health & lifestyle.

- ❑ Human body inherently possesses self-healing powers. These healing powers only work under the ideal environment including right foods, right cooking techniques, right thoughts, right actions, right living & right exercising.
- ❑ The human body has been blessed to get rid of toxicity & reverse decay, deterioration or diseases. The human body has the intelligence to repair, rebuild and renew itself. For example, a wound heals by itself, a bone reforms on its own and we recover from ill health under right circumstances based on body's inherent intelligence.
- ❑ Everything in the universe has a close connection irrespective of living or non-living status.
- ❑ Universe has fabricated the nature as well as all life-forms with the same basic material that is air, water, earth, metal & fire.
- ❑ Hierarchy of our health, happiness & well-being goes like this:

  Self-connect → Connect With People → Connect With Our Environment → Connect With the Universe.

- ❑ Nature strives for balance. It is always working on maintaining balance outside & inside the body due to its inherent intelligence.
- ❑ True health and healing involves 'whole' person'. It is not about treating only the diseased part. It involves time, effort and contribution from the sufferer.
- ❑ Nature & human body operates on an unseen energy that enlivens the body, mind & soul. If this energy gets blocked it leads to a diseased state of being.
- ❑ Human Beings possess an inner voice or conscience or intuition that directs us right at each step. It is important to listen to this voice as a guided path towards our goals.

- ❑ Food is not about counting calories and weight-loss. It is about body nourishment. Quite interestingly, when you stop counting calories and focus on nourishment, your most important health goal in life, that is the weight loss, is achieved automatically!

CHAPTER 26 - WHAT IS HOLISTIC HEALTH AND WELL-BEING?

'Despite of being alive we rarely experience liveliness. Many of us actually have no idea how good our body & mind are designed to feel. If you actually want to know what health, liveliness & happiness is visit a forest, observe animals, maintain silence & just listen to your heart!'

Merely the absence of a disease must not be considered as a state of perfect health. The absence of a disease is just a state of partial health, which means that at the surface level our body system keeps running and performing its routine jobs without any serious hindrances. However, the state of perfect health is much more than a temporarily fixed state of the body. Sadly, the entire world is running a marathon to achieve perfect health without knowing what health actually means. Further, the diseased individuals keep living in a state of partial health under the impression that our surrounding ecosystem is well-equipped to make us healthy. This ecosystem is the medical facilities! If this ecosystem had been the strength behind our health & wellness, no one would have been sick considering the existence of fantastic health ecosystem in modern times!

To define health simply, it is a perfect state of physical, emotional and mental health, where you are able to enjoy peace, calm & joy, irrespective of any external influences. Consider yourself physically and emotionally healthy if you experience:

- ❑ Disease-free body where you need not be on any kind of medications.
- ❑ Rare or nil incidences of falling sick. You are even free from minor health issues such as cold, flu, allergies etc.
- ❑ Enhanced energy, flexibility, strength and vitality.

- ❑ Happiness, joy, calm and peace as a natural state of being.
- ❑ Good appetite and regular bowel movement.
- ❑ Good biological functioning including strong immunity, ideal weight, good circulation, healthy digestion and balanced hormones.
- ❑ Radiant skin.
- ❑ Relaxed deeper breaths on a constant basis and a feeling of lightness in the body.
- ❑ The sense of comfort and harmony with yourself and driven by purpose in life.
- ❑ The sense of high self-esteem, self-trust, self-awareness, calm and comfort with oneself.
- ❑ Alertness, mental strength, and emotional stability.

CHAPTER 27 - PHASES OF HOLISTIC HEALING AT BIOLOGICAL LEVEL

'Actual healing is a slow & steady process & happens in phases. These phases may be troubling at times, not because healing is troubling, but because your own body abuse over years in the form of wrong dietary & lifestyle ways costs you a little hard when you get on to the right healing path. However, believe it, this trouble is for good! '

So, you worked hard to make your disease, expect some inconveniences when you work on a path of healing. When given an opportunity the human body will do its best to return to a healthy state of functioning, including the healthy state of cells, tissues, and organs. When you begin to transform yourself at any level be it dietary or lifestyle level, a process of physical change begins to take place. This transformation may include giving up processed, chemical-laden and artificial foods and adopting a whole and natural way of eating. It also includes beginning to listen to our body and performing rituals that support our life function. Exercising will further support this transformation process. Each person will have a unique response to this process. Your experiences at different levels of transformation will be as mentioned below:

Beginning Stage: The beginning stage of transformation includes a minimum of 3-4 months depending upon your body condition and health goal. When you give up your past poor dietary habits, sugar, saturated fats, animal fats and other past foods, and begin eating a clean diet consisting of whole and natural foods, your body will go through an internal transformation process where all internal health parameters begin to function better. During the beginning stage all toxins, accumulated fat, accumulated liquids, mucus, diseased tissues and other toxic elements begin to break and start getting out of the body. On breaking up, all these toxins look for rescue routes and enter the blood and other routes through which the elimination happens. Since this elimination happens through all body's detox channels including kidneys, colon, skin and lungs, initially you may feel few odd health symptoms. This is because at this point the toxicity of our body goes up temporarily when all toxins begin cleaning out from all corners of the body. For example, your skin condition may go worse initially and temporarily before it emerges as clear and radiant. This is a sign that accumulated toxins are trying to leave and the body has begun to prepare for a healthier state. However, where some people may not feel the elimination symptoms at all, others may feel sick initially. It all depends on how toxic you already and how your body decides to clean from within. Few common elimination symptoms may include hazy urination, skin rashes, and acne, aches and pains, headache, fatigue, insomnia, diarrhea, mucus discharge, loss of appetite of increased hunger, mood swings, bad breath, body odor, irritability and constipation. However, these are temporary elimination symptoms. By the end of 3-4 months, you begin to emerge as a somewhat transformed person. Your bloating and digestive issues begin to get better, immunity improves, skin becomes radiant, you begin to experience happy and joyous moods and your perspective towards life begins to change.

Intermediate Stage: The intermediate stage of transformation includes a minimum of 4-6 months. During this stage, the transformation begins to set in deeper and the signs of change experienced in the beginning stage stabilize. By this stage, you begin to get clarity on the balance and orderliness in all aspects of life and begin experiencing the positive energies of food in your physical and emotional states. The most important transformation that occurs at this stage is your blood quality begins to change and become clear and pure. With the blood quality getting better, your entire body gets to change at deeper levels. This means that your skin restores its balance without any signs of acne, dullness or rashes. You realize that you get lesser incidences of allergies, cold, cough, flu, and other regular health issues because the immune system continues to become stronger. The cessation of body bloating goes to a next level where the digestive issues get better good digestive health begins to gain permanence. Your bowels are working well at this stage, and the digestion process is happening smoothly. Healthier weight loss happens all by itself as it is an automatic response of healing process. Similarly, various other functional parameters of the body become much better in their functioning. The cumulative effect is visible in your settled physical and emotional health state.

Advanced Stage: The advanced stage of transformation goes beyond 6 or more months. During this stage, your transformation reaches a stable state. This stage is a typical example of healing from outside-in. When the changes become stable at the outer level that shows on the skin and general health and well-being, the healing sets in deeper inside. If you suffer from a chronic or any lifestyle disorders, the reversal may begin to happen at this stage, depending upon how chronic your condition is and how diligently you are working towards your transformation. By this time, though, you already know what is good for you, what works for you and what doesn't. This means any chronic health conditions begin to get better that shows in your medical tests!

CHAPTER 28 - BALANCE IN LIFE

'Balance is grounding. It helps you live life fully while enjoying all aspects of your life equally. From that equal focus on all aspects of life emerges satisfaction, empowerment, happiness & never ending zeal for life!'

Why do you crave salty foods after consuming too many sugary foods? Why do you feel the need to eliminate after a few hours of consuming hearty meals? Why do you sleep after days' work? Why does it rain automatically when the weather gets too hot? Why did the elders say that laugh less or else you will have to cry equally? Why do you need a break frequently even if you like your work? Why spending time with children, family and friends makes us happy after a day's of hard work? Why does silence follow anger? Do you feel at calm if you are pursuing any passiona long with work?

Think deeply and you realize nature's intelligence strives to maintain balance all the time. When any aspect of the universe, be it humans, other life forms or nature itself, begins to go out of balance, the other opposite force begins to dominate automatically. For example, we automatically crave salty foods after consuming too many sugary foods. Outside in the nature, it automatically rains when the weather begins to get too hot. These are all the balancing acts of nature and point to an important universal truth that nature sustains on balance. Even the diseases that we suffer from are a balancing act of our body, where, to balance internal functioning the body starts to compromise on certain other internal elements that lead to disorders. The concept of yin and yang in TCM specifies that everything in the universe sustains only on balance. If one force gets stronger even if it is positive, it will create a problem, like eating too many healthy sweets will rip off the body balance and will create deficiencies.

The term 'Balance' is strongly rooted in the ancient healing concepts. Balance simply means not overdoing anything and attending to all important aspects of our life equally. Balance is what human life sustains on. However, we live in an ever-changing world and maintaining a state of perfect balance may seem unachievable. It is important to understand what balance means to humans and how it applies to each sphere of our life. Each one of us sustains on various aspects of life. The balance of all these aspects is the key to perfect health and happiness. These important life aspects can be divided into following two categories:

Internal Balance

Internal balance refers to the balance with respect to internal body functioning. For example, osteoporosis is a classic case of acid-alkaline imbalance within the body. To keep itself alkaline, the body works against us and absorbs minerals from bones to maintain its functional balance. Causes of internal imbalances include nutritional deficiencies, internally weakened body state, tendency to get sick often, emotional upsets, feelings of irritation, loneliness, and fear. It is not a choice but an uncompromised need of our body to keep itself in balance all the time. The important aspects of internal balance include:

Mind: Mind is in balance when despite of negativities of life, we are able to rise above to achieve a balanced thinking state. It also means that we are able to challenge ourselves intellectually and keep progressing in life to achieve our goals. This balance is achieved by positive thinking, avoiding over thinking, accepting situation and life as it comes, meditating and by focussing on breathing right.

Body: Body is in balance when its internal functioning happens optimally and we are disease-free. The internal functioning is considered to be in the balanced state if we have stable body temperature, balanced blood sugar levels, balance acid-alkaline state, balance between consumption and elimination is maintained and balanced hormonal activity takes place. These internal parameters must be able to maintain balance irrespective of changes in weather, environment, foods, emotions etc. This balance is maintained if the organ functioning is efficient, hormonal system functions normally, theimmune system fights back infections strongly and lymph system gets cleared regularly.

Soul: Soul is in balance when we are able to attain a state of higher self, when our intuition guides up towards the path of righteousness, when we feel contended and unaffected by evens and odds of life, when we are able to understand ourselves and follow our paths of passion and when we become more giving, empathizing and loving towards others.

EXTERNAL

External balance refers to the balance that we maintain with our surroundings, our needs and aspirations, our professional life and in our relationships. We often compromise on external balance and end overdoing certain things by compromising on other important aspects. However, with right planning and awareness, we can completely take the control of our external balance and enjoy our life fully. This balance may begin to get disturbed when our work-life is out of balance, when we stay disconnected from nature in indoor environments day-in and day-out, when we give up our passions for work and when we stop growing at mental, emotional and spiritual level. The important aspects of external balance vary at the following levels:

Self-Time: Often underestimated, self-time is the strongest pillar of external balance. Pursuing passions, performing activities of interest such as gardening, reading, dancing, singing in continuum with our work profiles can keep us in balance to quite a large extent. Better still is to take time out for outdoor activities to be done amidst nature & experience a new realm of energy and vitality.

Personal Life: Work is never-ending, we must realize this fact intentionally. Breaking a never-ending work cycle and valuing other aspects of life equally, will help you live life in a balanced way. It will keep you in a stable state of mind and free of any guilt's and grievances. Family and friends are our backbone and time with them must be highly valued. Further, we are social animals too and living life without family and friends will surely put us off balance. However, social life can be sometimes pressurizing and one must consciously make sure not to get influenced by the thoughts, choices and the standards of modern society.

Professional Life: This is one area of life that gets out of balance way before one realizes. Never ending calls, stress, day and night work shifts, no time to enhance skills or self-growth, too much pressure and pushing oneself too hard for achieving goals just throws you out of balance. As humans, we were never born to work like machines. Rather, we are not machines! Plan and work out your professional life right.

CHAPTER 29 - WHAT IS VITAL LIFE FORCE – THE ENERGY?

'Universe operates on some unseen supreme force. The external universe comprises of rivers, mountains, oceans, volcanoes, plants, trees & other nature's elements; Our internal universe comprises of our body functions, thoughts & much more than the physical body. The same energy that makes the rivers flow externally makes our blood stream flow internally. The same energy that operates outside in the nature operates within us too. This force may be unseen & unexplainable in modern science, but it has a huge relevance in ancient sciences. Addressed as life-force, it is the source of moving & lighting-up the universe with vitality or aliveness!'

An interesting research study performed on a set of criminals and their dietary patterns reported that nearly all criminals were meat eaters and alcohol consumers. All of them showed typical traits of anger, violence, aggressiveness and thought patterns. The conclusion derived was that there is some aggressive energy about animal foods and alcohol that makes people develops animal type instincts such as aggressiveness. This aggressiveness may manifests into the crimes that they do!

Alternatively, consider the simple eating & living pattern of ancient monks, yogis, and saints. Their primary purpose in life is to meditate and achieve a state of higher self. And they very well realize that a state of higher self cannot be achieved without a disease-free body and a settled mind. So, as a part of their daily routine practices, they ensure to incorporate techniques that keep their body healthy and mind free of unwanted, disturbing thoughts. Their food habits revolve around freshly cooked seasonal foods, specifically of vegan type. Now, why is this specific eating pattern so common in all three meditative classes of people? What are these specific categories of food types providing them? And yes, you got that right! Through this specific food pattern, they are acquiring pure, freely circulating energy that helps keep their body disease-free, mind pure & promote their vitality or 'aliveness'. 'Aliveness' or vitality shows physically as healthy body, radiant skin, bright eyes, lustrous hair, shiny nails, strength, physical and mental strength, cheerfulness, zest, zeal for life, happiness, joy and overall reflects as the impressive positive aura of an individual. That explains why some people just glow from within and create a positive impact on others.

Modern science may take a few more years to realize that there is some kind of universal energy that gives us specific traits depending on what we choose to eat and how we decide to live. This energy system as understood by ancient sciences is much more than the currently prevailing nutritional system & calorie system. Ancient healing practices had a heightened awareness of this energy concept called 'life-force'. Life-force is known as 'Prana' in Ayurveda and 'Chi or Qi' in Traditional Chinese Medicine.

An electricity system best explains the concept of 'life-force'. Consider what lights up our houses, offices and electric gadgets. It is the energy in the form of power that is unseen, yet it is such an important aspect of our daily lives. Without electricity even for a few hours, our entire life comes to a standstill. Similar to this concept of electricity, there is an electric force that lights up our internal being, providing force for the functioning of our internal body system. It is the same force that operates outside in the universe that makes the river flow. The same force makes our blood stream flow throughout the body and helps it carry nutritional elements in its flow to be supplied to all parts, similarly like a flowing river carries minerals to be supplied to the surrounding vegetation areas.

Our body is a whole universe in itself.

Electricity System	**Life-Force in Ayurveda**	**Life-Force in TCM**
Lights/Moves the World.	Lights/Moves our Body.	Lights/Moves our Body.

(Continued)

Consists of a wired network & grid system at strategic locations. These grids act as energy centers.	Consists of an imaginary network or channels called 'Nadis, with energy centers at strategic locations called 'chakras'.	Consists of an imaginary network called 'Meridians networks' , with energy centers at strategic locations called 'Energy Centers '.
All systems shut off when the power goes off, whether it is lights, air conditioners, computers etc.	Life-force keeps us alive and when it draws out of the body, we become lifeless.	Life-force keeps us alive and when it draws out of the body, we become lifeless.

LIFE FORCE IN AYURVEDA

Life-force is called 'Prana' in Ayurveda. Prana enters our body when we are blessed with life in our mother's womb. It drives us throughout our lives and leaves the body at the moment of final departure. It keeps the physical and mental energies flowing inside our body. Physically, it is responsible for the flow of oxygen on inhalation, the flow of carbon-di-oxide upon exhalation, distribution of nutrients to various parts of the body, operation of metabolism and various other internal body functions. Mentally and emotionally it is responsible for the flow of positive or negative energies depending on what we eat, and how we live. These positive and negative energies form our thought patterns. Similarly like an electricity system, the life-force unites our mind and body and the quality of our life and health entirely depends upon the vitality that we have provided through the prana energy. This prana energy must flow smoothly through the body without any blockages. This is the ideal state of health at the foundation level.

Primary Prana Source for Our Body: Our lungs are considered to be the supreme seat of prana. From the fresh air we breathe prana that is the basis of our aliveness. Lungs absorb life-force from the environment (life-force absorbed in the form of oxygen preferably amidst lush green environment). We also derive a substantial amount of prana from our foods, water, sensory impressions and mental experiences. The quality of our vitality or aliveness depends upon this prana, and since in these times we are continuously depleting our body of vital prana due to our dietary, lifestyle habits and polluted environments, we possess weak prana that shows up in our physical and mental states as weak diseased body, lifeless appearance, dull skin and thinning hair, lack of will and power to accomplish aspirations in life. People, who are great achievers, have a will to succeed and keep moving forward in the areas of their interest generally possess that vitality that keeps them going.

Prana as a Body Fuel: Consider how a fetus develops into a full-fledged baby. Nutrition from the mother's womb acts as the building block and the life-force provides the energy to form limbs, organs, and liveliness in the baby. Prana travels through an imaginary channel or 'Nadis' , through which it energizes the building blocks of all life-forms. Prana acts as a fuel for our body at different planes. From the nose we inhale prana in the form of air and from our foods we extract prana. From the good quality of foods that we consume, good prana is extracted and from poor quality foods, poor prana quality gets extracted. At the foundational level, it is this good quality or bad quality prana makes all the difference between health and disease respectively.

At the psychological level, strong prana makes us receptive to all kinds of positivity. It helps us make right choices like including positive foods for nourishment and good prana, inculcate positive feelings and will to achieve a higher state of self-knowledge and self-understanding. Weak prana makes us attract negativity of all forms including wrong dietary habits, cravings, emotional vaccum, disturbing thoughts and wrong desires. Weak prana creates an imbalance at aphysical, emotional and mental level which, going forward, transforms into visible physical disorders.

Working on Prana: Air is the first and foremost element that must be worked upon to strengthen prana. This means that deep and fuller breathing pattern is an uncompromised need of our body as it draws prana from the outside air. This act of inhalation of fuller air will expand our energy, foster sense of peace and calm, creates alighter feeling in the body, keeps our thoughts grounded and stable, enhances vitality and maintains balance. Now, all those who meditate, perform breathing exercises or pranayama and exercise well, can relate to all the feelings that are just explained, due to the fact that through their physical activity they enhanced their prana quotient. After air, prana is majorly affected by the foods that we eat. Whole, natural, fresh and seasonal foods cooked lightly provide the best quality prana that reflects in physical health and vibrancy and radiance of a person. Other sources of good prana include what we take in through our sensory organs including good natural sights, good music, nice natural fragrances and how we think and perceive. The sound of 'OM' , which is an Ayurveda's meditative technique, is believed to create vibrations that can help instill the life-force into the subconscious and create more Prana in the mind.

LIFE FORCE IN TRADITIONAL CHINESE MEDICINE

The subtly rising vapors or steam in a pot of cooking rice is symbolic of life-force in TCM. Pronounced as 'Chi' or 'Qi' in TCM, it is considered to be the reason behind our aliveness. The ancient texts of TCM mention that the flow of chi is very much like the blood flow in our body. However, the only difference is that veins and arteries a physical and real channel through which the blood stream flows, whereas, energy channel is an imaginary channel existing on a different plane than physical, through which the energy flows and provides vitality to our cells, tissues, and organs.

Interestingly, in TCM the Chi is believed to be originating from the digestive system or the lungs and is believed to move in the body through acupuncture meridians that reach each and every organ and cell of the body. The theory is very much similar to what Ayurveda suggests. Rather, the originating points of chi both in Ayurveda and TCM are considered to be digestive tract and lungs. This also means that if we compromise on these sources, precisely foods and breathing capacity, our vitality is going to decline for sure. With the declining vitality, body imbalances shape up that manifest into our physical and emotional disorders.

As in Ayurveda, TCM considers that the life-force originates in the human body through following sources:

Prenatal Chi: This refers to the genetic life-force that you inherit through your genes from your parents. So, what your ancestors carried is passed to you as life-force, and that 'show we see how some people may be constitutionally weak while others are born strong. Prenatal Chi also depends upon the quality of food that mother consumes during pregnancy as well as her emotional health.

Air Chi: This refers to the life-force inhaled in the form of air. Better the quality of air better will be the chi that we inhale. Inhaling in a polluted environment means we are inhaling a poor quality chi that will impact our health negatively.

Food Chi: This refers to the chi that we take in in the form of food. The quality of food decides what kind of chi will be converted into our body after digestion. It also depends upon our digestive health.

CHAPTER 30 - OUR INTERNAL CLOCK

'Time is the key whether it is our external body activities or internal body functioning. There is no other bigger secret of health & well-being beyond this fact! '

Do you remember our parents and grandparents telling us to get up early and increasing our energy quotient through exercise during early morning hours, or eating dinner between 7 pm-8 pm?

Though our parents and grandparents may not have been successful to justify this logic to us, and so we may not have taken it seriously also, but there is a universal logic applying here – 'The Biological Clock' !

Talking about our internal body clock, all our organs have an active time associated with their functioning, during which the energy flows through that particular organ making it active. Activities performed in tandem with the body clock ensure optimal body functioning. For example, morning 3-5 the energy is active in the lungs, waking up at this time and exercising will give a new release of energy. If breathing, yoga or meditation is practiced during this time, it has maximum benefits. For asthmatics, this is the toughest hour and sufferers may feel breathlessness. Studies suggest many asthmatic attacks happen during this time.

Our connect with the nature is also tied-up with our timings & activities. Going against this connect creates body imbalances. Imbalances further lead to chemical disturbances in the body that over time becomes the manifestation of our disorders. Abiding by the right activity times as per our biological clock can help us keep fit and going for years! Detailed body clock timings are discussed in Part 5.

CHAPTER 31 - IMPORTANCE OF GOING ANCIENT IN MODERN TIMES

'Health & happiness is our natural state of being, and so, no new life on earth is born with a disease, a cough, a cold, an allergy, stress, depression or a cancer! It is how we connect with the universe that decides the fate of our health. We are all born healthy & our entire focus must be on maintaining our natural state of being. We must help ourselves with the right healing environment for our body, mind & soul. No property, no car, no fortunes, but perfect health is what we must gift ourselves day-in & day-out!'

What is our purpose or expectation from our treatment when we are diagnosed with any disorder? Rather, when you pop-in that small magic pill, what is your intent behind that?

I am sure the purpose of everyone is to heal, get better, feel better and be healthy for life. And, if your purpose aligns with this one, there is no safer, better, easier and cost-effective way to deal with your sufferings but to adopt aholistic approach to health & healing.

Health & well-being is not just limited to a few aspects of life, specifically diet or exercise that are considered to be the only modern standards of health & well-being. If that would have been the case, the entire world would have been healing and would not have been getting diseased, considering the entire world is dieting and exercising today!

Health is about you as a whole. The world is slowly realizing this and transitioning towards holistic ways of living! There has been a drastic increase in the number of students who pursue holistic studies, there are a lot of patients who are adopting macrobiotics, chelation, colonic therapy, homeopathy, acupuncture, nutrition therapy, Ayurveda, yoga, chiropractic, whole food supplements, exercise, stress reduction and other natural and other healing modalities. Many medical doctors are incorporating holistic methods into their practices, as they see the obvious failures of too many drugs. Even if the drugs work, they leave behind another league of diseases for you to handle later, 'the side-effects'. A subtle fundamental shift has already begun to show up globally. People today are more aware of the dark side of dairy foods, refined stuff and sugars. People are intentionally adopting and transitioning to vegan diets including foods such as whole grains, whole-grain products, beans, fresh vegetables, fruits, nuts and seeds as important part of their diets.

There is a great need to go holistic in modern times. We may be having the best medical infrastructure and the research studies may be evolving globally, still, the fact is that illnesses are increasing by the day. You never know one fine day you may get a massive heart attack without any signals, or you may get detected with cancer to shatter your life altogether, or arthritis or osteoporosis may cripple you for life, or worst still you lose your mind and senses to an Alzheimer's or Parkinson's, or your ability to enjoy food gets limited for life with a diabetes. This is a hard reality of modern times. Treatments are there and will be there always, but your quality of life will keep deteriorating if you do not put a stop to what feeds your roots and creates diseases. The life is no good with these irreversible body damages and it becomes a vicious circle of pain, suffering, limitations, unrealized aspirations, sadness, emotional upsets, ordinary life of struggle with something that we self-create. When we proceed towards treatments, all these important human aspects just get a miss, which are very much important for our happy existence in the world.

We come across so many cases of real-life stories of people who have come out of cancer with right thinking and the right approach to healing with holistic approaches. There also are people who are not ready to change their ways of thinking, eating and their ultimate resort is painful cancer treatments. Compared the after-treatment life of two, the cancer patients who have healed through a combination of holistic approaches and medical support not only have managed to cure themselves but their quality of life has enhanced than even before. And talk to a lazy cancer patient who has left his fate on treatment and recovered, the quality of life will be the same because they changed nothing about themselves after the treatment. Same ways of living, eating and thinking, and ultimately the same breeding ground for cancer!

The first line of health prevention begins with self. Further, the consumption of acidic foods is disturbing the fundamental elements of our body drastically. People who prefer prevention than suffering and treatment are actively adopting diets and lifestyles that are not only making them healthy but also helping them reverse their biological age making them feel better and become younger.

The little secret about health & wellness is 'Balance' , 'Prevention' and 'Awareness'. These three aspects help us maintain our internal and external balance. Talking externally, if you have created fortunes but are a workaholic, your balance is disturbed. In this case, your family life suffers. Internally, if you eat a lot but your body is constipated, you are again creating an imbalance that will result in a compromised state of health. Any internal or external imbalances will manifest into imbalances and will give rise to mind or body issues, that is the universal law of nature.

CHAPTER 32 - FOCUS ON MODERN MEDICINE – WHY?

'Western medicine is the highly developed, research-based treatment system that is growing along with our diseases! However, you must not be at rest considering that the treatments of your disorders are available. If treatments would have had cured us from the root, no one would have been sick considering we live in an age where western medicine is at its peak. No treatment or cure can beat what you yourself can create for yourself by adopting holistic approach to healing. Go holistic today, it may look like impossible initially, but your body & mind will thank you forever for adopting this way of life!

Now that you understand the in and out of your body functioning, and if a holistic approach to health seems to make sense, your next obvious question will be why does western medicine rule the healing world? Why it is that if there are potential natural mediums of health management already available, the people prefer 'pill culture' ? If we can revert back our health conditions with living right and eating right, why are people not adopting this culture? Why is this healing mechanism not adopted by everyone? Where are the gaps?

The answers to these questions are that Western medicine has come as a boon for the human race. For someone with a fractured leg or any sufferer of a chronic disease, nothing immediately works than the Western medicine. However, the gap here is that we have become way too much dependent on Western medicine as if our secret health is hidden in that small 'pill'. We have lost the sense of deciding how and when Western medicine must be incorporated into our lifestyle. Once a disease sets in, Western medicine along with holistic approach is a must to cure & heal the chronic conditions. However, for regular health issues such as headaches, allergies, seasonal flu, cold, cough, unexplained pains, sinus and other initially developing health issues nothing works best than adopting a holistic approach. Rather, adopting holistic approach at this first stage where diseases begin to crop, can save you from any big disorders that may be in the pipeline if we allow these nagging issues to grow. Somebody rightly said once, 'Prevention is better than cure' !

Though a lot of people are becoming aware and have started to adopt a balanced approach of combining the ancient healing modalities with the Western medicine, yet there are some practical reasons as to why people prefer Western medicine over the holistic approach to healing:

- ❑ Western medicine is a quick approach to treating our issues, whereas, healing is a permanent but slow and gradual approach.
- ❑ Western medicine works like a magic cure with all its solutions in a small pill. There is no expectation from you to change anything about your diet or lifestyle except in certain chronic condition.
- ❑ The unwillingness of people to change themselves. Getting out of the comfort zone and taking a step forward towards altogether a new way of life is unimaginable for our generation today.
- ❑ The inception of Western medicine has conditioned our minds to believe that no treatment happens without medical intervention. The thought has somehow created a deep-rooted niche within our psyche and our auto-response to any ailment is medication.
- ❑ The wide availability of medical facilities that further led to the rise of Western medicine as the first line of treatment for any disorder, minor or major.
- ❑ Western medicine reassures you a sense of confidence that all is well, though that reassurance is at surface level as the treatments are performed on the surface level of a disorder, we do not realize the roots still prevail!

PART 4

This section amazes you with interesting facts about how your face & body indicate your internal health & eating patterns. You will realize how your body, diet & lifestyle speak the story of your health that you may be knitting all by yourself over-the-years. This is an important as well as an interesting section that keeps you engaged through self-analysis.

INTRODUCTION - TELLTALE SIGNS THAT SPEAK OUR HEALTH STORY

'While each one of us is busy making our unique story in this crazy world, life is simultaneously creating its impression on us that shows up in our physical, emotional & mental health & well-being. The story of our life can be well read on our face, our body, our diet & our lifestyle!'

CHAPTER 33 - WHAT'S YOUR DIET & LIFESTYLE TELLING! – READING HEALTH IN YOUR DIET

'Your previous night's meal platter shows in your moods, behaviours & your general health the next day. If you consumed salad, you probably feel light, & if you had alcohol you may be feeling low, irritable & dizzy the day after. Similarly, your way of life may be your own choice but you do not have any control on the consequences that arise from your lifestyle choices. Your each choice & act is either taking you closer or away from a diseased state. Both your foods & lifestyle choices are actively forming you each single day & are visible in your looks, feelings, acts & daily experiences. '

Read how your diet & lifestyle is showing up on your face and body and how it may manifest into some disorder years later:

Dry, Rough, Falling & Thinning Hair: Dry, rough falling & thinning hair are a signal that body organs lack required nutrition. People consuming highly processed food diet, artificial sweeteners, too much of protein, lesser fruits & vegetables are more prone to hair loss or brittle hair. It also indicates kidney weakness and hormonal disturbances. Studies suggest that hair require a balanced diet consisting of adequate protein, vitamin C, zinc, iron and essential fatty acids to grow healthy and lustrous. This could also happen due to hormonal imbalance caused by certain dietary & lifestyle patterns.

Premature Aging & Troubled Skin Condition: This is a clear indication of high consumption of sweet, fried, oily, rich foods containing trans-fats or hydrogenated fats. Smoking and alcohol may further accelerate aging. This also means that the body lacks right nutrition. Alternatively, this may also indicate too much of internal toxicity and high need for the body to detoxify. A nutritious diet consisting of a diet rich in Vitamins B12, Vitamin A, Vitamin

C, Vitamin D, Vitamin E, essential fatty acids, antioxidants, and flavonoids is capable of reversing the skin condition and skin again.

Disastrous Oral Health: This could indicate high consumption of acidic foods, processed foods, chemical-based stuff, sweets, biscuits, and cookies, hard foods such as hard cookies or smoking. Even lot of sugary beverages and soda based drinks have been seen to have a disastrous effect on oral health. Rather, this could also be an indication of lack of Vitamin C. Eating foods such as apples, green leafy vegetables, strawberries help improve oral health.

Excessive Weight Gain: Eating too much high-calorie, low fibre, processed and refined category food leads to excessive weight gain. Lack of right hydration such as in the form of soda, sugar and caffeine drinks contributes towards weight gain. The first step to weight loss is opting for low-calorie, high fibre, unprocessed foods like fruits, vegetables and whole-grains, nuts, seeds, herbal teas and fermented foods.

Compromised Mental Health: Lack of good fats such as omega 3 & omega 6 fatty acids may drastically impact optimal brain functioning. Consumption of wrong fats in the form of trans fats and hydrogenated fats further creates a dull mind as these fats ruin the structure of brain leading to emotional manifestations in the form of low moods, depressive tendencies, and mood swings. Lack of hydration also impacts mental capabilities and overall it is an indication of nutritionally poor diet. Flax seeds, fish oil, walnuts and chia seeds help better the brain function.

Digestive Issues: High consumption of acidic foods, lack of enzymes in foods, lack of gut flora or good bacteria and consumption of heavy foods directly show up as digestive issues. Too much-refined foods, high consumption of cola's and sugary foods, drugs, medications, low-fibre foods, fried and oily foods and processed foods, all contribute towards compromised digestive health.

Compromised Immunity: Weak immunity has a direct link with a modern diet that is highly acidic, processed, and chemical based, highly salty and highly sweet. It also indicates severe nutritional deficiencies including minerals, vitamins A, vitamin C, vitamin E, zinc, selenium, iron, folic acid and vitamin B12. In the case of low immunity try consuming agood quantity of fruits, vegetables, whole grains, citrus foods and if need be, certain immunity boosting supplements such as vitamin C.

Feelings of Fatigue: Fatigue is a direct indicator of highly acidic and highly toxic body state. It indicates an urgent need to detox. It also indicates that your foods are getting heavy on your system and exerting pressure on your internal organs. It also indicates that you must include good-quality carbohydrate foods in your diet such as brown rice. Lack of nutrition especially anti-oxidants, vitamins and minerals may show up as physical or mental fatigue within the body. Vitamin B12 has been reported to fight the low feelings and help reduce fatigue. Other foods that you may be lacking include probiotics and food enzymes.

Lifestyle Disorders: Our lifestyle today is precisely about processed and chemical-laden foods, alcohol, smoking, sedentary, indoor, toxic, stress, smoking and disturbed general health. Our commonly consumed foods are sodas, alcohol, chips, chocolates, frozen & readymade meals, cookies, pastries, chips, bakery stuff, confectionery, refind flours and oils, refined sugar, bread, caffeinated drinks, tea, milk and milk products. What do you think will the outcome be? It is quite obvious, few of us will end up having diabetes, few will get affected with cancer, some will die of heart disease and others with something else. Ultimately that's the hard truth of what our lifestyle today that collectively speaks our health story.

CHAPTER 34 - WHAT'S YOUR FACE TELLING! – READING HEALTH ON YOUR FACE

'Our body & face are a mirror of our internal health. A beautiful & radiant person speaks good internal state of health. Similarly, a dull, lustreless & lifeless face & a diseased body has a story behind it that our doctors can read, why can't we!'

The 3000-year-old face reading heritage from ancient China - Face Reading, is still till used as a potent way to diagnose the internal state of health of an individual. It is believed that an expert Chinese face reader can read about 70% of an individual's health on their face. It is a great tool to figure any disease that may be in progress and helps diagnose them in their formative years versus Western medicine that diagnosis a disease only when it has reached its maturity. Hence, it can help people prevent any future health disasters. The most wonderful aspect of this diagnostic philosophy is that it can be used to prevent illness, as the initial warning signs begin to appear on the face and body.

Face: Dull, lifeless face indicates weak gland functioning, toxic liver and weak kidneys and weak digestive health.

Forehead: Forehead indicates weak digestive health and nervous system. Stress in these parts of the body may show up as breakouts on the forehead.

Nose: Nose is directly related to the circulatory health and circulatory organs that is heart. Red protruded tip of the nose could directly indicate an underlying heart issue or high blood pressure.

Cheeks: Cheeks directly indicate the health of the lungs. Ever wondered why your face looks fresh instantly after a workout? It is because with better lung activity remove the highlighted contant and shows on cheeks. Changing appearance or hollows on cheeks are a sign of lung and digestive weakness. It may also indicate that you must inhale oxygen deeply.

Chin & Jaw: The chin & jaw area indicates the reproductive health in women. That is the reason that near mensuration period a lot of women develop acne in mouth and jaw area. It is a strong indicator of hormonal disturbances as well.

Eyebrows: Thinning eyebrows indicate overall weakening health state. Two vertical wrinkled lines between the eyebrows indicate a toxic liver or pent up emotions.

Tongue: Tongue is the first and foremost organ that shows the toxicity of the body so clearly. The White color of the tongue indicates mucus accumulation in the body. Layered white coating on the tongue is a big indicator of high body toxicity, and indicates the need for a detox. Abrasions on tongue edges indicate probable lung issues and the importance of deep breathing exercise.

Eyes: Eyes and surrounding eye area may indicate varied health issues. Puffy eyes and eye bags indicate improper kidney functioning. It may also indicate a toxic liver state that needs detoxification. Yellow tinge in the eyes indicates a weak liver function.

Mouth & Lips: Mouth & lip area indicates the digestive health. Swollen lips indicate stomach disorders. Tight lower lip indicates weak digestion and weak intestines. Pink lips are an indication of good digestive health. Cracks on the corners of lips indicate vitamin B12 deficiency. Try incorporating probiotic foods and more green leafy vegetables in your diet for digestive health.

Ears: Ears are directly associated with kidney health. In TCM it is believed that kidney health shows up on the ears. A thick, well-formed ear is considered to be a sign of good health by birth. However, small ears are an indicator of weak health specifically kidneys and adrenal glands. Too much wax in the ears indicates consumption of foods high in fats and itchy ears indicate an allergy.

BEAUTY CONCERNS & THEIR FACIAL & DEEPER CONNECT

'Do you seek botox, medication or topical solutions for your skin concerns? Think logical when dealing with your skin. What shows on the outside of the skin is just what lies beneath. Similar to what a wrinkling orange looks like when its internal water begins to dry up, our skin begins to show aging signs when our underlying water begins to dry up. Your skin solutions lie in internal healing than external treatments!'

Acne: Acne is an indication of overactive oil glands that secrete excess oil through the skin and clogs pores. Blocked pores on the skin surface when come in contact with bacteria, may give rise to pus-filled acne, which is nothing but body's effort to get rid of excess oil through the skin. Acne could also mean poor bowel health, a diet high in unhealthy fats and impure blood. Cut down on high sugar consumption, unhealthy ways, processed foods, animal food and dairy for relief.

Excess Facial Hair: Particularly along the jawline, chin, and upper lip could be a symptom of polycystic ovary syndrome, a hormone imbalance in which male hormone levels are elevated.

Thin Hair: Thin and damaged hair indicate alack of minerals specifically silicon. Try consuming nutritious meals including more of fruits, vegetables, nuts, and seeds.

Crow's Feet: Crow's feet are a direct indicator of premature aging and acidic body state. Cut down on coffee, soda, tea and other processed and chemical-laden foods. Try consuming good quantity of fruits and vegetables.

Eye Bags: Eye bags or puffy eyes may happen due to lack of rest temporarily. If it is a permanent feature it indicates the need for a kidney detox. Drink plenty of water and cut down on chemical-laden foods including tea, coffee, soda, cold and frozen foods and artificial sweeteners.

Under Eye Dark Circles: Under eye dark circles have a connect with the liver and indicate toxic liver state. It also indicates that liver needs detoxification. It could also indicate iron deficiency. Cut down on chemical based food consumption and try to consume fiber rich diet.

Psoriasis: Psoriasis is a deep rooted skin problem that indicates toxic liver and gall bladder. It also is a sign of vitamin D deficiency. Try exposing yourself to early morning sunshine at least ten minutes a day.

Oily T-zone: Oily T-zone could indicate fat toxicity within the body. Oiliness on t-zone may just be the elimination effort of the body to get rid of excess oiliness. This condition is caused by over consumption of milk and milk products, consumption of poor-quality fats such as trans-fats and hydrogenated fats found in all commercial eatables.

Enlarged Pores: Enlarged pores could occur due to high consumption of white sugar or foods containing artificial sugars. It could also indicate overload on the pancreas. Cut down on sugar for relief.

Dry Lips: Dry lips could indicate dehydrated body. It could also indicate vitamin B12 deficiency. Increase your water and liquid intake for relief.

Sores Around the Mouth: Sores around the mouth or dryness or cuts on the corners of the mouth may indicate vitamin B12 deficiency. Try consuming vitamin B12 diet including potatoes with the peel, sweet potatoes, green vegetables and a b-complex supplement.

PART 5

This section guides you through the day to day activities that will help you strengthen your physical & emotional state of health. This section holds the key to the ancient art of self-transformation if followed routinely!

INTRODUCTION - DAY-TO-DAY FOUNDATIONAL STEPS TO HEALTH & HEALING

'The way you acquire your diseases because of your wrong dietary & lifestyle habits, similarly, you can help your body transform for good by again transforming your wrong patterns to the right ones. Learn to take the responsibility of your health on day to day basis, & over-time you will experience a healthier you. This is again a universal law that is unchangeable. Trust yourself; Strengthen your beliefs & get ready for transformation!'

Think about this self-reflective thought, 'How many of your family and friends visit hospitals frequently for disease-management? What lifestyles & eating patterns do they follow? What do they eat & how do they cook it? What food choices do they make & how do they think?

Radiant health is nothing more than true insights into these questions & taking small steps to transformation each single day.

Let's explore what your health & well-being is knitted from & let's try to knit it right.

CHAPTER 35 - DINCHARYA – AYURVEDA'S GUIDELINES TO LIVE THROUGH THE DAY

'Your daily choices determine how your future will unfold! Even nature follows a routine diligently. That is how nature maintains its balance. Night follows the day. Spring precedes summers, summers precede autumn, and autumn precedes winters. We must follow a disciplined routine, those who fail to do so, suffering precedes their life!'

Ayurveda focusses on the importance of a routine even before a healthy diet and a regular exercising routine. The very first rule while following a routine on day to day basis is to slow down. Making efforts to slow down your pace will keep your energy stable even if you keep working through the day. It will also keep you away from stress, anxiety, and tension of rushing into things that not just spoils the day out also creates body imbalances internally. Ever wondered how tired you feel if you are stressed, even if you do not work through the day. And how fresh you sometimes feel if you are relaxed, even after working through the day. Tiredness and stress deplete your energies from within, which causes mood swings and depressive tendencies. Your self-esteem goes for a ride in this emotional state and you feel self-empathetic and helpless. This impacts your attitude towards self and towards others. So, it is essential to practice peace and calm in daily routine and not to get carried away by the situations and happenings of life.

Ayurveda tradition further suggests that by following the ideal flow of dincharya, we delve into the best of what nature intends to offer. Dincharya has been practiced by ancient saints for thousands of years, not because they were bound to do so, but because they understood the body in a profound and respectful way. Let's explore what an ideal routine must be through the day as per Ayurveda tradition.

SAMPLE MORNING ROUTINE AS PER AYURVEDA

Dinacharya practice the importance of mornings as the most sacred time for self-rejuvenation, self-care and for setting the peaceful yet energetic pace of the day. Mornings in Ayurveda are much more than reading newspapers, having breakfast in a hurry and leaving for work. A rejuvenating flow of rituals in the morning lends you health, beauty, calmness, vitality and energy to begin the day with enthusiasm. Below is a sample dincharya as per the Ayurveda tradition.

Pre-Wake Up Time: As soon as your sleep cycle breaks, do not jump out of bed. Take a few deep breaths and stretch your body in the bed. It helps activate your bowels for complete elimination. Self-affirmations at this time will help your subconscious mind to focus on positivity through the day.

The Wake Up Time-5 a. m. : Ayurveda suggests that the ideal time to wake up is nearly 5 a. m. Our minds is fresh at this time and the life-force in the atmosphere at its peak during morning hours. It is recommended to consume a glass of warm lemon water. It activates the peristalsis movement that helps in cleansing the bowels. At this time the energy is active in the large intestines and so it is the best time to get rid of body wastes.

Rinsing Time: After bowel cleansing, one must brush the teeth and scrape the tongue to clean the mouth. Massaging teeth with a mixture of pure mustard oil and sea salt will keep teeth healthy. Splash cold water on the face will freshen you up. Wash eyes with pure cold water or rose water to brighten them up. As a precautionary measure against dust, pollen, germs or congestion in the nasal cavity, perform jalneti (the process is discussed in the further sections). It is a precautionary technique to be away from cold, flu or sinus related common issues.

Bathing: Bathing in Ayurveda is an elaborate ritual. Before bathing, you must rub your skin, toe to head with a coarse towel to activate circulation and calm the nervous system. Then you must oil the whole body with sesame or mustard oil and use a natural cleanser to wash off excess oil.

Yoga/Pranayama/Meditation: After the cleansing activities between 7 a. m. to 8 a. m., you must perform yoga, pranayama, and meditation. Sun salutations is a good yoga technique to stretch almost all muscles of the body. It is believed to have a calming effect on the whole body and gently massages all organs. It also regulates your breathing pattern and energizes you for the day. Alternate nostril breathing can be practiced after yogic exercises, followed by few minutes of meditation.

Eat breakfast: For a good digestion, Ayurveda recommends having breakfast between 8-9 am. During this time the energy is active in the stomach and foods consumed between this time will keep us safe from digestive issues, gastric issues and other stomach related troubles.

SAMPLE AFTERNOON/EARLY EVENING ROUTINE AS PER AYURVEDA

Work & Concentration Time: Between 9 a. m. - 12 p. m. it is considered to be the ideal time to perform the most important and decision-making activities of the day.

Lunch Time: Nearly by 1 p. m., Ayurveda suggests to consume a hearty, healthy, warm lunch.

Post-Lunch Time: Post lunch time in Ayurveda is considered to be a slow time as the consumed food goes through the process of digestion, making you feel relaxed and lazy as all energies get active in digesting food. A power nap during this time will make digestion do its job efficiently.

Back To Work Time: Time between 3 p. m. – 5 p. m. is again considered to be a good time to work. Concentration during this time is high and all important tasks to wind up the day must be performed during this time. A cup of non-caffeinated tea like ginger tea can help you get active and focus better.

SAMPLE NIGHT ROUTINES – AYURVEDA'S VIEW

Family & Relaxation Time: After 5 p. m., you must spend time for self-relaxation and be with the loved ones.

Dinner Time: Ideally, between 6 p. m. to 7 p. m., you must target to consume your dinner. Consume light meals at night, preferably soups and lightly cooked vegetables. At least 2-3 hours of gap between dinner and sleep helps the digestive system to be over with its tasks before sleep. This helps the digestive system to take a break and rejuvenate itself for the next day's digestion. It also helps the other body systems to perform their tasks in sequence.

Creating the Environment For Sleep: It is important to set the right mood for a good night's sleep. Dim the lights after sunset and refrain from using bright light during the night that confuses your system and sleep-producing hormones. This keeps sleep at bay.

Taking Warm Bath: Taking a fragrant warm bath before sleep relaxes the body and prepares it for sleep. You may use lavender, sandalwood or chamomile fragrances to relax your senses.

Gentle Walk & Foot Massage: Light walk at night freshens the senses. Also, pressing the acupressure points on the feet and massaging the feet before sleep is a great technique to relax the body and induce sleep.

Bed Time: Between 10 p. m. to 2 a. m. is the detox time of our body where various internal processes come together to detoxify you. For all those looking for enhanced beauty and strong immunity, 10 p. m. or before is the time to leverage the most out of it. The mantra is to be asleep before your body begins deep detox!

CHAPTER 36 - UNDERSTAND WHAT YOU EAT & WHY YOU EAT

'In a world where health choices are no simpler & retail shelves are full of health-foods, finding perfect foods is a big battle. Today's healthy food choices lead to confusion than health. The only way to choose right foods is to become empowered & Know thy foods. Remember the little secret - It is not the foods that you choose that make you healthy, but it is the foods that you understand take you on a healthier path. This is the forgotten message of traditional times!'

So, are you confused about your foods? Yesterday you read something about some healthy food that does not hold much relevance on health cards today based on latest studies and research!

Newspapers, articles, magazines, books, TV shows and a whole lot of media is centered around finding a magic diet that heals, cures, beautifies and provides anti-aging benefits. Some studies specify dairy is good, while others say it leads to toxicity. Some studies mention that animal protein is important for health while some discard it as the cause of heart disease and kidney problems. However, does it happen to you that despite of a whole lot of information available everywhere, you are still struggling to find that perfect diet that works for your specific health goals? Actually, we all are struggling to find our centering diet. And too much of research and studies on foods have killed the simplicity, originality, and purpose of consuming food. The segregation of diet types has mechanized the way we look at food, and has deviated us from the sole purpose of eating and nourishing ourselves. Today, we are struggling with the basics of diet and food to maintain our health. We are unaware what it takes to be healthy; we are unaware what is nutritious balanced diet for our body in the long run; we don't know what good foods and bad foods are and why; we don't know how to find the best diet. The simple answer here is listening to your body, eat what your body is most happy with and live in accordance with nature's rules!

Before entering the world of holistic health & wellness, I had been in a state of constant conflict with myself to balance my carbohydrates, proteins, and fats to achieve that optimal weight, clear skin and perfect health. I had been on a super healthy diet for years in hope to achieve my health goals, yet, I had been bloated, fatigued and had been continuously struggling with some nagging body issue or the other. On top of that, I had been an avid health & wellness reader and did not leave any recipe or remedy that I came across that could support my health goals. I have spent years strengthening my understanding on fats, calories, vitamins, free radicals, antioxidants and exercise. Sometimes it was soups and salads and someday it was fasting. Someday it has been a juice diet and someday a protein rich diet. I have tried it all, and all in vain! I call my efforts vain as the results were still not what I wanted. My knowledge of TCM, Macrobiotics, and Ayurveda laid a defined set path and right understanding about food and its applicability on our body.

The fact is there is a specific pattern to eating right, eating at the right time, cooking right, consuming it rightly and it is all set by the nature's cycle. Just by ensuring right nutrients in varied ways you cannot ensure the expected health goals…It simply does not work like that!

Advanced research and studies have managed to understand nutrition to its core. However, modern science did not ever understand why the natural foods like fruits, vegetables, grains, pulses, and legumes naturally have their specific measurements of nutritional elements. For example, why Vitamin C and Bioflavonoids are born in a combined package in a lemon. What is it that makes a plant grow and get its nutritional strength from? Why fruits and vegetables are considered to be the best food sources despite of all kinds of healthful foods available worldwide?

The modern understanding of foods is limited to taste and laboratory-prepared artificially nutrition fortified foods sold in appealing packaging. This is what we have been eating and thinking as healthy for over the years now. For example, corn flakes when sold with extra nutrition added in appealing packaging appeals to our senses as perfect healthy diet food. So then, if such laboratory-made nutrition-infused foods are such a health rage, then why are we not able to achieve our health goals? Why are we more diseased than ever before? Why people in olden times who did not have laboratories to create the healthy foods lived more healthy lives than us? If laboratory made foods are well-researched healthy foods then why are we getting sicker? Do artificially made foods lack something?

So now we have reached a point that emphasizes the concept and importance of 'live foods ' versus 'dead foods' & 'nutritious foods' versus 'non-nutritious foods'. Ancient healing systems including Ayurveda, Macrobiotics, and TCM never talked about broken nutritional elements. Did you ever come across the concept of carbohydrates, proteins, minerals, fats and vitamins in ancient sciences? No, the concept did not exist in ancient systems and the break-up of nutritional elements is the concept of Western medicine that originated just a few decades back.

The fact is, today we are feeding our body such foods that either we are not designed to consume or that our body does not relate to. The outcome is internal deficiencies, imbalances & a diseased state. Further, we do not understand our foods logically today. Some of the thought-provoking questions that we must be addressing for our own benefit are:

What is nutrition?

Is nutrition the only component that our body needs through food or is there anything else to it?

Why is it that there is so much discrepancy in research studies about food and nutrition?

And lastly, should we take away every good information about any food blindly as published in media and at various other places?

The right approach to understanding our foods must be logical. We must further understand that there exist two mutually-exclusive theories about food that have originated in different eras. These two theories are:

Biochemical: This theory describes the modern view of nutrition and looks at food as a fragmented break-up of nutrients such as carbohydrates, proteins, fats, minerals, vitamins, antioxidants etc. This theory considers ideal nutrition as a sum total of its parts. It considers the basic nutritional elements the whole sole building blocks of our body at the cellular level.

Natural: This theory describes the ancient view of food and nutrition. It considers 'whole' as healthy and complete, and important for total well-being. It considers that the foods that originate in nature are complete in nutritional elements and must be consumed as is. It does not focus directly on the nutritional elements. Rather, this theory considers that more than nutrition, 'life-force' or liveliness of the foods matters the most.

Let's try to dig deeper into understating the two different views of our daily foods.

NOURISHMENT & NATURAL NUTRITION VERSUS TASTE & LABORATORY-MANUFACTURED NUTRITION

'When thinking foods & nutrition, taste is just our tongue's requirement. However, good nutrition is our body's important requirement. Ironically, foods that appeal to the tongue may most often become the cause of our physical downfall, while foods that appeal our body will help us achieve a higher state of satiety. That being said, it is important not to confuse the requirements of the body with that of your tongue!'

For a holistic health & wellness practitioner, the definition of healthy diet and lifestyle is very different from that of a clinical nutritionist, dietician or a common man's understanding. Where the focus of clinical nutritionist is fully on balancing nutritional elements and calories, a holistic nutritionist thinks about foods that provide nourishment and life-force. As per holistic nutritionist, the definition of right foods is:

- Energy or vital life-force providing foods that keep us healthy, lively and well.
- Dense nutrition providing foods that help our body carry out its biological processes optimally.
- Clean foods that keep our system clean internally.
- Whole and natural foods coming from the nature directly without any processing.

The modern view of nutrition lacks the understanding of food from vital life-force perspective. Hence, the very first point is invalid in case of modern nutrition. Though it is the major differentiator that makes all the difference between a healthy or unhealthy and sickly state!

OUR PERCEPTION OF FOOD

'Unless you know what you eat & why you eat it, it is no use following even the best diet plan ever, because our body perceives food in a very different way. Food for body means cleansing, nourishment, growth, healing & satiety in that order. Any food that stagnates the body is not what it needs, even if the food in question is the most potential health food on the retail shelf!'

'Nutrition is the foundation of our whole existence'. That is what we know in modern times. Our whole focus is to balance the nutrients within our body and we leave no stone unturned to count calories and balance proteins with carbohydrates. We know fats cause high cholesterol, and so, we ensure to eliminate it from our diet altogether. And yes, vitamins, the most important pill of the day is what we think will keep us beautiful and healthy. We also know it is the quality of nutrition that helps us achieve our health goals, and we are quite choosy in that sense. We will not pick up a normal biscuit packet from a retail store, rather an oats cookie pack makes much more sense. Or, early morning muesli breakfast is much healthier than a bread toast. And our understanding stops there! So, despite of all this are you able to achieve your health goals? Do you feel energized through the day, is weight-loss happening to you? Are you free from common health issues? Is your Skin speaking your internal health? Most importantly, do you feel light and happy through the day? If your answer to all these questions is no, it's time to look at foods from your body's understanding perspective that your own understanding perspective.

When it comes to food, we often come across this saying, 'You Are What You Eat!'. In its literal sense, the meaning of this saying is as simple as it sounds, yet its impact is as complex as providing nutrition to nearly 10 trillion 'cells', which are the smallest functional units of our body. Nutrition quality provided to all these cells determines our physical, emotional and mental health.

HOW YOUR DIET TRANSFORMS INTO YOU?

Within the body, food converts into elements that nourish us, help us grow, keep our body in optimum working condition, strengthen us physically and emotionally, and provides us the most cherished experience called life. How our diet converts into what we are is simple to understand. From the body's perspective, that's what food means:

Diet → Blood → Cells → Tissues → Organs → Feelings → Emotions = Health & Well-being

Now, let's change the scenario by introducing 'Poor Diet' that represents processed items, trans-fats and hydrogenated fats, artificial sweeteners, chemical-laden stuff, high protein, animal fat, soda based drinks, caffeinated drinks, dairy, high salt consumption, frozen foods, bakery, confectionery and other commercial stuff. Now the chain goes like this:

Poor Diet → Toxic Blood → Diseased Cells → Worn-Out Tissues → Disturbed Organ Functioning → Disturbed Feelings →Unstable Emotions = Physically & Emotionally Unhealthy You.

Now, let's again change the scenario by introducing 'Healthy Diet With a Life-Force' that represents fruits, vegetables, nuts, seeds, sprouts, herbal teas, whole grains, fermented foods, enzyme-rich foods and fiber-rich foods. Now see how the chain goes like:

Healthy Diet With a Life-Force → Clean Blood With Pure Nutrition → Healthily Functioning Cells → Tissue Strength → Organs Functioning At Their Best Capacity → Happy & Joyous Feelings → Stable Emotions = Holistically Healthy You With a Fit Body And Sound Mind.

MODERN VIEW OF NUTRITION – THE BIOCHEMICAL NUTRITION

'Modern diet & lifestyle habits have become a threat to our existence. By giving up on our traditional ways of eating & living, we are ourselves destroying our health & wellness. At the foundational level, It is not the lifestyle disorders, but our perceptions & choices of food & diet that are becoming a medium of our destruction!'

The theory of modern nutrition originated less than 100 years ago after medical science realized that few diseases could be prevented by including certain foods or food extracts. The food constituents and extracts that were found beneficial to prevent certain diseases were later termed as 'Essential Nutritional Elements'. Alternatively, some nutrients that did not seem to be causing any harm to human health were termed as 'Non-Essential Nutritional Elements'.

The theory of modern nutrition considered foods and the human body as a mechanical laboratory objects to validate what food constituents work on human body and what not. Overtime the nutritional theory replaced the ancient theory of foods and their applicability for treating nutritional deficiencies. It created nutritional standards based on calorie system and formulating regulations around food standards and food consumption. As the nutritional therapy evolved and it was realized that nutrition does not work in isolation, for example, the relationship between Vitamin D and Calcium was researched, new theories around nutrition and their food sources started to resurface. That's where even the milk industry gained limelight as a true source of calcium, and for Vitamin D milk powder fortified with Vitamin D was launched in the market. It was further seen in nutritional science that a few nutritional elements cannot be directly ingested and made within the body by some other source nutrients. For example, the eatable amino acids in protein are incomplete and get completed in the body by using these essential amino acids consumed from the diet. By now, the world already had its focus on nutritional theory. For the convenience addicts, nutritional elements got launched as small pills as easy sources of balancing nutritional deficiencies.

The major reason why we see research discrepancies on foods and their goodness is majorly because:

- ❑ Firstly, the nutritional science is still evolving.
- ❑ Secondly, our body does not connect to nutrition in its individual form.
- ❑ Thirdly, all people are unique with unique constitutions, metabolisms, and body functioning. A standard dietary system for all has been raising questions about nutritional theory's efficiency for complete health.

The nutritional theory considers the human body as a mechanical functional unit like a factory where food acts as fuel for the factory. The modern system then tries to monitor the visible physiological functions of the body and validate the right fuel type for each function. However, the problem is that this factory is quite complex with various fuel types at play for various functions. Further, the machinery in the factory is so closely interacting with other functional parts having different fuel requirements. Moreover, this factory carries its own intelligence and functions accordingly. Millions of cells in the factory die every minute and the new ones are born. Even if there is no worker to attend to this factory, it keeps running on its own with available means for quite some time. There exists a maintenance system in the factory known as the immune system, which is strong as a protector but weak if it is not provided the right strengthening powers. However, if this maintenance system breaks, it does not take much time for the factory and all its units to begin breaking one after the other. Where the modern nutritional theory fits here is to try to provide each functional unit the right fuel by monitoring each unit's functionality and requirements. It is incomplete in a way that human factory is vast and some of its aspects are still to be unfolded, and so there are a lot of research theories coming up every now and then around foods, diseases, and nutrition. Secondly, the interconnectedness and interactions between individual functional units and the apt role of nutrition during this interaction phase is a complex research, also because each factory works based on some basic elements using which it was constructed. These basic elements are termed as 'Constitution' in ancient sciences. And the problem does not end here. The third most important issue with modern nutritional science is that it considers fragmented nutrition as a solution to the factory needs. However, we are still to reach a stage where the modern science is fully clear of the interactions of fragmented nutritional elements completely with each other. This is also because trillions of cells that form us, their interaction with each other, body organs formed by grouping the cells and functions of each smallest and biggest body unit is a highly complex system. Further, our body functions holistically! There is another problem that arises in nutritional science. The sources of nutritional elements are plenty. For example, both lemon and guava contain Vitamin C. How does one decide which Vitamin C from which source is better for their specific body condition. Further, the world has been confused after industrialization due to thousands of nutritionally fortified industrialized health foods are available in the market that contain all kinds of nutritional elements. For instance, corn is sold as corn flakes with added salt, fat, sugars, and fortified nutrition.

The bottom line is we are consuming high quantity of industrialized health foods in the form of dairy products, cereals, refined sugars, refined vegetable oils, candy, ice cream, alcohol, muffins, crackers, chips, snack foods, pizza, soft drinks, condiments, cookies, cake, bakery foods, salad dressings etc. Such foods are depleting us of our nutritional requirements and further adding the burden of artificially loaded stuff on our body. Even if we follow a diet plan, we still end up consuming a lot of industrialized stuff considering healthy due to added nutritional elements. And that could point some clues why are we getting sicker even after following well-laid out diet plans.

FOOD CONSTITUENTS IN MODERN NUTRITION

At its core, the theory of modern nutrition boils down to breaking up the nutritional elements in two broad categories: 'Macronutrients' and 'Micronutrients'. Let's explore them further.

MACRONUTRIENTS

The three nutritional elements namely carbohydrates, proteins, and fats constitute macronutrients.

Carbohydrates: Carbohydrates inside the body breakdown into glucose which acts as the fuel for body and brain and provides energy for internal body processes. It is the primary energy source of the body. Carbohydrates can be of a simple type or complex type. Sources of simple type carbohydrates are sugars in commercial products, fruits, dairy products, honey etc. Simple type carbohydrates are attributed to be the prime cause of major modern lifestyle diseases. Sources of complex carbohydrates include grains, starchy vegetables and legumes and contain fiber along with sugar. This is a good form of carbohydrates that aids digestion and helps lower bad cholesterol and other health conditions.

Protein: Proteins form the building blocks and all structural elements of the body. We need protein to repair the wear and tear of our body, to aid growth, to build and repair your muscles, skin and bones, to form internal structural elements and to support certain biological functions. The very first signs of protein deficiency can be indicated by looking at your skin, hair, and nails. The protein metabolism process converts the consumed proteins into amino acids which is the usable form of protein internally Protein break down in the digestive system into amino acids. It is important to consume essential 8 amino acids through foods and rest other amino acids are made within the body using the primary 8 amino acids. Proteins have the capability of being converted into energy by the body when you lack the primary energy producing source i. e. carbohydrates. The protein may replace the energy conversion task of carbohydrates. However, this is not the ideal scenario within the body, and too much protein may show up in the long run in the form of gout and kidney issues, cholesterol issues etc. The waste leftover of protein is nitrogen and sulfur waste and the body must get rid of this waste through kidneys. If not eliminated, you may end up with a host of diseases like high uric acid, gout and kidney problems. Animal protein is the concentrated form of protein, and the burden of expelling its waste is way too high for the body as compared to plant-based protein. Higher the concentrated form of protein that you consume more is the nitrogen and sulfur waste and more is the burden on your kidneys to expel it. Protein sources include nuts, beans, legumes, meat and certain grains. Protein is much required by our body beginning from the smallest and innermost unit of the body (cell) to constructing you physically, including your skin, hair, and nails. Even blood, enzymes, hormones, saliva are the by-products of proteins. Right forms may include egg whites, legumes, pulses, nuts, seeds, dairy, and soy products. These sources not just supply proteins, but fiber and other nutrients as well. Whereas animal based sources may overwhelm your system with proteins and also lack in fiber and other nutrients.

Fats: Fats are not the primary source of energy but can be used by the body to convert into energy, if the primary source of energy i. e. carbohydrates is missing. Fats help our body absorb vitamins and aid our growth and development. Healthy fats can be found in food sources such as nuts and seeds and help control the cholesterol levels. Other fat types including saturated and trans fats can prove to unhealthy if eaten too often. Sources of saturated butter include butter, solid shortening etc. Sources of trans fats include vegetable oils, margarine, cookies, crackers etc. Eating too much of saturated and trans fats may lead to high cholesterol levels and cardiovascular problems. Right fats are important for our body functioning and when you do not consume fats at all, you also are not able to nourish yourselves with vitamins, in spite of taking them in plenty. It could be a Vitamin D supplement or carrots for Vitamin A or a Vitamin E supplement. This is because Vitamin A, D, E and K are fat-soluble and need fat in your body to be absorbed.

Unsaturated Fats: These types of fats are referred to as essential fatty acids because they match the composition of fats that exist within our body. Two important fatty acids namely linoleic acid and alpha-linoleic acid cannot be synthesized in our body and must be essentially consumed through our diet in the form of omega-3 and omega-6 fatty acids. Sources of omega 3 & omegas 6 fatty acids include flaxseed oil and walnut oil. Consumed in moderation, this fat category is an important fat category, not to be cut down at all as it provides fuel for the brain and lowers the cholesterol levels.

Saturated Fats: Saturated fatty acids constitute a substantial part of the modern diet. Studies have shown that this fat type may increase the risk of cardiovascular diseases. Foods of regular consumption that are rich in saturated fatty acids include butter, milk, cream, cheese, ghee, processed meats, pork, lamb, sausages and the skin on chicken. Ghee, Coconut oil and Palm oil.

Trans Fats/Hydrogenated Fats: Commercial food items, baked products, biscuits, cookies and anything on the retail store shelves is loaded with these fats. Most widely used fat category in today's times, has a direct connection with lifestyle diseases.

MICRONUTRIENTS:

Vitamins & Minerals: Our body requires various vitamins and minerals such as calcium, sodium, phosphorous, other trace minerals in limited quantities to perform its internal functions including growth, nerve functions and digestion. Though our body's requirement of vitamins and minerals is relatively small as compared to macronutrients, the deficiency of these may lead to serious health problems as they are the core components of our internal functioning. A major source of vitamins are fruits, vegetables, nuts, and grains. Consumption of milk to counter calcium deficiencyis a much-hyped topic in our society today. We have been made to believe that the only promising source of calcium is dairy it is a must in our diet. This is untrue as other vegan sources of calcium are equally promising and include sources such as sesame seeds, green leafy vegetables, almonds, broccoli etc.

COMMON FOODS STAPLES OF MODERN TIMES

Dairy foods: Dairy enjoys a special place in each household. However, the ancient wisdom mentions that we need milk only till the weaning period. Rather, new studies are emerging that mention dairy as a contributory factor behind cardiovascular diseases and few cancers such as breast cancer in women.

Cereals: Our breakfast today primarily consists of commercialized cereal products. Cereals in their raw form have also served as staple foods in various ancient cultures such as wheat and rice in Indian culture and rice specifically in Chinese and Japanese cultures. However, when we began to process grains and started to add sugars, salt, colors and other additives to our gain products, that's where cereals began to become a matter of serious concern for our health.

Refined Sugars: The entire world is under the havoc of refined sugar. Any food products on the retail stores have sugar as their major additive, be it candy, cookies, energy bars, sweetened yogurt, ice creams and others. Our modern diet is highly dependent upon sugar. Sugar creates dampness in our digestive tract and makes it a perfect place for bacteria and viruses to thrive. The proliferation thus leads to digestive and gastric issues. Refined sugars are also responsible for immense weight gain.

Refined Vegetable Oils: Refined vegetable oils form an important part of our cooking and dietary styles. Interestingly, the world is always on a look-out for a perfect oil, even after they get diagnosed with heart or other diseases. The only change that we see in people when diagnosed with a disease is that their hunt gets directed towards finding a better oil to suit their current condition, as the previous one has been marked dangerous by the doctors! However, if you get into the history of refined oils, it was about 5000 and 6000 years ago that the world began extracting oils from walnuts, almonds, olives, sesame seeds, and flax seeds and other seed sources. In those times the oils were directly pressed to be consumed with meals. However, as the industrialization progressed, oils from all other sources began to be extracted. Even vegetable oils came into existence. The problem with vegetable oils was that they were too watery to be consumed for cooking and their shelf-life was much lesser. So, through the process of hydrogenation, the vegetable oils were processed to gain oily consistency and to last longer on the shelves. The problem with this processing was that it altered the chemical bonds of the extracted oils and the altered chemistry does not gel well with our body chemistry. This started to show up in coronary heart ailments after over consumption of hydrogenated vegetable oils.

Alcohol: Alcohol is one of the major constituents of the modern diet. Specifically in the modern lifestyle, alcohol holds a very prestigious place. However, alcohol is high sugar and when mixed with the blood it gives a sudden rise in blood-sugar levels, and so we immediately tend to feel light and better after its consumption. The problem with alcohol consumption is over-consumption specifically in nutritional deficient bodies that are also highly burdened with the constituents of modern foods. The consolidated effect of alcohol, nutritional deficiencies, and burden of processed foods shows up as quick aging and other health issues.

Salt: The culture of consuming excess salt is a mandate in the food world nowadays. As our body strives for balance, the more sugars we consume, the more salt we crave and vice versa. However, salt was not supposed to be consumed the way we consume it these days. The property of salt is to help cook food so that it dissolved and pre-digests foods for easy digestion. Good quality salt is also needed for certain internal body processes. The problem with our modern salts is that they are too commercial for our body requirements. They are creating internal imbalances versus creating internal balances.

Fatty Animal foods: Animal food also largely forms the modern diets. Animal foods are a source of concentrated form of nutrients, which means they fill us up with macronutrients relatively largely specifically protein. However, that may sound good and so we see a lot of people consuming excessive protein in the form of animal diet, the question here is whether do we need that much protein? Though the negatives of high protein diet do not show up immediately, over-time high consumption of protein may lead to kidney issues. Moreover, Animal diet is rich in fats, providing us with an excessive amount of fat to be handled by our body. Not to forget the way animal husbandry is done these days, it is no surprise that we are also taking in a lot of preservatives and additives in anindirect form that are being fed to the livestock.

WHAT'S WRONG WITH THESE MODERN FOOD STAPLES?

These modern food staples including dairy, cereals, sugars, refined oils, animal food, salt and various other food combinations, may though seem nutritionally promising, yet they seem to be creating diseases in humans. If you join the dots, this is what we majorly consume today and our combination of nutritional elements gets derived majorly from these sources only, yet our diseases are increasing. For example, we are very particular about milk consumption, yet, our calcium deficiency is increasing. What could be the cause?

Our main modern staple foods, though being nutritionally sufficient, have played around with some other nutritional characteristics in our diets leading to negative effects on our health and well-being. These other important nutritional characteristics include glycemic load, fatty acid composition, macronutrient composition, micronutrient density, acid-alkaline (pH) balance, sodium-potassium ratio and fiber content. Let's explore each one of these other ignored nutritional characteristic one by one.

Glycemic load: Glycemic load or glycemic index is a mechanism to measure how quickly or slowly the carbohydrates and sugars mix with the blood and create blood-sugar fluctuation or blood-sugar stability respectively. This is important as abrupt blood-sugar rise leads to a lot of metabolic health issues including diabetes. It is important to choose foods with average and low glycemic index versus consuming a lot of high glycemic index foods, to keep blood-sugar stable. Our modern food staples being of refined category increase the glycemic load and play havoc on our blood sugar levels. Overtime this converts into Diabetes or any other metabolic issue. This may further trigger some hormonal changes related to insulin production. Diseases related to insulin resistance include obesity, coronary heart disease (CHD), type 2 diabetes and hypertension. It is quite likely that metabolic disturbances may be the cause of modern chronic illnesses such as gout, acne, polycystic ovary syndrome, breast, colon or prostate cancer. However, this trend of the disturbed glycemic load was rare or absent in ancient societies living by the ancient theories of food and diet.

Fatty Acid Composition: Fatty acid composition in our western diet staples majorly consists of wrong fatty acids. Research studies now indicate that to prevent the risk of chronic diseases, the type of fat being consumed is of more relevance than the quantity of fat consumed. Today, we are consuming fats from wrong sources such as trans-fats & hydrogenated fats. Our body needs good fat that can be consumed from flaxseeds or chia seeds.

Macronutrient Composition: The macronutrients in our diet including carbohydrates, proteins, and fats have evolved over time due to industrialization. Our original carbohydrates, proteins and fats based foods such as whole grains, pulses, legumes, nuts, seeds, vegetables, and carbohydrates have been majorly replaced by their refined and processed versions. Today, our body does not receive macronutrients in their original forms. The fragmented and processed nutrients thus play around with our internal chemical chemistry and gives rise to deficiencies and other functional issue inside the body such as blood-sugar imbalance, constipation and broken integrity of the body elements.

Micronutrient Density: The macronutrients in our diet include vitamins & minerals. We are severely low on micronutrients today, and so we see a severe rise in vitamin & mineral deficiencies. As minor issue as it may sound, the issue is highly deep rooted because even though vitamins and minerals are used in lesser quantity by the body, still they have varied uses in various important internal functions. The deficiency of vitamins and minerals in carbohydrates, proteins, and fats have evolved over time due to industrialization. Our original carbohydrates, proteins and fats based foods such as whole grains, pulses, legumes, nuts, seeds, vegetables, and carbohydrates have been majorly replaced by their refined and processed versions. Today, our body does not receive macronutrients in their original forms. The fragmented and processed nutrients thus play around with our internal chemical chemistry and gives rise to deficiencies and other functional issues inside the body such as blood-sugar imbalance, constipation and broken integrity of the body elements.

Acid-Alkaline (pH) Balance: Like our cars perform best in an optimal internal environment, when, the machinery is oiled properly, right air pressure is maintained in the wheels, there is enough & right kind of fuel to run the car; Likewise our body is meant to work in an ideal internal environment which is calculated in terms of body pH. The pH level is a numeric measurement of the acid-alkaline balance inside the body. Acid-alkaline pH Level is the numeric measurement of the ideal working conditions for enzymes, cells and various other internal functioning elements. It is measured on a scale of 1-14, where 7 is neutral, but the pH of a healthy body is considered to be 7. 4 and this measurement cannot afford to vary vastly. Even the variation range of 7. 35 & 7. 45 means highly, chronically troubled pH. The pH of 7. 35 is the state of high acidity or even cancer! The pH balance is auto-regulated by the body and comes under the umbrella of homeostatic state, where, body strives its best to maintain its pH of 7. 4, even if it has to compromise on the internal mineral reserves of the body.

The connect of acidity with our body is not just what we experience in terms of gastric & digestive issues. On the physical level, a common person may realize the acidity symptoms in the form of gastric issues, but the term 'Acidity' is a much bigger problem.

Acid inside the body could be a consequence of shallow breathing pattern or could exist due to too much intake of acidic foods, it could accompany stress, it can just arise due to consumption of chemical laden foods, cosmetics & other products. Once inside, the acid state can ruin your body fully. Too much acid enters the fluids running into your body & changes their chemical composition so that the body cannot function ideally. The impact could be:

- ❑ Gastric issues - The only feeling that we relate to when we talk of acidity!
- ❑ Inflammation - For example, arthritis & heart disease are inflammatory conditions.
- ❑ Weakening of Internal Mineral Reserves to Neutralize Acid - Osteoporosis & lesser bone mass is the consequence in this case.
- ❑ Weakened Immunity - Seasonal allergies, flu, cold & cough & respiratory issues, headaches are the prominent symptoms in this case.
- ❑ Other impact on the outer surface of the body includes fungal infections, bad breath, foul body odor, unexplained aches pains & headaches to name a few.

In our daily lives, the acid-alkaline concept is quite at use internally when we feel active, energetic, healthy with no aches & pains, no allergies, strong immunity, free from cold & cough; Conversely, it is equally at use when we suffer from as simple as unexplained headaches, pains, cough, cold, allergies to as complex as a heart disease, osteoporosis, low bone density, cancer and other lifestyle disorders. With high acidity inside you will age faster, degenerate faster, become sick, fatigued, irritable & dull frequently. The body needs an alkaline pH to maintain clean blood, good enzyme reserves and healthy immune function. Maintaining a healthy pH is extremely important for good health, well-being, and prevention of diseases. Factors that affect pH include stress, diet and lifestyle, environmental factors, use of chemicals and synthetic dyes. Optimum pH balance is important for the body cells to be able to work efficiently. Acidic /Alkaline fluctuations within the body may lead to imbalances. If the body is too acidic, you can start to experience feelings of imbalance including gas, constipation, bloating, acne, heartburn, acid reflux, indigestion, mild headaches, gastritis, candida and frequent flu. Advanced symptoms of over-acidity include Crohn's disease and even cancer (all forms). Even modern science now acknowledges the importance of alkaline diet to treat health issues as minor as cold & coughs, skin problems, unexplained aches & pains, headaches; and as major as life-threatening diseases!"

All we need to do is, provide the body with right means, i. e. right foods, therapies & exercises to make our bodies alkaline. It is important to realize that most of the foods that we consume & activities that we perform daily cause a lot of acidity inside our bodies, and the reasons are plenty, including, poor dietary choices, environmental factors & anti-nature lifestyles.

Sodium-Potassium Ratio: Salt consumed through fast foods or processed foods rips off pour sodium-potassium balance within the body. Our major source of salt these days is manufactured salt or sodium chloride, that is bleached and ripped off trace minerals that are important for our body functioning. Further, the commercial foods also make us deficient in potassium. Some experts hold a view point that this sodium-potassium ratio imbalance is causing us cardiovascular issues. Excess processed sodium causes fluid retention and may expand the blood volume causing high blood pressure, stroke, and other heart diseases. Precisely this imbalance may be a cause of everything from heart diseases, kidney issues, chronic health issues, gastric issues and even cancer.

Fiber content: The plain simple fact, we lack sufficient fiber in our diets today. Our common food staples such as flour-based items, refined sugars, cooking oils, dairy, animal foods and alcohol, all lack fiber. The only good sources of fiber include plant foods, specifically foods and vegetables. Good quantity fiber is important for digestive health and helps to reduce freely moving toxic elements in the body and pushes toxins out. Health issues that arise due to lack of fiber includes constipation, gastritis, hemorrhoids and varicose veins.

CALORIE SYSTEM - IS IT THE RIGHT MEASURE?

A lot of youngsters today survive on junk food while restricting the intake to required calories, thinking that health is perfect as long as calories are within the standard range. It is important to understand that calorie wise, things may be in control, but the harmful effects of foods containing those calories cannot be underestimated just by keeping the intake of calories in control. For example, considering that today morning your breakfast choices are 100 calories either from a slice of brown bread or a bowl of whole oats. What would be your choice? Do you think it will make any difference to choose any specific item to consume 100 calories in your breakfast, or do you think both sources are good because both foods contain equal calories?

If that question is to be answered correctly, the effectiveness of calorie system seems to take a back seat! We believe that our caloric requirements can be any irrespective of the quality and type of food that we choose. For example, 100 calories from a bowl of whole oats are much better than 100 calories from a slice of brown bread because within your body the breakup of nutritional elements goes like this:

100 Calories From Whole Oats: Provides complex carbohydrates, fiber, better mood, better digestive health, lowers cholesterol, no added colors and oils and above all longer satiety.

100 Calories From Brown Bread: Provides additives, preservatives, and commercial oils, bloating, digestive issues, thesluggish start of the day and make you feel hungry quite sooner.

Calorie counting system should be just considered as a scale to keep a check that you are not consuming more than required quantity of food in a day. It is equally important to focus on the quality and type of calories that you are consuming and not just blindly banking on calorie counting.

INGREDIENTS OF PROCESSED FOODS & THEIR IMPACT ON OUR BODY

According to a study published in 'The American Journal of Clinical Nutrition' , processed foods increase the risk of high cholesterol, diabetes, obesity, cavities, gastrointestinal disorders, infertility and can damage our organs. All commercial foods come under the category of processed foods. 'Processed' means food products created using food colors, artificial food additives and preservatives. It may also mean food irradiation such as milk pasteurization and fruit and vegetable canning. Processed foods can be one of the major sources of toxins. Commercially processed foods contain over 3000 chemicals, additives, pesticides, herbicides, growth hormones and other additives that get accumulated in the body as toxins or fats. Chemicals & food additives enhance food flavors, preserve food for long, reduce manufacturer's cost, make food highly palatable & boosts sales. Some of these chemicals, colors, and additives are known allergens, carcinogens, mimic hormonal activity or weaken immune system. Many of them are banned in various countries but still freely used in some other countries.

For our body, the processed food mean the following:

Hidden Sugars: The most commonly used additive, it acts as taste and texture enhancer to make commercial foods palatable. This additive is associated with hyperactivity, blood sugar spikes, alteration of cell chemistry leading to hyper behavioral patterns. The common food sources include Juices, Colas, Sodas, bread, bakery items, confectionery items, milk additives etc. It is associated with increased risk of heart disease, weak immunity, obesity, cavities and type 2 diabetes.

Trans-Fats: Trans-fats are associated with a risk of heart diseases, cancers, and inflammatory conditions. This fat type increases the shelf-life of a product and is found in pizza, margarine, salad dressings, chips, biscuits including diet biscuits, cookies, snacks etc. It is banned in a lot of countries due to its ill effects. Trans-fats are associated with high risk of heart diseases, cancers, including breast cancer. The common sources include margarine, vegetable shortenings, crackers, cookies, snack foods etc.

Antibiotics: Some foods have also been found to contain antibiotics and are associated with weakened immunity and interfere with biological functioning. The tested food source includes honey.

Artificial Coloring Agents: This additive is associated with hyperactivity disorder (ADHD) in children, allergies, asthma and inflammatory skin conditions. The common food sources include confectionary items, cakes, pastries etc.

Butylated Hydroxytoluene (BHT): A widely used additive that is suspected to be a possible carcinogen and retards rancidity.

High-Fructose Corn Syrup (HFCS): A widely used primary & cheap sweetener added to all commercial foods such as soft drinks, cereals, yogurt, cakes, and sauces etc. It contains mercury that is linked to tooth decay, migraines, diabetes, obesity and cancer.

Monosodium Glutamate (MSG): It is found in many products and enhances food taste. It has been seen to cause excessive nervous system stimulation that leads to the killing of nerve cells, causes nausea, cramps, dizziness, rash, heart palpitations, numbness, migraines, mood swings, and confusion.

Sodium Benzoate: A food preservative and common additive in soft drinks, it reacts with vitamin C that is commonly added as an antioxidant in some fruits juices like oranges, lemons, cranberries.

Artificial Food Colorings: This additive is used to make processed foods look bright and appetizing. It is synthetically derived from coal tar and petroleum and is extensively used in junk foods and soft drinks. It is found in confectionary items and used in a lot of restaurants. It causes hypersensitivity, ADHD (attention-deficit-hyperactivity disorder), asthma, and inflammatory skin conditions such as atopic dermatitis.

Sodium: This salt additive has been associated with an increased risk for heart disease. Found in all salty foods, junk foods, burgers, pizzas and other common food items.

Other Additives to Make You Hungry, Fat & Fast Food Addicts: Few other food additives have shown to make you hungrier and addict to processed foods. Few additives are also added intentionally to make you fat and increase your appetite. Even 'diet foods' are not spared!

AYURVEDA'S VIEW OF NUTRITION

'Food & nutrition are not standalone Concepts. Unless a food processing unit with good burning capacity exists inside our body, even the best foods lose their effectiveness. Ayurveda's understanding of food begins with 'Agni', which is the digestive fire. Then, the importance of right foods is emphasized. However, even the most healthiest foods will not help us if they are not burnt properly in the burning chamber called Agni!'

Ayurveda's viewpoint on food and diet holds a totally different point of view than the modern view. Unlike the modern understanding of food and nutrition that has its emphasis on food completely irrespective of individuals who need it, Ayurveda believes that our entire focus on foods is of no use unless our digestive system is in the right order to digest, absorb and assimilate what we eat. Ultimately, it is the nutritional extract that gets assimilated becomes a part of us, provides us energy and forms our consciousness. If our foods fail to reach the stage of assimilation, you are rarely helping your body with any soup or salad diet that you may be consuming! That is a probable reason, why some people even after consuming healthiest still feel bloated all the time. Their Agni is weak! Rather, in Ayurveda, there is no standard term as 'Ayurvedic food' that focusses upon a specific kind of diet plan. This is because in Ayurveda it is believed that each individual is different, the individual capability to digest, absorb and assimilate nutrition is different and metabolism of each individual is different. The view of right or wrong food begins with understanding a human being than the foods. Further, Ayurveda suggests that the life-force in natural foods cannot be produced in the laboratory made foods, though nutrition can be replicated in the laboratory. Live foods that have the power to regrow are of utmost importance in Ayurveda and dead laboratory made foods are considered to be providing negative energy despite of providing complete nutrition. Also, there is no concept of calorie counting in Ayurveda.

'AGNI' – THE DIGESTIVE FIRE

Before focusing on food, Ayurveda focusses on 'Agni' – the digestive fire which is the force behind burning what we eat. Digestive Agni can be compared to a burning fire. If the flame is very low, then it will take a long time to cook the food and vice versa. If we put a huge log on a low fire, it will extinguish it. Similarly, if we put a burden of a lot of wrong foods on a low burning fire, the result will be partially burned food. So, our digestive fire must be balanced so that we can digest our meals efficiently and smoothly.

Agni is of utmost importance in Ayurveda, as, if it is weak, it could become the breeding ground for many chronic illnesses of modern times. Foods that get broken down fully by the Agni get separated into nutrition and waste. The separated pure nutrition traverses through the body along with the blood to irrigate the tissues and provide energy, strength, good appearance and internal nourishment. Water plays a crucial role in this entire process as blood needs ample water to flow well, and hence, hydration is very important. The left over wastes are passed out through colon and bladder.

TIPS TO STRENGTHEN THE AGNI – THE ULTIMATE DIGESTIVE FORCE

So, if you are following a diet plan, ensure that your Agni is strong to reap the benefits of your healthy diet. Few tips to strengthen Agni include:

- [ ] On waking up, the Agni must be stimulated. A cup of warm ginger tea does the job well. You may add lemon, if required.
- [ ] Ayurveda recommends consuming the heaviest meal of the day during lunch, for the simple fact that Agni cycle follows the cycle of the sun and is strongest during mid-day.
- [ ] By evening the cold hours set-in, also slowing down the Agni, as well as our digestive ability. So, you must consume a light meal in the evening.
- [ ] Apply the Japanese 80/20 rule. Eat until 80 full and stop.
- [ ] Chew your food very well.
- [ ] Do not starve yourself and eat at regular intervals.
- [ ] Have dinner at least 3 hours before sleeping.
- [ ] Avoid skipping meals and do not fast without preparing your body for fasting.
- [ ] Try to maintain similar eating time each day. Our body likes discipline!
- [ ] Use digestive spices in your cooking such as turmeric, ginger, fennel, coriander etc.
- [ ] Do not drink water with your meals, specifically cold water. Cold water acts as a fire extinguisher for the Agni and may keep foods undigested in the stomach.
- [ ] Eat consciously, enjoying the taste of each food. Tastes have a healing relevance in Ayurveda.
- [ ] Do not overeat and do not eat at odd hours, specifically later at night.
- [ ] Eating slow is the key to eating less yet ending up feeling full.
- [ ] Consume right food combinations, for example, do not combine fruits with dairy.
- [ ] Light walk after dinner helps digest the food.
- [ ] Try not consuming raw fruits and vegetables if your digestive system is weak.
- [ ] Avoid eating leftovers.
- [ ] Use herbs and spices in your cooking techniques to balance cooked food.

- ❑ Warm food is suited best for stimulating Agni and digestive enzymes.
- ❑ Do not eat at a small gap after consuming your meals, maintain the interval.
- ❑ Try eating with a calm and peaceful mind. Negative emotions affect digestion and impact the mind negatively.

BALANCED DIET IN AYURVEDA

Unlike the modern concept of balancing nutrition, the concept of a balanced diet in Ayurveda is about balancing 6 tastes. It is believed that each specific taste including, sweet, sour, salty, pungent, bitter and astringent nourishes and stimulates specific organs of the body, ensuring that organs work optimally. When organs work optimally, your probability of falling sick goes drastically low. A balanced diet in Ayurveda must consist of all these 5 tastes in all meals. The order of tastes in Ayurveda diet goes like this: Sweet, sour, salt, pungent, bitter and astringent.

'Madhura' or Sweet: Sweet taste is meant to soothe the digestive system. If must be an important taste of all our meals. Probably, that's the reason that our ancestors and even we are in the habit of consuming sweet after meals. However, if sweets are consumed through refined and commercial foods, it may lead to high acidity, obesity, congestion and other diseases.

'Amla' or Sour: Sour taste is known to stimulate Agni and prepare the body for digestion including stimulating the appetite and enhancing the secretion of various digestive juices such as saliva and digestive enzymes. We must begin our day with a glass of lemon water because it is sour and helps cleanse, awaken and energize us. Though, anexcessive quantity of sour foods may cause indigestion and heartburn.

'Lavana' or Salty: Salty taste helps maintain the water and electrolyte balance of the body. This taste is associated with kidney functioning. Excess salt causes high blood pressure and water retention.

'Tikta' or Pungent: Pungent taste has warming qualities and helps clear sinuses. It also aids digestion and blood circulation. In excess, pungent taste causes fatigue and excessive thirst.

'Katu' or Bitter: Bitter taste is considered to be a blood and body cleanser. It aids digestion by enhancing the release of digestive enzymes and juices. It helps break accumulated fats and toxins. It contains all anti-bacterial and detox properties such as killing germs, clearing congestion and purifying blood etc. It works wonders for the skin and helps relieve itching and swelling.

Astringent: Astringent taste acts as a binding food, and helps bind toxins and fats from nook and corners of the body to be thrown out of the system. Examples of astringent foods include raw bananas and chickpeas.

TRADITIONAL CHINESE MEDICINE'S VIEW OF NUTRITION

'In context of modern lifestyles, our foods, food habits & cooking techniques that are supposed to form & heal us, are working against us destructively. It is now the time to look at our foods & cooking from age old perspective!'

Not so long ago, our ancestors lived on local and natural produces, ate seasonal foods, and used to cook food to convert it into healing energy. Cooking was an art that was passed from generations to generations. However, due to industrialization today, our perspectives towards food have changed and so has our body chemistry. The negative results of our dietary and lifestyle patterns are quite clear in the rising incidences of lifestyle disorders such as heart diseases, osteoporosis, cancer, arthritis, diabetes etc.

For a TCM practitioner, a traditional 'healthy' diet is very different from the modern concepts of nutrition. The basic dietary premise of TCM is based on balance. The TCM dietary principles apply food energetics to create and maintain an internal balance that also ensures clean metabolism and a well-functioning body.

To be precise, the TCM's theory of nutrition revolves around foods containing life-energy, 5 tastes, healing cooking techniques and a balanced body state.

UNDERSTANDING FOOD ENERGY – THE LIFE-FORCE FROM FOODS

Do you feel fresh, light and lively after consuming sweet fruits? Or Do you feel dull and sluggish after consuming oily, heavy and fried foods?

Whatever you feel, it is no coincidence, there is a whole psychology running behind your feelings - "The Food Energy"! Sweet foods are nourishing for the stomach, provide quick energy and release feel-happy hormones. Further, sweet taste consumed from fresh foods such as fruits carries a fresh, light and lively energy and have the power to lift up moods and feelings.

As per the concept of food energetics, food is not just meant to fill the stomach and provide fuel for lasting energy which is the concept of modern nutrition. However, Ayurveda recommends that consuming good foods have the energy to improve mood and thoughts apart from strengthening the body. They make you feel light and keep you active through the day. Alternatively, poor diet may fill you up but provides negative energy making you feel dull and lazy. Specific energies released by specific foods are listed below:

- ❑ To feel warm consume carrots.
- ❑ To feel light and fresh consume green leafy vegetables.
- ❑ To feel relaxed consume corn, tofu, vegetables.
- ❑ To feel calm and at peace consume pumpkin and naturally sweet foods.
- ❑ To feel energized consume brown rice and ginger.

As per TCM, foods can be categorized into two main categories: 'Cooling' and 'Warming' foods. Warming and cooling foods can be used to balance the body which may be deficient in the extremities: 'yin' or 'yang'.

Cooling Foods	Warming Foods	Balanced Foods
These foods impart a cooling effect to the body.	These foods impart warming effect to the body.	These foods impart balanced energy and hence are neutral foods.
These foods help to cool the heated body state and clear toxins from the body.	These foods create an effect of a rising energy and provide warmth. These are good foods for improving blood circulation.	These foods create a neutral energy and can be consumed in any condition.
In the case of thirst, heated body condition, perspiration, anxiety, mouth ulcers, hot flushes these foods can be helpful.	In the case of cold hands and feet, stiff joints, lack of energy and fluid retention these foods can be helpful.	These foods are the safest to consume in any condition.
Examples of cold foods: Lettuce, Lotus Root, Mushroom, Spinach, Buckwheat, Millet, Tofu, Orange, Pear, Pineapple, Strawberry, Watermelon, Alfalfa Sprouts, Apple, Banana, Kiwifruit, Lemon Bitter Gourd, Celery, Cucumber, Green leafy vegetables, Seaweed, Green Tea, Peppermint Tea and Sesame oil.	Examples of warm foods: Pistachio Nut, Cherry, Cumin, Apricot, Peach, Mustard greens, Onion, Pumpkin, Coffee, Coriander, Mustard, Nutmeg, Spring onion, Fennel seed, Garlic, Ginger, Ginseng, Jasmine tea, Coconut milk, Guava, Mango Black pepper, Cinnamon, and Clove.	Examples of neutral foods: Chinese cabbage, Corn, Potato, Figs, Black sesame seed, Black soybean, Sunflower seed, Sweet potato, Adzuki Bean, Almond, Goji Berries, Grape, Olive, Papaya, Carrot, Pumpkin and Shiitake mushroom.

BALANCED DIET, EMOTIONS, BODY ORGANS & TASTES IN TCM – THE CONNECT

TCM's view of nutrition is based on the concept of 'extremities' and 'balance'. The two extremities, 'Positive' and 'Negative' energies are categorized as 'Yang' and 'Yin' respectively in TCM. Yin foods in TCM are considered to be cooling, while yang foods are considered to be warming. TCM diet theory believes that we must maintain a balance between these two extremities through the consumption and combination of right foods. Also, as considered in Ayurveda, a balanced diet in TCM is about balancing the 5 primal tastes including sour, bitter, sweet, pungent and salty.

Sour: Sour taste in TCM is associated with the liver. In its disturbed state, the emotions of anger and impatience govern an individual. For example, an angry and irritated person by nature may have liver issues from a TCM perspective. To soothe liver issues, TCM suggests incorporating sour foods for a calming effect on the liver. Such foods include kiwifruit, tomato, kiwi, grapefruit, olives etc.

Bitter: Bitter taste TCM is associated with the heart. In its disturbed state, the emotions of heat, hatred, and lack of joy govern an individual. For example, a permanently sad person who is never joyous may have heart issues which may also show up as heart palpitations, anxiety, red face, ulcers in the mouth etc. Bitter taste soothes the heart and the sources include bitter gourd, mustard leaf, and other bitter green vegetables.

Sweet: Sweet taste in TCM is associated with spleen and pancreas and digestive area. In its disturbed state, the emotions of worry and anxiety govern an individual. For example, a person who worries and remains anxious may have digestive and absorption issues, which may show up as insomnia, lack of energy and digestive issues. Sweet taste soothes the spleen and pancreas and has a positive impact on digestion. It acts as a tonic and provides a cheerful and lively energy. Good sources of sweet foods include starchy vegetables, whole grains, nuts, fruits, sweet potatoes etc.

Pungent or Spicy: Pungent or spicy taste in TCM is associated with lungs. In its disturbed state, the emotions of depression and grief govern an individual. For example, a person who holds a lot of grievances may have respiratory issues which may show us asthma, blocked and runny nose, headaches, bronchitis and sinus issues. Spicy foods provide an upward rising energy and help open up sinuses. Good sources of pungent foods include ginger, black pepper, and other herbs.

Salty: Salty taste in TCM is associated with kidneys. In its disturbed state, the emotions of fear and insecurity govern an individual. For example, a child who is often scolded wets his pants out of fear. This is a typical example of fear affecting the kidneys. Kidney issues may show up as high blood pressure, tiredness in legs, back pain, lack of energy and water retention. Salty taste strengthens the kidneys and acts as a purgative to clear stagnation and drain off the toxins. Good sources of salty foods include sea salt, soy sauce, and sea vegetables.

HOLISTIC VIEW OF NUTRITION VERSUS MODERN VIEW OF NUTRITION

Holistic nutrition focuses on food nutrition and food energy as a whole and does not separate it as individual nutritional elements as carbohydrates, proteins, vitamins, mineral etc. Rather, it considers all these nutritional elements as a whole and believes that each one has a role to play in biological functioning, but, in co-ordination and not separately. It also considers food as energy and does not perform energy measurement from calorie counting perspective. It focuses on eating foods in their most natural form, where all nutrition is intact in the right proportion and right combination. It also believes in the kind of energy that each food provides. For example, green leafy vegetables provide a vibrant energy apart from just providing the goodness of their inherent nutrients.

Most importantly, holistic nutrition does not believe in exchanging nutritional components for energy requirements, such as replacing protein diet with atraditional diet consisting of all nutritional elements. When we begin exchanging one nutrition to meet body needs that some other nutritional element must provide, like proteins for energy than eating carbohydrates, body imbalances are bound to occur.

The modern view of nutrition looks at food majorly from calories perspective. It also looks at nutrition individually, without taking about how holistically or in combined form all these nutrients function within the body. It justifies that how if you do not consume carbohydrates, proteins and fats can compensate for body's energy requirements. And that is a major reason that despite of being on 'n' types of diets, we still do not feel perfect physically and emotionally.

THE POISONOUS WHITES/REFINDS & THE RIGHT SUBSTITUTES

'The modern food industry is under the grip of 3 white poisons. Sadly, about 80% of our diet today is formed from these white poisons!'

SUGAR

'Think & name any major disease & you will find its direct connect with sugar. Do you still need more reasons to realize why sugar is harmful? Sugar is destroying our children, it is making us toxic & acidic leading to sickly states. And, we are happily relishing it's delightful yet artificial taste at the cost of our health. Is the deal worth?'

Right carbohydrates or sugars are essential requirements of our body and are much required for biological functioning. If you learn to master the art of using right carbohydrates or sugars, sweet taste can be tonifying for our body. However, today we are not consuming the sweets that our body is meant to process. We associate the sweet taste with white sugar, and that's what marks the beginning of our health issues. Even the quantity of sugar that we are consuming is making us sick like a slow poison. You think and name any major disease, and it has a connection with sugar. Do you still need reasons to know why sugar is harmful!

Understanding Sugar From Our Body's Perspective: Our body needs the energy to function. The primary source of energy for the body is glucose. Glucose is derived from carbohydrates and sugar based foods that metabolize and convert into glucose to release energy.

What We Don't Know About Our Sugars?: Our body needs glucose only in small quantities for optimal functioning. Sweet in excess makes our blood toxic, acidic and make us obese. If acidic state hits the body and our blood becomes toxic, our immunity gets weaker and we cannot escape health issues such as frequent colds, flu, coughs and in the long run degenerative diseases such as diabetes, inflammation, arthritis, osteoporosis and cancer. Also, what we don't know about our sugars is that we are consuming sugars in large quantities intentionally or unintentionally. We intentionally add sugar to our morning tea or coffee but have it unintentionally in our diet biscuits. Bakery items consume a lot of sugar and even our oats in the morning go in with at least 2 teaspoons of sugar. A bite of chocolate after meals, rather even fruit is sugar. Not to forget the cola's, sauces, dips, ketchup's processed items and ice creams that have become an inseparable part of our lives, all contain cheap quality sugar. Our body is not designed to handle that much sugary sweetness. Initially, the sweets may provide a quick burst of energy, but, over time high consumption causes fluctuating blood sugar levels. So, when you feel cheerful after consuming chocolate high, you may also become prone to lows as when the high sugar effect fades it leaves you depleted, dull and low on energy. Ideally, the sugar consumption should be such that you not only feel energetic but also are able to sustain that state rather than going into sudden sugar lows. High sugar does give you high energy momentarily along with elevated moods, but when the effect crashes it leaves you restless. As a matter of fact, those who understand carbohydrates well, use right carbohydrates as a sedative to calm mind and relax.

Right forms of sweets foods that provide sustained energy include whole grains, sweet potatoes, pumpkin, fruits in limited quantity and raisins. Always remember, higher and more refined the sugar, more quick spike in your blood-sugar levels will begin to occur, more energetic you may feel till the effect sustains, and more depleted you become when the effect fades away.

REFINED OILS

History of Refined Oils: There has been a lot of confusion about oils, its usage and right kinds of oils. This is because we do not understand our requirements of fats well. Let's first understand how ancient people used to consume oil when oil mills did not exist. In traditional times people consumed oil in its raw form directly through the sources of oil such as nuts, seeds, whole grains etc. As industrialization happened, and oil milling began for commercial purposes, the idea of oil extraction gained importance. However, initially, it were just oil rich sources from which the oil used to be extracted, such as sesame seeds, mustard seeds, almonds, walnuts etc. As technology progressed, the plant's sources of oils were being used for oil extraction. For the oil extraction industry, the good part was that plant oil sources were readily available without going scarce such as sunflower oil etc. However, the concerning part for the industry was that plant oils did not have an oilý texture, looked watery and became rancid in short time. It was not possible to preserve them for long. Then came the process of hydrogenation that processes the oils to a level oily concentration and increases its shelf life. The problem with hydrogenation was that it changed the chemical structure of oils, and the changed chemical structure does not match our body chemistry, thus interfering with our body functions. That's the history of commercial oils. To be precise, hydrogenated vegetable oils such as canola oil, cottonseed oil, and others are unnatural oils created through the hydrogenation process for longer shelf-life and commercial use. These oils disturb the original chemical composition of oils making them unhealthier for use. In various studies, these oils have been found to cause serious health issues such as inflammation, arthritis and cardiovascular diseases.

Why Do We Need Oils?: Firstly, we do not need oils, we need fats! Some important organs of our body are majorly made up of fat. More than two-third of our brain is all fat and the brain cell membranes are made up of EFAs (Essential Fatty Acids). So to keep the brain functioning optimum fat is required. It is also essential for energy, growth, metabolism, healthy eyes, skin and bones, to keep body lubricated and for reproductive health. Rather, some vitamins like Vitamin E, Vitamin A, Vitamin D and Vitamin K are all fat-soluble, which means that unless you have fat in your body, these vitamins will not be absorbed by the body and can be toxic if the right amount of fat is missing.

Which Oil to Buy?: Should you be using rice bran oil, mustard oil, canola oil or some other? It's too much of confusion unless you know how it is used by the body. Our requirement of fats must be adhered to based upon its usage in our body, and not by choosing the best oil from the retail shelves. We need Omega 3 and Omega 6 fatty acids for our brain health. Saturated fats can increase the HDL (good cholesterol levels) significantly. Unsaturated fats provide energy, considered to be good for heart health and support cell wall structure. Before deciding the right oil, think your health state and your body requirements. Ideally, there is nothing like consuming oils directly from their sources. For cooking purposes, prefer cold-pressed oils preferably sesame oil and mustard oil. Flaxseeds and walnuts provide us with Omega 3 & Omega 6 fatty acids that are a must for proper brain functioning.

REFINED FLOURS

Refined flours are the processed form of whole grains and much widely used processed item for commercial products such as bakery items, pizzas, hamburgers and others. Studies in recent times have shown that the more we are consuming refined flours, the more we are getting deficient in essential nutrients, specifically vitamin B12, iron, folic acid, and fiber. Gluten is yet another recent epidemic from the flour world.

White flour is produced by removing the outer layer of grains which is the bran and wheat germ. Both these ripped elements of whole grain contain healthful properties. Where bran is the fiber part of the grain, the bran contains essential oils much required for our body functioning. White flour has been reported to increase the risk of modern lifestyle diseases such as diabetes, weight gain, inflammation, arthritis, heart diseases etc.

CHAPTER 37 - CONNECT WITH NATURE

'The virtual world is producing beautiful visuals & awe-inspiring replicas of nature on screens using technology. However, the real world still possesses something that the virtual world can never replicate – The life-force in nature! Virtual beauty cannot ever replicate the sense of healing, balance, peace & calm, that the spectacular nature naturally possesses!'

Feeling sluggish?

Do you live in a big city in some tall building where sunlight has to find it its way to enter your home or home? All sorts of unnatural noises keep you devoid of supreme silence? You spend your entire day in a fancy, well decorated closed boxes called buildings? How many times a day does it happen to you that while sitting in closed, indoor, air conditioned environments, you feel like rushing out? Rather, when you are already comfortable sitting in a cozy environment, way at all would you crave for that break? Why does a simple walk in nature all the power to rejuvenate you?

Life under unnatural set-ups, away from the direct connect with nature in any form causes a myriad of physical, mental & emotional ailments. With the advent of technology and machinery, we may have created fancier closed boxes for ourselves, but it has resulted in our major disconnect with the nature and the results are directly visible in the rising number of people visiting therapists office often.

'Nature Deficiency' is a term that is now being used by the therapists to address such people who are totally disconnected with nature the and show up in clinics as cases suffering from unknown sadness, low moods, and other psychological issues. Today, the connectedness of individuals with the nature has got limited to occasional visits to a nearby park or travel to a hill station or a beach area. Nature has lost its presence in the lives of many people globally, and subtle signs of that disconnect often show up in people's thought's, behavior's and physical health.

Remember the times when children used to play outdoors in parks, mud, grass and amidst the whole day, totally unbothered of food, hunger or attention needs of theirs. The children of today belong to a set of parents who aspire to provide them the best of the environment, education, lifestyle and food, all unnaturally! Environments have grown indoors, education is all bookish, lifestyles are more about indoor and virtual conveniences and foods we already know, are artificial! Simultaneously, the children today seek more attention, are disturbed by nature, are hyperactive and nowhere close to what children in the past used to be like; natural, happy, joyful and happy-go-lucky. One major gap that differentiates the children of today and the children of the past, is the time that children in the past used to spend amidst nature watching the sky, listening to birds, chasing domestic animals, having a direct connect with the earth, playing on the grass and amidst trees, observing and chasing butterflies, absorbing the varied beauty of flowers, enjoying the rains and talking to the stars. The children of today hardly spend quality time in the nature because, we as parents want them to eat, live, see and experience the best!!! And, the definition of that best is air conditioned environments, instantly calming foods, instant happiness tactics such as a Mc Donald's burger or a pizza party, learning through gadgets, entertainment on televisions and secured closed environments where even the fresh air is banned!

As the ancient healing systems suggest, we have a direct connect with the nature because we are formed out of five important nature's elements, namely, earth, water, fire, metal, and air. All structural composition of our body is considered to be the Earth element, our body liquids signify the water elements, metabolism and digestive process signifies the fire elements and air within us resembles the air element. Understanding ourselves by this theory, we are a human manifestation of nature itself, and it is already inherent within us to be deeply connected with the nature. Ancient Indian, Japanese, Chinese, Australian Aborigines and Native American populations traditionally showed the acts of respect towards the nature by living in total harmony and connectedness with the nature. No wonder, their children, women, and adults never visited a phycologist's clinic!

So, next time when you feel sluggish, try connecting back with the nature and observe and experience the wonders of nature. Get out of your unnatural life mode and gain the earthly experience. Observe the wonders of nature, the life forms, feel the healing vibrations and look around and admire the different forms of beauty in the nature.

RESEARCH-BASED FACTS ABOUT NATURE & ITS IMPACT ON HUMANS

- Research done in Finland reported that the people who strolled through a park for nearly 20 minutes reported much lesser stress than the ones who strolled in the busy city.
- Series of studies published in June 2010 issue of the Journal of Environmental Psychology mention that being out in the nature makes people feel more vitality not just at the physical level but freshness at the mental level too.
- In an experiment conducted in Japan, where two groups of people taking walks of equal length and difficulty in a forest and in an urban center walk were monitored. It was reported that the ones who walked in forests had significantly lower heart rates, better cognitive abilities, lesser stress and anxiety, and were more relaxed as compared to the ones who walked in the urban center. It was concluded that something in the nature has the power to reduce stress.

THERAPEUTIC REASONS TO SPEND TIME AMIDST NATURE

Natural Colours: Research suggests that looking at flowers of different colors helps create a sense of happiness and calm among individuals. It acts as a power medicine for the mind and enhances its cognitive abilities. It has also been seen in researches that children spending substantial time in nature during school hours or otherwise tend to possess better cognitive skills. Interestingly enough, a common pattern among dull, unenthusiastic people is their habit to stay indoors. Colors have the power to brighten us up instantly. If you look closely, nature is all full of soothing colors in its different life-forms. The therapeutic relevance of natural colors is justified as different wavelengths of light that strike our eyes, makes our brain interpret these light wavelengths as colors. So, precisely, these soothing light wavelengths act as a healing energy as our body needs exposure to a diverse array of this energy (light) wavelengths to be healthy and at peace.

Connect With Other Life Forms & Learn Subtle Traits of Life: Connect with different life-forms existing in the nature can make us realize and accept the realities of life quite closely. For example, a commonly found ant in each household never gives up. Observing an ant helps trigger your thought process about how they keep moving ahead, without stopping to keep their livelihood on. Living with a dog automatically surface outs feelings of love and compassion hidden within you, even if you come across as the toughest person on the outside. Dealing with a cat teaches you the other aspect of life and think over whether selfishness and self-love are co-related for good. Watching a bird fly instantly provides a break-free feeling. To be precise, connecting with other life forms makes you realize the vastness of the world, helps you get out of your small inner world and build a larger perspective towards life. All such broadening experiences help stimulate the brain to perform at the peak of your cognitive ability.

Natural Sounds: The natural sounds refer to soothing sounds of the nature, such as the chirpiness of the bird, or the breezy voice of the flowing air, or the water gushing down a stream. Sound therapy is all about getting connected with the natural sounds that generally become audible in a state of silence, and imagine they are freely available in the nature! Sound therapy has its relevance in ancient texts of Ayurveda, where the supreme vibration of 'OM' is considered to be the most powerful healing force due to its vibration effect on different energy channels of the body. Sound therapy has shown to produce drastic results for stress reduction and lowering the blood pressure. For the gushing sound of a waterfall, there are a lot of electric fountains available in the market that try to produce the similar sound by rotating water. It is a good idea to surround your house with such replicas of nature's sound for a positive energy within thehome environment.

Connect With Microbes: Try relating to this. When in olden times, the children used to play in the mud and on earth almost the whole day, there used to be lesser incidences of sickness being reported amongst children. Today, when our children are highly protected and mostly spend time in clean indoor environments, our children get sick quite often! We want to live in a totally sterile environment and kill off all those microbes through anti-microbial soaps and sanitizers. Though it is important to kill some of the microbes that are detrimental to our health, not all microbes are bad! These exist a host of microbes that are essential for our survival and exposure to them is highly important for the healthy functioning of our immune system. The best place to get exposed to good microbes is out in the nature, connecting with the earth, playing on grass and taking all that muddy dirt positively.

Leisurely Movement: Who can underestimate the power of that leisurely walk during the wee hours of morning or evening. Nature automatically has the power to relax us, and you let yourself loose in the nature, you realize your movement automatically becomes fluid and free-flowing. Being out in the nature acts as a power capsule full of fun and health benefits. While your senses are engaged in the beauty of nature, your are automatically doing your body a favor by boosting your circulation, increasing flexibility, enhancing the functioning of the lymphatic system and helping your bones gain density and muscle strength. Not-to-forget the contribution of nature to enhance your beauty and skin health while you are enjoying your power capsule.

Fresh Air: Fresh air an important requirement of our body & gives us vital life-force. Indoor environments are all full of toxic air if there is no vent to recycle the stale air. People working in corporates or any other closed room environments are highly subject to allergies, cold and flu, because of the quality of air inside. I often come across corporate people who are permanently sneezing and suffer from allergies who prefer being on medications, but do not want to understand what may be causing them this issue. Rather, I have had experience with some colleagues in the past to whom I tried explaining the stale air concept of indoor environments, but he simply do not intend to relate to the concept and are happy in their own medication zone! The fact is that indoor environments are frequently contaminated with chemicals in the name of room fresheners. Further, the synthetic material or carpeted rooms hold onto a lot of toxic matter that we inhale day-in and day-out. The reason for your health issues may seem quite unrelated initially, but you can realize the change when you move out of the city environment and enter a clean, pure natural environment specifically on the hilly sides. Your health issues just fly off in the air.

Bio-energy: Bio-energy literally means living energy. It refers to the positive healing energy emitted from natural light, sound, air, stones, crystals and other natural forms of elements. Simply stated, bio-energy recharges our body, mind, and energies. The world knows that spending time in nature is rejuvenating, freshening and has the power to bring us back to life. Acts of accumulating bio-energy within you include experiencing these natural energies such as touching a flower, lying down on the grass, walking barefoot on the earth, hugging a tree or listening to the sounds of nature. We may have developed the best running shoes with all the comfort embedded, but the energy that walking barefoot can provide, no shoe brand can provide, be it Adidas or Nike!

ENLIVEN THE CHILD WITHIN YOU – THE NATURE THERAPY

'Nature Therapy' is an upcoming Western concept that focusses on experiences in the nature versus reading them in the book or watching them virtually! It intends to recreate a sense of conscious connect with the nature, specifically among children and sickly people who are on a healing path. Research studies suggest that direct exposure to bio-energy results in increased energy and an enhanced sense of well-being. If you come across any adventurous people who often go out on nature's trips such as wilderness excursions, hiking, swimming in deep oceans and mountaineering, you experience a sense of liveliness and feelings of health & well-being. Such people live to their full potential and research suggests that the connect with nature helps them ward off feelings of exhaustion. Rather, such people report enhanced energy levels, better cognitive function, and performance, even after hours of activity in the nature.

Most of us spend half of our life indoors today. A child has a natural instinct to connect with the nature. As we grow up we form various important relationships, while forgetting the most crucial relationship with the nature. Our modern society does not focus a lot on connecting with the nature, and the people who are nature-lovers are so because of personal choice. That forgotten relationship with the nature shows in modern offices, schools, families and even public gatherings.

Nature-Deficiency is very much a reality, specifically among urban dwellers. The natural areas and parks are limited, even if they exist they lack lush greenery, life is more about television and computers, children do not get to play our with a fear of stranger-danger and ultimately we end up being modern unnatural beings, that nature never created! And the impact shows in the emotional and physical health of children and adults. Our brains over-work and over thinking has manifested into our habit. Stress is widely accepted killer of our times. However, researchers believe that nature never intended our brains to work like that. Mental tension, fatigue, burned-out feeling, overwhelming nature was never intended to be inseparable aspects of human mind.

Try to think and see things in a broader perspective and there lies a great opportunity with everyone to enliven the child within themselves by adopting 'Nature Therapy'. Be a child again with your children and get back to the nature, the root of our existence! Making few simple changes in your routine can yield radical differences in your mental and physical state. Right from better moods, improves thesense of well-being, better self-esteem to results in terms of better performances, improved memory and clear thinking anddecision making, all reflects as soon as a person gets closer to the nature.

Few tips to enliven the child in you:

Consciously Observe the Cycle of Human Life: It all begins with consciously questioning some facts of nature. Why do we feel sleepy at night? Why do we work through the day? Why do we feel awful in a pattern at certain times of the day? It is all about consciously observing the cycle in which human life operates. How this cycle is so closely associated with nature, day, night, weathers, natural sounds, fragrances, and tastes. Observing nature helps us grow easy yet strong and accept transitions of life gently and come to terms with the realities of life with a broader perspective.

Go Barefoot on Sand, Soil, Earth & Grass: Ever wondered why walking barefoot on the sand near the ocean becomes a memorable experience. It is much more than good memories! Our body contains positive ions that are not good for health. For the body to keep its balance, it must constantly be in touch with the negative ions that neutralize the effect of positive ions. Earth and ocean sand contains negative ions. Scientifically, walking barefoot on the mineral-rich sand of the ocean is believed to have a healing effect on our body, as the negative ions from sand help neutralize the positive ions in our body. However, even soil, grass & Earth is believed to have the similar rejuvenation effect on body and mind. So, the next time you see your child walking on the soil barefoot, do not force them to wear footwear, rather, join them barefoot! Children are more intuitive than us and clearly take clues of nature that are in their favor. Trust their instincts!

Soak Up Some Sunshine: Sun is considered to be the supreme source of energy. All life-forms on earth derive their energy from the sun. Plants get their vitality in the form of chlorophyll through a process called photosynthesis that utilizes the fire, earth, air and water energy of the nature to foster growth. As plants have a direct connect with the sun, even human being are directly connected to the sun's energy to health & well-being, specifically the mental health. Rather, in Western countries, where the sun does not shine frequently, a lot of people report unknown sadness, feelings of sadness and depression. Rather, sun-gazing is an ancient practice where it is believed that there are times through the day and night cycle where gazing at the sunlight can increase energy, vitality, and eyesight of an individual. Spend some time each day under the sun, preferably early morning hours to experience the powers of this supreme energy.

Count the Stars & Observe the Power of Silent Moon: Ever wondered why you are advised not to go to the oceans during evening and night time. Ever wondered how the sea and ocean tides get rough as the day progresses towards the end? Moon is powerful enough to create fluctuations in the oceans on Earth. However, a walk in a moonlit night has an adverse effect on humans and makes us relaxed. That's a fabulous example of how everything in the universe is so closely connected. Observing and learning about the moon, counting the stars helps us take into a world of infinite. It is a great way to expand consciousness and imbibe broader perspective in life.

Bring Nature at Home, Plant Trees at Home: If your cribbing point is that you do not have time to go out in nature, try bringing nature at home. Plant more trees and plants at home, water them, observe them grow, and you are already are engaged with the nature at the comfort of your home. It creates positive energy, helps you delve into your own world of peace and slows the pace of your life.

Travel Often to Places Where You Find Rivers, Mountains and Oceans: Make yourself and your children experience the nature directly versus understanding nature in the book or watching it virtually on a television of a computer. It is not just experience but a heightened sense of awareness and knowledge that you come back with.

Create a Connect with Other Life Forms: Visit natural reserves, zoos, get a pet or just watch homely insects. The idea is to observe other life forms and their activities, their natural healing sounds, their postures and just engaging with them. Focus on other life forms help us shift focus from ourselves temporarily and bring back our thoughts in perspective. Ancient art forms like Indian classical music and dance, energy movement forms in Traditional Chinese Medicine like Tai Chi, Kung Fu and Qi-Gong have adopted their movement forms by observing nature and other life-forms.

Learn the Energy of Bio-Energetic Elements: Crystals, natural stones, transcendental natural sounds, flower touching, animal talking, feeling the water, swimming in streams, make one feel nature. Each of these earthly elements possesses a healing energy and knowing about them will help you strengthen your belief in the unseen powers of nature.

Bring Back the Wildcraft & Scrapbook Culture: Bering back the scrapbook culture. Collect plants, leaves, natural food types, other naturally existing elements and store them in a scrapbook. It is a great bonding and emotionally releasing activity both for adults and children. And it does have an element of nature.

CHAPTER 38 - FEED YOUR BRAIN

'Like we feed our body with the best foods, we must feed our mind too with the right foods. Food for mind!!! Yes, there are foods for mind too!'

While the entire world is becoming highly aware of the importance of good diet for physical health, no one gives a second thought whether there could be any foods at a rescue that could help us strengthen our mind as well. Actually, we do not relate to mind and foods, the idea is just too hidden for us to think about it and incorporate in our daily routine.

However, an even mind needs food to think better, feel better and live positive. From the scientific perspective, about 80% of our brain is formed of essential fatty acids that include omega 3 and omega 6 fatty acids. These essential fatty acids are not produced inside our body and we must continuously consume foods that provide omega's for a perfect mental health. Our brain structure and neurotransmitters that that act as messengers between our body and mind are highly dependent upon dense nutrients. Chemicals namely serotonin, dopamine, and norepinephrine are the three neurotransmitters that could become a cause of mental diseases such as depression and physical diseases namely Parkinson's disease and Alzheimer's disease. To keep the brain structure intact, we must feed ourselves the right fats and for neurotransmitters to perform their signaling function efficiently, we must provide them good quality vitamins and minerals. Furthermore, a healthy gut can help our brain function optimally and keep our mental health stable. Yes, there is a connect between the gut and mental health! The brain chemicals serotonin (90%) and dopamine (50%) directly related to our mental health are produced in the stomach.

KEY NUTRIENTS FOR BRAIN HEALTH

B12 Vitamin: B12 deficiency has been reported to have a direct association with depression. Vitamin B1, B6, B3, and folate are directly associated with mental health. Vitamin B is found in whole grains, nuts and seeds, dark green vegetables, animal meat and can be taken in the form of supplements specifically by vegetarian people.

Vitamin C: Even Vitamin C deficiency has been reported to be a causative factor for depression. The good sources of Vitamin C include lemons, citrus fruits, guava, kiwi, bell peppers, and strawberries.

Omega-3 Fatty Acids: Good fats are essential for brain structure and mental health. Omega 3 & 6 fatty acids are the ideal fat forms for a developing or weak brain and are found in fish, flaxseeds, walnuts and omega-3 fortified eggs. Even supplementation can be used in the diet to counter its deficiency. Bad fats such as trans-fats and hydrogenated fats found in all commercial products may rupture the brain structure and are the leading to inflammation and emotional disorders such as mood swings & depression.

Iodine: Metabolism is dependent upon iodine and it has been reported to improve the brain health. Good sources of iodine include seafood and iodized salt.

Selenium: Selenium has been shown to reduce the symptoms of depression and inflammation. Good sources of selenium include chicken, liver, and fish.

Zinc: Zinc is an important nutrient for neurotransmitter functioning. Good sources of selenium include legumes, meat, and multivitamins with minerals.

Magnesium: Magnesium can help reduce anxiety, depression and help in dealing with other mental disorders. Good sources of magnesium include whole grains, dark green leafy vegetables, nuts, seeds and dark chocolate.

Iron: Iron is also a potential nutrient associated with good mental health. Good sources of magnesium include eggs, chicken, and dark green leafy vegetables.

Vitamin D: Vitamin D, the most talked about vitamin of our times has an impact body-wide. Our brain loves this vitamin and it is known to reduce the depression symptoms. It is an essential vitamin for optimal brain functioning. Good sources include sunlight, cod liver oil, eggs, and vitamin D-fortified foods.

CHAPTER 39 - KEEPING CHECK ON BASIC PARAMETERS OF HEALTH

'A blood pressure meter or any other mechanical gadget may be signaling the internal condition of only the body symptoms. However, to get the true picture of your optimal body functioning & to know where exactly your health is heading, it is important to keep a check on basic wellness parameters. Most probably you will never need a blood pressure meter there after! '

Today, we do have blood pressure meters to keep a check on our blood, we also have equipment's to keep a check on our heart, kidneys, lungs and what not. However, we are so dependent upon technology today, that at the core level, we have gone away with the sensibility to understand and recognize timely inconvenient signals that our body communicates. Like, recurrent incidences of cold and cough may someday manifest into a sinus issue, bronchial issues, asthma. And we know that with the people today, cold, cough, allergies is a generic norm! And popping pills is next to eating food. Rarely, do we realize ultimately where we may land up. With the blood pressure meters we are tracking our blood pressure and with the pills, we are controlling it, but the reasons that are causing it are still there! Blood pressure is just a symptom that we intend to cure, deep within lie a host of troubles manifesting to emerge someday as our focus is just symptom treatment and not the elimination of blood pressure's root cause! How much you control or suppress the symptoms, unless the underlying cause is targeted, you can never be healthy, happy and free from diseases.

To judge the state of our health daily, we need not visit a doctor unless it is too late! Learning the art of decoding our body signals can save us from losing our health. These simple self-tests are great clues about your true picture of your health. Followed on a daily basis, our body may give interesting clues about where our health is heading towards:

Waking Up Fresh: When you wake up in the morning you are fresh and full of energy, ready for the new day. You jump from the bed rejuvenated. If you feel otherwise, the body may be under some kind of stress.

Regularity & Time of Your Bowel Movement: Timely bowel movement indicates that toxins are continuously removed from the body. Ensure this by increasing your fiber intake to normalize your bowel action and push out toxins as much as possible. Bowel movement must happen at least once a say and must not stink, should eliminate without winds, flatulence.

Gut Health: There is a saying, 'Way to health & happiness goes through the stomach'. Any issues in your gut like bloating, gastric issues, abdominal pain, indicate compromised gut health. Any feelings of lethargy, tiredness, and heaviness after meals also indicate digestive issues. Ensure good digestive health by focusing on chewing foods well and consuming gut-friendly foods like probiotics and enzymes.

Energy Level: Depleting energy levels may mean your compromised cellular activity. If not taken care in time may lead to further weakened cell activity and further health deterioration. Ensure this by regular exercising to provide oxygen to cells, reducing acidic food intake, relaxation, and healing therapies.

Food Cravings: Specific food cravings are nothing but your body's way of communicating that you lack specific nutrition. Ensure this by consuming balanced nutrition and not gorging on comfort foods when cravings strike.

Unexplained Aches & Pains: The major causes of pain in the body could be for some reason. However, if unexplained it may mean inflammatory issues or muscular pains. Ensure this by figuring our dietary & lifestyle reasons that could be giving rise to inflammation. If muscular, better get your muscles to use by exercising.

Happiness Quotient & Stable Moods: Much neglected area when it comes to understanding individual health, at a biological level any stress in any area of life may have a chemical reaction within, really creating acid inside, remember those butterflies in the stomach! Ensure this by indulging in following your passion each day, giving time to yourself & family/friends each day, practicing meditation and just being in the moment. If happiness without reason defines you, you are definitely in a good and stable state of emotional health.

Robust Immune System: Rare instances of falling sick, colds, flu, infections, asthma, allergies and other illnesses indicate a well-functioning immune system.

Natural Vitality & Skin Radiance: Brightness in the eyes, lustrous skin and hair and shiny nails indicate a good state of health.

Sound Sleep: Quantity & Quality of Sleep: A strong indicator of your physical and emotional health, if you do not sleep well, or sleep less that 7-8 hours, and if you do not get up fresh in the morning, it may indicate or lead to compromised state of immunity, liver & kidney function. Ensure this by going off to sleep at a regular time and sleeping for good 7-8 hours, relaxing your body so that the internal organs are rested too, indulging in relaxation therapies and feeding yourself light foods. Undisturbed sleep through the night without waking up is a strong indicator of good health.

Other Signs of Overall Good Health: Other signs of good health are indicated by good body circulation, no feelings of lethargy and fatigue, pleasant body odor, no bad breath and clarity of thought and direction.

CHAPTER 40 - RETHINK BEAUTY

'The old charm of grandma's beauty recipies has somewhere lost in the world of artificial chemical-based beauty industry. However, true beauty reflects from within & need not be dependent on external treatments to reflect its radiance. Modern beauty products not only sell dreams, but also carry health threats due to their extensive chemical composition. What goes in reflects on the outside. Do not aim for a plastic beauty, let it shine through from within...And, it's time to get back to the grandma!'

Do you seek beauty solutions at a dermatologist's doorstep or at beauty salons?

Do you wonder how do celebrities manage to look beautiful forever?

Do you believe that celebrities who endorse on-the-shelf beauty products get beautiful using the same products?

And most importantly, just think:

Did Cleopatra ever visit abeauty salon or a dermatologist's clinic?

The modern beauty industry is highly dependent upon chemicals to make us look beautiful. However, the ill-effects of these chemicals have begun to show up in the health issues of not just women but young girls too! Imagine a 6-year-old girl already in her puberty! Yes, it is a reality. Chemicals in cosmetics including lead and others have been highly linked to hormonal issues, PMS, mood swings and other physical and emotional issues in clinical tests. It is not just what we eat but what we apply too, that gets into our body and creates toxicity. It all started with industrialization when marketers started launching ready-made solutions to long beauty rituals followed in ancient times. As we have fully given in into industrialization, our sensibility to think what is right for our skin has totally gone for a toss. We would rather trust a dermatologist than our grandma for beauty fixes.

Just think why do you buy beauty products?

Is it because you hope these products:

- ❑ Will make you look beautiful
- ❑ Smell good
- ❑ Are value for money
- ❑ Are endorsed by celebrities

Now think, what are your beauty goals?

- ❑ To have a soft, glowing and fresh skin.
- ❑ To have ageless skin with no acne, freckles or wrinkles.

And, what do commercial beauty products give?

- ❑ Dreams!
- ❑ Strong fragrances that can irritate your skin and make it dry and rough.
- ❑ Strong chemicals can create a lining on the skin that may block pores.
- ❑ Cleansers with strong chemicals that rip off your skin of essential oils and disturb skin's pH balance.
- ❑ Toxins may get removed to a certain extent by dead cells still exist
- ❑ The softness that you seek is all gone as soon as you dry your skin and ultimately you need moisturizers

Food For Thought – Are you able to realize your beauty goals using commercial products or just concealing your skin superficially to look beautiful? Further what else these beauty products are giving you that your skin is taking in?

Try out this experiment & you know by yourself what I mean when I say that you absorb what you apply on your skin!

Apply neem oil on your head & body for 20-30 minutes. Try focusing on your taste buds after 30 minutes and the bitter neem oil tastes on your tongue! Don't worry, this experiment is organic & apart from a bitter taste it will also give you anti-bacterial properties and will detoxify your skin! However, my purpose here is to give you a real demonstration of what we feed to our skin is all being absorbed within. In short, every chemical that we apply, ingest or inhale, the chemicals get into our body. How you got a taste of neem oil on your tongue was that neem oil got absorbed through your skin, got mixed in your blood stream and the taste was passed on to your tongue.

Biologically, skin in itself is an elimination organ of your body waste. It needs to be scrubbed, massaged and stimulated to remove toxins effectively and keep it healthy. The best way to get the best skin absolutely free of cost is to rub your skin with a coarse towel to remove dead cells and toxins. Claims from any cleanser product company about their product cannot make your skin feel clean as this technique can!

Physical beauty is not dependent upon chemicals and other commercial beauty products, it need not! Rather, beauty was never an external matter in ancient times, nor is it today. We must understand the beautification facts first before going for chemical based solutions blindly. Peek into the lifestyles of a lot of celebrities and you realize their beauty secret is not about commercial products but about strict natural lifestyle and natural foods and products. We must understand that 'Beauty' is very much synonymous to 'Vitality', and is only reflected outside as a reflection of the strength and optimal functioning of our internal body organs. The very basics of having a beautiful, glowing skin lie in the following facts:

- ❑ Having a regular bowel action.
- ❑ Having a strong internal body detox system.
- ❑ Cleansing body regularly using various therapies.
- ❑ Water is the best friend of beauty.
- ❑ Clean, pure diet adds radiance to our beauty.
- ❑ Exercise, or even dance, that involves body movement can be stimulating and cleansing for the skin.

- ❑ Stimulating/Activating body organs through exercises/ Yoga/Pranayama/Stimulating and cleansing foods.
- ❑ Having properly functioning kidneys, as Kidney's impact body vitality to a great extent.
- ❑ Having lungs functioning at their optimal level as lung health shows on the face.
- ❑ Being stress-free and happy and consistently working towards it.

When you start looking beauty from such perspectives you will realize how what our grandmothers thought us makes perfect sense if you seek permanent solutions for your beauty issues. And, for all those who are looking for beautiful body, skin, hair and nails solution in a dermatological clinic, healthy diet and good lifestyle is a must try. Beauty is skin deep and resembles a wrinkled orange when it gets dry and toxic inside. By the way, that wrinkled orange gets its wrinkled state when the liquids under its skin begin to dry out, same happens with our skin! Deep below under the skin, the body components are deprived of nutrition to keep your assets in good condition. If our internal organs are deteriorating, our skin speaks the impact with dullness, wrinkling, and uneven skin tone. If you are anemic, your skin speaks the impact by showing pale and lifeless skin. If you are prone to pimples, most probably your are too much of a junk food eater including refined oils, fried stuff, processed foods etc. If in-spite of your doing everything you still have lifeless skin, most probably your lungs are not in good shape, or your kidneys are not processing the fed nutrition the right way.

Rather, when it comes to flawless skin and lustrous hair, any discussion is incomplete without the mention of Traditional Japanese women. Flawless skin, lustrous hair, low frequency of degenerative diseases, seems like traditional Japanese people never age.

But how do they manage to live through years being young and ageless?

Take some clues here, Japanese eating habits are considered to be one of the healthiest due to the following reasons:

- **Green Tea:** Japanese people consume a little green tea with their meals and throughout the day which provides potent antioxidants that help in countering the continuous decay of the body.
- **Eating Posture:** Japanese people kneel down on their legs while consuming meals (the same way as we do Vajrasan). It is a highly effective posture for improving digestion, and it is traditional Japanese posture for consuming meals.
- **Small Servings:** Japanese eating bowls are half the size of our bowls. They believe in eating less and small bowls serve the purpose (when you have less on your plate you eat less, simple!). Even modern science states that apart from junk and processed, overeating is the next major cause of body deterioration world-wide. The ideal balance is eating till 80% full and leave 20% empty space to enjoy optimum health.

CHAPTER 41 - DETOXIFICATION – THE RIGHT APPROACH

'A famous quote goes like, 'Cleanliness is next to godliness'. While we leave no stone unturned to keep our houses & environment clean, ironically, we do everything that makes our body become unclean. As our house demands regular cleansing, even our body craves for regular cleansing. Detox regularly!

What goes in must come out! Elimination is the key to optimal health and the concept of detoxification is quite common these days. A lot of wellness centers and health & food chains offer detox solutions and it sells more like a fashion statement than a body necessity.

So, what is a detox and how to go about it? Let's try to understand the phycology of a detox.

Firstly and most importantly be aware, if your colon is clear and you are not constipated, it does NOT mean that you have eliminated all your body wastes. Colon is just responsible for throwing away about 25-30% for your total body wastes. About 70 % still resides within and toxins keep on accumulating all the time as a leftover of body functioning.

The toxin in simple terms is nothing but a poison that either develops internally or gets into our body externally. Internally our body produces it as a result of overeating, impartial digestion, acidic foods or because of consumption of processed and chemical-laden foods. Externally we take in toxin through our breathing, polluted environment, cosmetics, self-care products, home-cleaning products, synthetic clothes, cellular radiation and through any other toxic source that we come in contact with.

Elimination is not just about having a non-constipated body. Our body is eliminating and detoxifying all the time through various channels. Dead skin cells are eliminated through the skin, sweating is yet another toxin release that happens through the skin, liver eliminates toxins internally, kidneys eliminate uric waste, bladder eliminates liquid wastes, bowels clear solid wastes and lungs eliminate volatile wastes from the body in the form of carbon-di-oxide. When we practice pranayama or any other deep breathing technique, basically we are trying to eliminate toxic gasses by deep and fuller breathing. If done properly and regularly, breathing is an important source of elimination that protects us against toxic gasses that reside within our body. Before thinking of a healthy diet, you must think of elimination and getting all detox channels right, as the best of foods will also become toxic internally if not thrown out by the body in a timely manner.

Detoxification is a mechanism to get rid of body wastes. The purpose of a detox is to push out toxins in the form of faeces, urine, sweat, bacteria's and viruses within the body. When approaching a detox our entire focus is either on a fiber-rich diet or on making sure that one does not get constipated. Avoiding constipation is like working on just one elimination channel. However, the fact is any activity undertaken to purify the body, body organs, body's passage channels and energy channels is a detox. It could be a:

Fasting Detox: Through a fasting detox, the body is able to break down the toxins in the absence of food.

Diet Detox: Through a diet detox, the body gets right foods to clear out existing toxins, and side-by-side it receives nutrient-rich foods that strengthen the body from within.

Exercise Detox: Through an exercise detox, the body gets rid of wastes in the form of sweat.

Breathing Detox: Through a breathing detox, we get rid of body wastes in the form of carbon-di-oxide.

Meditation Detox: Yes, it is a detox too for our mind! Through a meditation detox, we get rid of emotional and mental wastes that pollute our mind.

All these are connected areas that need to be targeted together for a total body and mind detox. If you are doing everything for a body detox, but not focusing on right breathing pattern, you may not be getting rid of toxins even after consuming the best diet in the world!

TOXIN ENTRY CHANNELS

'Cancer is a result of highly toxic body state. It develops when due to uncontrollable toxicity, the body gives up on its efforts to cleanse internally. This should be enough reason for us to take our detoxification efforts seriously!'

Toxin entry points:

- ❑ A poor diet containing chemicals, artificial sweeteners, preservatives, added colors or any other additives.
- ❑ Polluted water specifically from plastic bottles that is exposed to high heat, example, water in aplastic bottle in your heated car.
- ❑ Polluted environment specifically if you spend hours on polluted roads.
- ❑ Fumes from log burning, or through any other source specifically in the case of people working in industrial environments.
- ❑ Indoor environments where oxygen levels are compromised like air conditioned rooms/halls.
- ❑ Cosmetics that you may be using, for example, deodorants, lipsticks that contain lead which is a known carcinogen.
- ❑ Personal care products and as simple as your daily care soaps and shampoos.
- ❑ Smoking.
- ❑ Synthetic clothes that do not let the skin breathe.

SIMPLE ACTS OF DETOXIFICATION

There following channels of elimination are active organs that purge waste and toxins from our body. Dedicating yourself to simple acts of detoxification can ensure good health & a long lite. Incorporate these detox organs strengthening tips in your daily routines.

LUNGS

Lungs expel carbon-di-oxide which is the volatile form of toxin in our body. The best way to detox lungs is to utilize 100% of lung capacity by performing deep breathing exercises. Irrespective of whether or not you smoke, you must cleanse your lungs regularly. We accumulate a lot of toxins in the lungs from our environment including dust, metal particles, toxins from artificial fragrances. Due to these toxins, the elasticity of our lungs gets compromised and the ability to inhale fully gets limited. Cleansing lungs regularly help you safeguard yourself against any infections and lowers the risk of other lung and respiratory disorders such as lung cancer. Lung detoxification is a great way to aid smooth nasal airflow and maintains optimal functioning of the respiratory tract.

Tip to detoxify lungs:

- ❑ Dairy acts as the rival force for lungs. It is important to refrain from dairy products when you decide to detoxify lungs.
- ❑ Pure herbal green tea acts as a great detoxifier for lungs, specifically if consumed at the bed time.
- ❑ Begin your day with lemon water. Use the juice of 2 lemons in 300 ml of water and have it before breakfast.
- ❑ Take nasal steam with a few drops of eucalyptus oil added in hot water. Eucalyptus oil is known to purify lungs naturally.
- ❑ Nasal steam with camphor added water also helps cleanse the lungs. It acts well on congestion & sinus problems.
- ❑ Practice deep breathing for at least 20 minutes daily. It not only opens up lungs but also helps push out body impurities in the form of carbon-di-oxide.

- ❑ Ginger and lemon tea also helps to clean the lungs. You can make this powerful ginger tea by boiling some ginger, chopped onions, and some turmeric together for a few minutes. Drinking this twice a day helps clear lungs.
- ❑ Try not to smoke and try to be in smoke-free zone whenever possible.
- ❑ Try consuming pineapple juice in the morning. It contains natural antioxidants that help clean the respiratory system.
- ❑ Carrot, ginger and lemon juice also helps detoxify lungs and it also acts as a great detoxifier.
- ❑ Keep hydrated and consume a lot of herbal teas to detoxify lungs.
- ❑ Foods such as grapefruit, cabbage, beets, parsley, coriander, dates, and figs are great lung detoxifiers.

SKIN

Skin expels toxins in the form of dead skin and sweat. A famous saying goes like this, 'If you cannot eat it, do not apply it on your skin'. This is quite true considering how the host of chemical-laden beauty care products we use these days. Our skin is the worst sufferer as far as toxins are concerned. We feed toxins to our skin in the form of processed and chemical based foods that form our skin with poor nutrients, our skin further battles with environmental pollutants and toxins. On top of that, we add the burden of toxins on theskin by applying all kinds if chemical products. Skin detox is the first and foremost step towards the radiant and glowing skin. Though during the skin detox you may experience skin getting worse initially, this means that the detox is working. Initial worsening of on skin indicates that the internal toxins are breaking and getting out of the body causing temporary symptoms ranging from acne, breaking out of skin, fatigue etc.

Tips to detoxify skin:

- ❑ Foremost step for skin detoxification is to consume a lot of water and consume clean foods.
- ❑ Yoga or any other relaxation exercising techniques can help skin look and feel fresh.
- ❑ Sweat out to remove impurities from the surface of the skin.
- ❑ Focus on breathing exercises to get instant glow and radiance.
- ❑ Keep yourself hydrated with water and non-caffeinated herbal teas like ginger tea, chamomile tea etc.
- ❑ Take a detoxifying bath several times per week. You may add Epsom salt to a tub of warm water and soak yourself for 20-30 minutes.
- ❑ Steer away from dairy, poultry, meat, processed foods, food chemicals, artificial sweeteners, if you are seeking a porcelain skin!
- ❑ Clay is known to absorb skin impurities and holds a special cleansing relevance in naturopathy. Applying clay mask on skin helps absorb impurities from the skin.
- ❑ Avoid using chemical-based cosmetics as much as possible. Rely upon grandma's beauty secrets to beautify your skin.
- ❑ Rub your skin with a coarse towel before bathing. It helps remove dead cells.
- ❑ Clean your skin with a natural chemical-free cleanser. Check the ingredients of the products that you use to ensure they are chemical-free.
- ❑ Avoid sugar as much as possible. It is one of the major causes of aging skin.
- ❑ Include healthy fats in your meals including nuts, seeds and omega 3 and omega 6 sources such as chia seeds and flax seeds.
- ❑ Focus on consuming analkaline diet consisting of lots of fruits and vegetables.
- ❑ Exfoliate your skin frequently to ward off dead skin cells.

KIDNEYS

Kidneys filter the blood to extract the wastes in the liquid form. Dehydration is the worst enemy of kidneys that may hamper the optimal functioning of this important elimination organ. Kidney function gets impacted by medications, chemicals, preservatives, self-care products, processed foods and house cleaning products. Kidneys are responsible for regulating a lot of internal processes including acid-alkaline balance, blood pressure, minerals, hormones and watering the blood stream. In the modern world, we are inhaling, ingesting and absorbing too many chemicals that weaken kidneys. Weakened kidneys are unable to process waste products from the blood. If blood does not get cleaned-up, it leads to toxic build-ups in the bloodstream and causes damage. Toxin overload in the kidneys may show up the physically as dry skin, hair loss, inability to focus, urinary tract infections, high blood pressure, frequent urination at night time, skin rashes, feelings of fear, fatigue, lethargic feeling, drowsiness, sleep troubles, back pain and feeling cold. If you suffer from any of these symptoms, consider going on a kidney detoxification:

Tips to detoxify kidneys:

- ❑ The first line of defense against kidney malfunctioning is keeping away from processed foods, alcohol, caffeine, extremely cold foods, artificial sweeteners, preservatives, antibiotics, hormones, and additives.
- ❑ Believe it or not, high-protein foods have been proven to be detrimental to health. The best forms of proteins include vegan sources such as soy, beans, and lentils. Animal protein is too overwhelming for the kidneys.
- ❑ Hydration is one of the best things that you can do for your kidneys. Keep yourself hydrated through the day and try including herbal teas like lemon tea, ginger tea etc. to keep flushing the kidneys on a routine basis.

- ❑ An alkaline diet rich in fruits and vegetables supports kidney functioning. Cleansing juices made from vegetables and fruits facilitate toxin removal from kidneys. Foods that support kidney detox include celery, carrots, kale, spinach, cucumber, apples, zucchini, pineapples, peaches, and lettuce.

COLON

Colon expels toxins in the form of solid wastes. Though the concept of colon cleansing is there since the 1920s and 1930s, recently enough the concept has gained popularity. The techniques used for colon cleansing include colon irrigation, probiotics, herbal teas, and enzymes. The importance of colon detoxification has begun to gain popularity because of the toxic state of the colon. Overall, the digestive health of the world is declining. Undigested foods, mucus, bacteria, and other toxic elements sit in the colon for years and give rise to diseases gradually. Some of the symptoms of the toxic colon include weight gain, bloating, foul body odor, fatigue, irritability, heaviness in the body, ulcer, headache and low energy. At least one bowel movement a day is a must for each individual to ensure that toxins are being released from the system regularly.

Tips to detoxify colon:

- ❑ Enemas have been used anciently, specifically in Ayurveda as a means of colon irrigation. It is one of the most promising technique to clean the colon of any accumulated wastes. An enema is done by injecting fluid in the colon that stimulates the bowel movement and flushes colon of impurities. It must be done under expert intervention.
- ❑ A fiber-rich diet is yet another important source of colon cleansing. Some good sources include green vegetables, fruits, apples, berries and whole grains.
- ❑ It is important to consume good quantity of water along with a fiber-rich diet to clean and flush the colon.

- ❑ Laxatives are yet another remedy for colon cleansing.
- ❑ Probiotics help keep the digestive system in order and support the colon cleansing activity. These are a must when you are on a colon detox.
- ❑ Foods that toxify colon must be eliminated from the diet when colon detox is performed. Such foods include refined foods, sugar, dairy, flour-based items, alcohol, chemical-laden foods, processed foods, and caffeine
- ❑ Foods such as cauliflower, cabbage, broccoli and Brussels sprouts support the colon cleansing activity of the body.

LIVER

The liver is the hidden cleansing organ of our body. It acts as a gate keeper against any toxin that the body contains be it toxins from alcohol, medications, supplements, preservatives, fats, processed foods, sugar, even the self-care beauty products and cosmetics and toxins that we inhale, the liver must process and purify it all! And liver health is important for weight loss too! The liver is responsible for performing around 500 crucial activities within the body. It is responsible for chemically breaking all foods that we consume and filter them to remove any toxic matter from foods. If you consume healthy diets, it supports liver functioning immensely, if you consume a poor diet, it destroys liver functioning like nothing else. So, whether it is your salad, or soup or juice, medications, supplements, junk foods, cookies, bread, biscuits, alcohol or any other food, the liver must process it all! Now you see how much our liver is under pressure all the time, as we are busy feeding our taste buds. It is after liver's purifying activity on foods that the separated nutrients get mixed in the blood. However, over the years we have burdened our liver with wrong dietary choices and poor diets. Too much of toxicity overwhelms the liver and it is not able to perform its function efficiently. That leads to unwanted toxins getting accumulated inside. So, when it comes to weight loss, the more toxicity you accumulate, the more intoxicated liver becomes and does not perform its function well leading to toxic build-up, and ultimately more weight gain. And, this becomes a vicious circle!

A liver cleanse can not only help liver perform well but can also break down more fat, help you absorb more nutrients, reduces strain on the digestive system and immune system and relieves the body from the toxic burden. Precisely, liver cleansing can help the entire body functionality and organs, by efficiently filtering toxins at its barrier and not allowing them to freely float around in the system. Liver cleanse also acts as a potential beauty aid, making skin lustrous and appearance radiant.

Tips to detoxify liver:

- ❑ Alcohol and processed foods are great rivals of liver and weaken its functioning.
- ❑ Loads of antioxidant-rich foods such as mustard leaves, broccoli, parsley, broccoli sprouts, daikon, kale, green leafy vegetables are recommended to naturally support liver functioning.
- ❑ Fasting is yet another important medium of liver detoxification.
- ❑ Drink plenty of water for supporting liver's detoxification.
- ❑ Avoid excess dietary fats, artificial sweeteners, refined carbohydrates, white flour, gluten, packaged cereals etc.

CHAPTER 42 - GET THE BODY MOVING MINDFULLY – MODERN & ANCIENT VIEW

'Body movement techniques have evolved over years to be called as Yoga, Tai-Chi or Qi-Gong in ancient times, & to be fancily called cardio, cycling or swimming in modern times. However, whatever be the exercise name & type, what makes the dfference is getting started. It is important to move the body & techniques are just the medium!'

The concept of exercising is not new. In each ancient and modern era, the concept and techniques of moving the body have evolved to suit the needs & requirements of that particular era.

Do we ever realize what differentiates modern and ancient exercising forms? If we are empowered to know what benefits or weaknesses each exercising form carries, we are in a better position to choose right exercising forms based on our health goals. Where ancient exercising forms had a focus on mind primarily, the modern exercising techniques have their total focus on the body. Awareness about each aspect of life is the key to health & well-being, and it applies to our exercising routines as well. Both forms of exercises offer their own set of benefits, and combining the two is the best approach to achieving mind-body balance.

MODERN EXERCISING VERSUS ANCIENT EXERCISING

Ancient Concept of Exercising	Modern Concept of Exercising
Ancient exercising techniques have a strong focus on mind, body & soul	Modern exercising techniques focus entirely on the body

(Continued)

Here an individual aligns thoughts, self-reflects, and performs breath-control and physical postures to attain oneness of being	Here, since the entire focus is body, an individual may end up thinking or listening to music or just observing while exercising
The ancient exercising practices build concentration, strength, and flexibility	The modern exercising practices build muscle strength
Ancient exercising practices include postures that require the involvement of the whole body	Modern exercising practices may offer exercising options for specific parts of the body such as building up of abdomen or arm or leg muscles
Ancient exercising practices aim at reducing stress and eliminate pain in specific parts of the body	Modern exercising practices only aim at achieving defined health goals, be it weight loss or muscle building or any other
Ancient exercising practices are connected in a way that they flow from one posture to another and help regain energy, stamina and loosening up muscles and help develop fluid free flowing breathing pattern	Modern exercising practices are stand-alone exercise patterns. Breathing may or may not be an important part of these exercises
Ancient exercising practices help support the skeleton and even out the body mass proportionately. They help body become strong, lean, supple due to bending, twisting and stretching moves	Modern exercising practices help make body stronger, but too much focus on muscles may sometimes make body inflexible specifically in case of weight training
Ancient exercising practices energize you and keep you active and cheerful through the day	Modern exercising practices may tire you

(Continued)

<table>
<tr><td>These may not induce that much sweat, but keep body functioning specifically hormonal and digestive functioning in order</td><td>These help sweat a lot and improve circulation, digestion and toxin elimination</td></tr>
<tr><td>These provide techniques for gradual weight-loss that mostly is permanent</td><td>These provide techniques for quick weight-loss, that may bounce back again</td></tr>
<tr><td>These are apt for weak people, senior generation or and women</td><td>These are apt for youngsters, actors, and sportsmen</td></tr>
<tr><td colspan="2">For the people who have sedentary and stressful lifestyles, a combination of both forms of exercises is considered important to regain balance.</td></tr>
</table>

MODERN EXCERSING FORMS

GYMMING

The concept of gymming may have picked wave in the modern times, but the concept had been very much there since years. Holding a 3,000-year old relevance, the term 'Gymnasium' originally referred to a place to exercise naked. Today the meaning has taken a new significance of transforming the body through exercise. Its history dates back to the ancient Greek culture, where the purpose of gymming was ideally to improve physical appearance and become fit. It was all about maintaining an ideal body shape and the thought process has been continuing since the ancient Greek times. So, ideally for anyone who seeks physical endurance as a priority, gymming is a good option. The gymming exercises stimulate blood flow, heart rate and the rate of respiration and make the body work harder to expel toxins through enhanced respiration and sweating. It is effective to the extent that it can help one change their physical shape by shaping and developing muscles intensely. It induces deep sleep but makes one tired after practice.

WEIGHT TRAINING

Weight training helps tone the body and build muscle mass. It is one of the best ways to enhance strength and endurance. It is one of the important components of gymming exercises and helps shape and sculpt the body by increasing lean muscle tissue and density. Weight training also dates back to the ancient Greek times when Olympic athletes used weight training to gain physical strength and endurance.

SWIMMING

Swimming is an aquatic form of exercise and helps one burn calories effortlessly. When in water, the swimmer just does not get aware of how much energy and stamina they are using to push through the water. It is only after swimming that one realizes how tiring it had been. As an exercise, swimming is good for joints and helps lose weight. It is one exercise that is equally good for all age groups including children, women, youngsters and elder people. It is an excellent form of exercise for cardiovascular health, builds muscular balance, increases circulation and improves body flexibility.

AEROBICS

Aerobics is also a form of cardio exercise that helps better circulation and maintains body's oxygen levels. It is a strenuous kind of exercising regime that makes the heart stronger and strengthens circulatory system and lungs. It requires a lot of stamina to be able to perform aerobics efficiently. Due to its special cardio and circulatory benefits, aerobics facilitates proper circulation of nutrients and oxygen through blood to all parts of the body. It also helps the respiratory health due to the regulation of breathing pattern leading to deeper and fuller breaths. Maintaining aerobic health is essential to be able to carry out daily routine and tasks effortlessly. Other benefits of aerobic exercise include relief in muscle pain and soreness, strengthened the immune system, increased energy levels, weight loss, increased bone density, better joint health.

CYCLING

Cycling is a fun way of being connected with nature, yet performing good-quality exercise effortlessly. A lot of Western cultures have started to adopt cycling as a commuting source at the workplace. That is because the corporate employees end up sitting whole day long, and fun exercising option outdoors can help raise the health status. Cycling yields the same benefits as aerobic exercises and helps prevent various lifestyle disorders including arthritis, heart disease, obesity, emotional disorders etc. It is a viable exercising option for all age groups.

ANCIENT EXERCISING FORMS

Whether it is Ayurveda or TCM, the concept of body movement in these two ancient sciences involves uniting body, mind, and soul through physical postures and focus on the breath. In ancient times people used to create joy prevent diseases, alleviate pain and improve vitality by practicing a set of fluid body postures derived from observing the nature. The focus of mind-body exercises in these modalities was internal. It involved being aware of body movements, postures and body sensations while performing postures and connecting with oneself fully to relieve oneself of any physical or emotional pain.

AYURVEDIC EXERCISING REGULATIONS

- ‘Asans’ or exercises must be practiced daily early in the morning after morning cleansing and bathing rituals.
- Exercising during the day and towards the end of the day must not be performed as it oppositely interferes with the body functioning and disrupts sleep rhythms.

- Exercise must not be performed on a full stomach, and neither on a fully empty stomach. Few recommended foods before exercising include fruits, soups, and light warming foods.
- Exercise must be stopped as soon as body signals tiredness or else the effects will be counter productive.
- Breathing must be properly regulated as per the postures being performed.

YOGA

'Yoga is a living tradition that helps one unite with one's physical, mental & spiritual self by practicing body & mind discipline attained through 'Yogasans' & 'Breath control'. Yoga is an effective ancient science of self-exploration & personal growth at body & mind level. Practiced for centuries, Yoga still has the power to heal the world. With Yoga's steady practice, one can experience radiant health irrespective of age, health condition & stress levels!'

Yoga is an ancient body and mind wisdom having its roots in centuries-old yogic Indian culture. Going by its literal meaning, 'Yoga' means 'To Unite', and practically that's what yoga practice does. It works on the entire system - body and mind, to increase the 'prana' or the 'life force' within your body. Ancient yogis introduced the concept of 'Prana' - the invisible cosmic energy that is vital for optimum functioning and health of human body and mind.

The origin of yoga postures dates back to the times of ancient Yogis who took the clues from nature and created posture patterns that were in sync with nature's cycle. And so, yoga postures are meant to be slow considering the slow pace of transformation of nature from light to darkness and from infant to an adult. The postures have also been derived from the fact that movement is the basic nature of human body and this need begins to raise signals as soon as we wake up. For example, on waking up we have a natural instinct to stretch, revive and invigorate our bodies. In modern times, yoga has gained importance for its ability to make one toned, lean, flexible and sexy.

When beginning the practice of yoga in daily routine, it is important to realize that biologically our body is designed to move, and sedentary lifestyle is bound to cause diseases. However, movement in a particular yogic fashion is the apt state of movement for the body.

Yoga practice during morning hours not just rejuvenates us physically and mentally, but also brings us in a more conscious, calm state of mind to live through the day energetically, positively and happily. Yoga directly works on all crucial vitality and rejuvenating centers of the body - the brain, nervous system, spine, glands and organs, and from there originates a united holistic you who is in complete harmony with body, mind, and soul. Happiness, confidence, vitality, health, emotional balance, will to realize dreams and energy to work hard, all originates from this harmonious state of being.

Unlike the Western concept of exercise that focuses upon dissipated exercise mechanisms such as aerobic exercises and jogging for cardiovascular health, weight lifting for muscle strength etc., yoga asana and pranayama work on you as a whole, benefiting not just the cardiovascular system but nervous system, brain, spine and all other parts of the body. Yoga keeps our body and mind engaged together to such a level that you tend to visualize and concentrate on the body part that you are working on. From this originates the sense of unity of body mind and soul, resulting in a more calmer, happier and joyous you. Additionally, unlike western exercises, Yoga does not tire you but provides ample energy due to stimulation of energy centers of the body. Yoga must not be confused with merely as a set of physical and breathing exercises; at a higher state of self-achieved through body and mind discipline, more of a way of life that guides you to live in sync with nature and includes practices of breath control, meditation, adoption of specific bodily postures and relaxation posture to attain health physically, mentally and emotionally.

Benefits of Yoga:

- Improved vitality due to yoga's effects on crucial vitality and rejuvenation centers of the body.
- Balanced body weight is achieved naturally through yogic stretches that tend to move the deeply-accumulated fat from the remote corners of the body.
- Younger appearance mainly due to deep stimulation of body parts deep inside.
- Natural beauty specifically achieved through inverted postures that work against gravity to provide you a natural face-lift, reduce wrinkles, take years off your appearance, provide more blood supply to hair follicles, toned body, and calmer emotional state.
- Longer Life as yoga primarily works on the important determinants of long life including brain, glands, spine and internal organs.
- Sound sleep and enhanced relaxation that helps in the complete restoration of body and mind. Meditation and breathing techniques practiced before sleep can ensure deep relaxation, the release of body tension and a calm and fresh mind.
- Increased resistance to diseases, be it common cold or cancer. Whether you are fighting off a cold or flu or just seeking to maximize well-being, yoga may aid your immune system. By stimulating your lymphatic and endocrine system and soothing nervous system regular yoga practice can help you become radiant.
- Gland, spine & nervous system rejuvenation through yoga promotes a feeling of well-being, prevents premature aging, provides mental & emotional stability, helps one feel more confident, enthusiastic and optimistic.

- ☐ Yogic practices naturally detoxify the body through asana that not just stretch but also provide compression effect that massages the internal organs. Regular yogic practice can help you keep clean and clear from within.
- ☐ Yogic practices help increase cardiovascular and respiratory efficiency, normalize endocrine and gastro-intestinal function, and improve posture strength and endurance.
- ☐ Yoga benefits mental health by aiding improvements in mood, concentration, better productivity and higher creativity.
- ☐ Practicing yoga can help you be away from the clutter of everyday stress and worry, allowing your inner calm to shine through.

TAI CHI

'Who could have imagined how deeply ancient humans observed nature that they devised exercising moves based on animal movements. We are surely losing touch, not just with our ancient wisdom, but also with everything that heals. Undoubtedly, we are rapidly adopting what makes us diseased! Tai Chi is an ancient Chinese exercising form that helps balance our internal energy or 'Chi' by performing slow movements derived from animal moves!'

'Chi' the life-force or energy and the 'Movement of animals' are the two keywords in Tai Chi practice. Orientalists people experimented with breathing patterns of different types and imitated the movements of animals to create a healing modality called Tai Chi. Walking like a bear, stretching neck like a bird, twisting and swaying the waist and moving joints like a crane defines the movement postures in Tai Chi. The following animal movement forms are believed to have formed the core practice of Tai Chi: Tiger, Deer, Bear, Monkey and Bird.

Tai Chi movement form holds a meditative importance in the Chinese culture. It consists of smooth flowing movements that help to stretch muscles, and promote deep breathing. Tai Chi has been used in China since ages as a healing therapy to cure gastrointestinal tract issues, strengthen legs, regain physical and emotional balance and improve complexion.

QI GONG

Qi-Gong practice is believed to be originated by Taoist hermits more than 8000 years ago in ancient China. In its literal sense, the term 'Qi-Gong or Chi Gung' signifies 'Energy Work, Practice and Effort'. With these three important elements of work, practice, and effort on one's body, it is believed that the universal life-force gets developed and imparts health and vitality. Qi-Gong is believed to be a unique combination of health, wellness, and fitness, making it a complete mind-body rejuvenation program that detoxifies, energizes and strengthens. Breathing techniques have a special relevance in Qi-gong practice. It is believed to balance energy imbalances and be able to strengthen body organs individually with certain slow moves. The keywords that define the Qi-Gong practice include 'slow coordinated fluid body movements' , 'breathing techniques' and 'mindfulness practices'. The powerful combination of these aspects creates a cumulative effect of calmness, mindfulness, internal and external beautification, positivity, groundedness and complete rejuvenation. Medically, Qi-Gong has been proven effective for curing eye problems, digestive issues, degenerative diseases, tooth ache and skin disorders. The set of Qi-Gong exercises are broadly categorized into three categories:

- ❑ Exercises that regulate body organs
- ❑ Exercises that regulate breathing
- ❑ Exercises that regulate heart and mind

Qi-Gong practice is very common in China. The effectiveness of these exercises is believed to be multi-fold if performed amidst nature, preferably in lush green parks, in the fresh air and direct early morning sunlight. The practice involves standing, seated or lying down positions. In any of the chosen position, the purpose is to perform slow, fluid and rhythmic movements and slowly transitioning from one posture to another. Slow twisting movements hold a special relevance in Qi-Gong and work quite effectively to drain out stagnant blood and toxins from the organs. These slow looking set of Qi-Gong exercises are very powerful in restoring vitality, balance, lightness and aliveness of the body.

CHECKLIST FOR RIGHT EXERCISING – AYURVEDA's & TCM's VIEW

Exercise in ancient view is considered to be yielding benefits if:

- ❑ You are able to sweat.
- ❑ Your breathing gets enhances, deep and fuller.
- ❑ You do not feel tired and exhausted after exercise.
- ❑ Your body feels light and you feel a sense of rejuvenation and brightness.
- ❑ Your work capacity is increased and you feel that your stamina has developed.
- ❑ Your digestive health is improved.
- ❑ At the emotional level, you feel happy and joyous through the day.

CHAPTER 43 - BIOLOGICAL CLOCK IT IS QUITE A LOGICAL CLOCK – LIVE BY IT!

'Timing is important we know that. What we do not realize is that internal timing is equally important. The cumulative effect of continuously disobeying the biological clock culminates into lots of health issues triggered by these tweaks in time!'

How often it happens to you that you look at your watch and find yourself late for work, or for a party or for any other important occasion?

Next time when you think of getting late for work, do not forget to remind yourself that here is another clock which is seeking your attention – 'Your Internal Clock' ! Rather, you never know following your internal clock may be the solution to a lot of your physical and emotional health issues.

So, why it important to live a disciplined life and perform daily activities during specific times of the day?

Because nature intended humans to perform in a particular fashion. You cannot change the rhythms of this clock as it is regulated by the day and night cycle, precisely by sunrise and sunset. Breaking this natural cycle of the body is something like breaking the nature-set rule, whosoever breaks it has to face the consequences.

Each organ of our body goes through an active, high-energy state for 2 hours each through the day rotationally. It is ideal to synch our activities accordingly to support the body functioning when this energy traverses in order throughout the body. Research studies now suggest that following the body-clock is one of the sure-shot ways to keep body functioning in place and keeping lifestyle disorders at bay.

In ancient Chinese practice, the biological clock has an important significance. Even Ayurveda considers the importance of time discipline for health maintenance. Decoding health issues by understanding a person's routine and activity performing times is a great clue for a Chinese Medicine practitioner to decode the roots of their health issues.

The following interesting facts will make you wonder how closely our mind, body, and nature are correlated! Facts suggest that majority of heart strokes happen in the daytime around 11 am. If you regularly wake up at night for urination between 1 am to 3 am it is a direct indicator that the kidneys may not be functioning optimally. This kidney weakness also shows up in your bulging eye bags. Waking between this particular time frequently could also signal that liver is under pressure to detoxify too many bodily toxins. If 3 am to 5 am is your regular sleep hindrance time, beware, you may be under some grief, sadness or stress which is a directly lung related emotion. Waking up at this time may also mean lung weakness, bronchial issue. Rather, research suggests that many people face asthma attacks during this time of the day. If back pain bothers you by the end of the day after work, it could mean kidney weakness or you may have some fears and pent up emotions within you.

Every now and then we hear that we must wake up early and our ancestors have been explaining this to us since ages. But, we simply ignore, specifically the children of today! Thought from a long-term perspective when a disease strikes, we just think of the treatment and not the causes that led us there. If we can follow the biological clock of nature and the rules that nature has set for us, we can escape from landing up in a messy health situation. Next time when you think of your disease, before thinking of the treatment, think of the biological violations that led you there. And still, if you are not able to figure out, go and compare your lifestyle and energy levels with the ones who rise early, follow a disciplined healthy routine at any cost, go out in nature and exercise or meditate. You will get to see the differences and reasons for yourself.

IMPACT OF WRONG MEAL TIMINGS

Are you one of those who believes in creating your own meal or sleep timings?

For example, you wake up at 9 am, prefer to have your breakfast by 10 am, lunch at 3 pm and dinner by 9 am, you are absolutely violating your internal clock. Internally, our body functions as per the biological clock, and violating the rules creates internal imbalances. Our body is designed to consume breakfast in the morning nearly between 7 am to 9 am. This is because the energy or life-force traverses in the stomach region during this time. It stimulates the stomach and prepares it for digestion by starting the production of hydrochloric acid in the stomach that aids digestion. This acid is very strong and is meant to act on the food considering that you will feed yourself at the designated time. And you fail to do so. The impact is that this acid begins to eat you up, as it was expecting food but you failed to provide it the food. Physically this shows up as gastric issues, blood-sugar malfunctioning, acidity, fatigue, dullness and irritable feelings. Over time this may lead to metabolic disorders, such as diabetes or a thyroid.

Another example, if you are a late sleeper, say you sleep at 12 pm, at 8 am, so-called, you take your 8 hours of nap, still, you may wake feeling dull, fatigued and lazy. Over time you will become prone to obesity and may not feel as active as compared to someone who completes 8 hours of nap between 9 pm to 5 am. These ignorable symptoms could just be the beginning of body signals that something is disturbing body functioning, these symptoms along with other dietary and lifestyle factors may get converted into lifestyle disorders. By not following the nature's way of operating, you may yourself be opening up the perfect channel for diseases to seep in.

Now, do you know ignoring the ideal times for various vital activities of life such as bowel movement, breakfast, sleeping time etc. may affect you adversely and you CANNOT avoid the consequences! Believe it or not, you want it or not, your body is designed biologically to follow nature's rhythm, and it will work accordingly, whether you listen to it or not! If you listen, you enjoy good health and are free from bothering body issues, if you do not listen, be prepared for body troubles! If you are a late riser and skip your breakfast or consume it late, you may feel fatigued, stressed, irritated, non-focused, leg weakness and few other symptoms. If you feed yourself during this time, all other biological body activities get in sync automatically for the day. If not done, the biological rhythm gets disturbed early morning, leading to body complaints! No wonder, if you are a constant morning time nagger or worrying personality, it is because you have already upset your biological rhythm. As per TCM, the biological clock may yield the following health benefits for you:

- ❑ Better moods and control on unknown worry and irritation. Worry is an emotion originating in the stomach due to high cortisol levels early morning and to some extent can be controlled by feeding good food to the stomach.
- ❑ Better concentration and focus.
- ❑ Much better energy levels.
- ❑ Improved food cravings.
- ❑ Lesser digestive issues and better digestive health.

RHYTHMS OF LIFE CHART

Our biological clock and ideal activity chart:

Time	Energy Zone	Activity Code	Detailed Activity Sequence
7. 00 am – 9. 00 am	Stomach	Have Breakfast!	The code to define this time is 'Beginning' and signifies the beginning of day's cycle. This is the ideal time to consume breakfast which will yield many benefits.

(Continued)

			Your moods will be stable, gastric issues and other digestive issues will not surface and you will be active through the day. Warm meals that are highly nutritious are ideal to begin the day perfectly.
9. 00 am – 11. 00 am	Spleen	Be Active & Begin the Work!	The code to define this time is 'Action' and signifies getting back in action. During this time spleen converts food to blood and energy. The enzymes are released by the body to be able to digest foods and release energy. Metabolism and mental powers get boosted if you follow the cycle aptly. This is the most crucial time of the day to make important decisions and perform high precision tasks with concentration and focus. The most crucial work of the day must be performed at this time.
11. 00 am – 1. 00 pm	Heart	Socialize & Have Lunch!	The code to define this time is 'Socialize & Prepare for Lunch'. During this time perform light, joyful tasks, interact and communicate with people and get ready for lunch.

(Continued)

			The blood circulation gets boosted at this time that further control blood pressure and heart beat.
1. 00 pm–3. 00 pm	Small Intestine	Time to Look Into Problems & Solve Them!	The code to define this time is 'Go Slow' and signifies slowing down by the time body is digesting lunch. This time imparts mental clarity and a slow walk amidst nature can freshen you up for other half of the day.
3. 00 pm – 5. 00 pm	Bladder	Time to Wind Up Serious Work in a Relaxed State!	The code to define this time is 'Be Relaxed & Prepare to Wind up The Work'. During this time you tend to be more relaxed and still possess the ability to perform serious work of study. Consuming herbal teas during this time can greatly enhance your capability to concentrate and focus on your work. Herbal teas at this time help detoxify the body.
5. 00 pm – 7. 00 pm	Kidney	Prepare Yourself for Dinner	The code to define this time is 'Switch Off the Serious Mode'. This is the time to socialize, spend time with family, unwind and just be yourself. During this time it is recommended to be done with your dinner.

(Continued)

7. 00 pm – 9. 00 pm	Circulation	Continue Socializing and Begin Preparing for Sleep!	The code to define this time is 'Switch Off the Serious Mode'. During this time, keep moods light and perform activities that help you relax such as listening good music, a gentle walk in a park, massage or stretching that may relax the physical body. Try to avoid any mental activities that may lead to stress at this time. This is also the best time to conceive.
9. 00 pm – 11. 00 pm	Triple Warmer	Sleep Time is on!	The code to define this time is 'Sleep'. During this time your body functioning is all set to rejuvenate you and is waiting for you to get in the relaxed, unaware mode. All repairing work of the body, strengthening of the immune system or replenishing of the body happens at this time. Sleeping by this time will ensure you have enough energy for the next day.
11. 00 pm– 1. 00 am	Gall Bladder	Rejuvenation During Deep Sleep!	The code to define this time is 'Rejuvenation'. This time is supposed to be the time for deep sleep.

(Continued)

			However, your body is at serious work at this time by clearing all toxins, rejuvenating body cells and performing other cleansing tasks. You can best support your system here by being into a deep sleep and not interfering with body's activities during this time. Deep sleep at this time is important for you to feel energized the day after.
1. 00 am– 3. 00 am	Liver	Deep Rest!	The code to define this time is 'Deep Rest'. Until this time body's cleansing activities are on. The body detoxifies, recovers and thought cleansing process happens at this time. It is a crucial time for new blood cells generation.
3. 00 am – 5. 00 am	Lung	Sound Sleep & Time to Prepare for Waking Up!	The code to define this time is 'Slowly Transition From Deep Sleep to Wakefulness'. During this time the body begins preparing for wakefulness. It is the peak time for lungs to detox during this time. Performing stretching & breathing exercises at this time have a special relevance in ancient healing practices.

(Continued)

			It is time to absorb the life-force from the nature that shows in your activeness and good moods throughout the day.
5. 00 am – 7. 00 am	Large Intestine	Wake Up Time!	The code to define this time is to 'Be Wakeful & Transform'. This is where the cycle for the new day begins. It is time to get rid of wastes from the previous day and consume water to facilitate the elimination activity. You must clean and freshen up your body during this time for a perfect start of the day. An interesting belief points that combing during this time helps release mental tension. Keep this time as pure, alkaline and natural as possible.

RESETTING INTERNAL CLOCK

You must try your best not to play around with the biological clock if you want your body to perform at its peak through the day. However, in current times there is a great possibility that the biological clock may get disturbed as people are working 24/7 and traveling in different time-zones. Below are a few tips that can help you reset your internal clock back if it gets disturbed:

- ❑ Avoid napping at odd hours.

- ☐ Try to maintain sleep time and wake-up time discipline. Rest of the activities will be adjusted automatically.
- ☐ Prefer waking up early in the morning for work versus working late night.
- ☐ Begin preparing for sleep by dimming the light around sunset, be away from gadgets, listen to light music, use relaxing aromatherapy fragrances and avoid exposure to bright light.
- ☐ Try to avoid eating meals or exercises later in the evening.
- ☐ Try having a warm bath at night.

CHAPTER 44 - DO NOT COMPROMISE ON SLEEP

'If you are continuously depriving your body of sleep, you are interfering with your body's ability to rejuvenate & detoxify. Analogically, it is similar to a situation of chaos & confusion, where the cleansing activity is also on side-by-side!'

SAP CEO CASE

SAP CEO, Mr. Ranjan Das, CEO and MD of SAP Indian subcontinent died after a massive heart attack in Mumbai in October 2009. He is considered to be the promising youngest CEOs to have suffered a cardiac arrest. The news of his demise came as a shock to the entire corporate fraternity, more because he was believed and practiced a healthy lifestyle. He was an active sports guy, a marathon runner, and a total fitness freak. The question still haunts the corporate fraternity as to how such a healthy individual could die of a heart attack so early, despite of practicing all modern norms of health & well-being. Well, a peek into his lifestyle suggests that he slept just 4-5 hours a day and had been concerned about his sleeping habits. One fine day it costed him his life!

The misconception that we live by in modern times that the only two drivers of health are 'healthy diet' and 'fitness' , are costing us more heavily. With our total focus on these two aspects of health, other important health factors get a miss altogether. When we discuss sleep, there is another misconception that people live with. Sleeping between 9pm-5pm or 12pm-8pm is a similar case for a lot of people, as they anyways are completing 8 hours of 'scientifically-proven' ideal sleep numbers. It's not the same, numbers do matter but the sleep at the right time matters equally. Sleep timings directly are linked with our internal body functioning that is responsible for rejuvenation, restoration, detoxification, cell renewal, hormone production, enzyme production and keeping organs at rest.

So, when it comes to sleep, the following things matter in that order:

1. **Time to Go to Sleep:** Our natural sleep cycle must begin with sunset and must end before sunrise.
2. **Number of Hours of Sleep:** Each individual has different sleep requirements and anything between 6-8 hours is considered to be an ideal number. However, if you practice sleeping for less number of hours and compensating sleep over the weekends, this system does not work right for the body. Remember, body functioning does not happen unevenly depending upon weekdays or weekends!
3. **The Quality of Sleep:** The quality of sleep is something that we tend to focus on the least. Many people experience disturbed sleep waking up at midnight for urination or their sleep just breaks. It does not happen without reason. Broken sleep in a pattern indicates suboptimal functioning of liver and kidneys.

As per the ancient wisdom, it is believed that if a person does nothing for health, but just get proper sleep and rest, they are able to maintain high energy levels and positive moods through the day. They may also experience lesser incidences of falling ill.

IMPORTANCE OF SLEEP

Emotional & Mental Health: Nothing benefits better than our emotional and mental health, in a deep sleep. Scientifically, our thoughts are also processed and filtered during a deep state of rest. The brain filters negative and positive thoughts and memories when we are asleep in a deep state of rest. Probably that is the reason that even if we sleep being angry, we wake up all fresh and normal. Sleep sorts it all!

Normalized Breathing: Slow, deep breathing is the requirement of our body and through the day due to a lot of activity and stress, our breathing pattern automatically gets fast, shallow or incomplete. Sleep gives us a chance to normalize our breathing pattern as we slip into the state of rest slowly. This creates some balance of our breathing pattern.

Beautified Skin: The term 'Beauty Sleep' is used in reference to the importance of sleep for healthy skin. The science behind this is that our skin on the outside is composed of dead cells that accumulate on skin throughout the day. And so you feel dull skin if not scrubbed frequently. However, during deep sleep, the body cells build up due to high metabolic rate during night hours. The newly built cells also form the fresh skin that shows up early in the morning as glow. The daytime sleep may not be as effective as cell renewal activity is performed majorly at night. So, for all ladies looking for a beauty solution, it all starts with a good night's sleep!

Strong Muscles: 'Repair and Restore' is the word for muscles during a deep sleep. Why is it that when we have tensed muscles, nothing works better that a good sleep? It is because in the state of deep sleep, our muscles get a chance to relax completely. The tissues forming the muscles thus get a chance to revive muscles back in their original state during this resting phase.

Strengthened Immune System: Why are the ailing patients throughout the world suggested to rest and preferably sleep to recover? Sleep is a state of deep relaxation. However, for our internal body functioning, it is a chance to be active and get at cleansing and repairing work when the office is closed! No disturbances, no distractions, only serious recovery, detox, and cleaning! Our immune system silently fights the battle with infections when there are no disturbances.

Better Hormonal Health: Why have the cases of infertility gone up around the same time when the culture of working 24/7 became a trend? Sleep at the right time is important for our hormonal system to work efficiently. Specifically, the fertility hormones are tightly coupled with good night's sleep. Leptin is the hormone that affects ovulation and if it is disturbed it leads to an irregular menstrual cycle. Irregular sleep patterns impact ovulation negatively.

Detoxification: The concept of detox is not new to our body. Our body detoxifies all the time. However, the peak detox period for our body begins at night time, specifically between 11 pm to 5 am. The only pre-requisite for this natural detox system of our body to work efficiently is a deep state of rest, which is only possible through deep sleep.

Optimal Digestive Health: Sleep is a great way to keep obesity and weight gain at bay. During sleep, our digestive system slows down and gets the required rest from exhaustive digestion process. If you sleep early, you close all your chances of eating late at night and accumulating all the probable fat and toxins, thus helping with weight management efforts. Rather, research suggests that lack of sleep makes us eat more as it suppresses the hormone responsible for creating a feeling of satiety and fullness. So, in the case of lack of sleep, we end up eating more leading to weight gain.

ANCIENT TECHNIQUES TO SLEEP WELL

- ❑ Avoid the consumption of caffeine or any other nerve stimulating food or beverage at night.
- ❑ Consume chamomile tea before sleep as it is known to induce relaxation.
- ❑ Foot massage with sesame oil or lavender aromatherapy oil before sleep helps stimulate certain acupressure points that help relax the whole body in just a few minutes.
- ❑ Focus on your breath and intentionally make it slow, deep and diaphragmatic in a lying down position. Try 4-6-8 breathing pattern, which means inhale to a count of 4, hold for a count of 6 and exhale to a count of 8 to bring your body back to relaxed state before sleeping.

- ❑ Avoid sleeping till late in the morning. Between 5am to 6 am is a good time to wake up.
- ❑ Do some light, motivational reading before sleep to relax and to set focus on the positivities of life.
- ❑ Create the right environment for sleep by creating darkness in the bedroom, having an aroma bath, dimming the lights few hours before sleep, keeping away from entertainment, infuse relaxing fragrances in the sleeping room.
- ❑ Light stretching will help open up and relax the body for a good sleep.
- ❑ Do not consume solid foods at least 2-3 hours before sleep.
- ❑ You can tap into a relaxing sleep by getting into bed between 9pm-10pm.
- ❑ Wear comfortable and preferably cotton clothes while sleeping to let your skin breathe.

CHAPTER 45 - LLMIT GADGET TIME AND USE GADGETS SMARTLY

'Technology is at its peak, & so are its side-effects. Sadly, our 100% focus is just on technology and its side-effects are enjoying a leisure time by creeping into our body and creating abnormalities at a subtle level. We need to be balanced than ever before, & support our body with dense uutrition to steer away from the negative effects of radiation'

Electromagnetic radiations from cell phones, electrical appliances, computers, power lines, tower transmitters, Bluetooth devices, Wi-Fi installations, microwave oven have been reported to be impacting physiologic functions and tissues of the body significantly. Research suggests that children born to mothers whose cell phone usage had been high during pregnancy showed adramatic increase in hyperactivity and other behavioral and emotional problems.

The foundational elements of our body including cells, tissues, and organs function based on their communication with their internally connected elements. This communication is based onsubtle electromagnetic signaling between cells. Research suggests that radiation from cell phones causes oxidative stress and has been found to cause diseases ranging from fatigue, irritated skin, headache to cancer.

TIPS TO DEAL WITH RADIATION SIDE EFFECTS

Maintain Distance from Gadgets: Try to reduce radiation impact on the head. Try hands-free, talk on speaker phone or from a distance. You must switch off the wireless router when not in use to minimize radiation. Best is to limit the usage of cell phone all together through the day. Pregnant women are advised to keep cell phone away from their abdomen and children must not be allowed to play with a cell-phone. They are highly at risk.

Mineralize Yourself: Give up acidic foods and adopt alkalinity, it is the only way to mineralize yourself. If possible, go out and swim in the sea water, it is highly mineralizing.

Use Herbs Frequently: Herbs are plants with medicinal value that have been seen to expel heavy metal toxins from our body. Sulfur containing foods such as garlic and onions and green and dried herbs such as cilantro, chives, aloe vera, tulsi (Holy Basil) and parsley are known to be heavy metal detoxifiers. Research on animals indicates that curcumin is a potent antioxidant and anti-inflammatory compound that exists in turmeric that helps to protect against radiation.

Consume Green Leafy Vegetables: Green leafy vegetables are great for detoxifying heavy metals. They are also high in minerals including calcium, B vitamins, and antioxidants.

Activate Lymphatic System: Exercise to stimulate your lymphatic system, which is the sewer system of our body. With a lot of metallic and other toxicity surrounding our cells, our lymphatic system becomes stagnant, due to which toxins do not get an outlet and our cells keep struggling in the acidic and toxic matter that must be eliminated. Exercising induces elimination of toxins through sweat.

Iodine to the Rescue: Adequate iodine levels act as a potential prevention against radiation. The rich sources of iodine include potato with peel, seaweeds, and eggs.

Probiotics: Probiotics have been found to provide protection against the effects of radiation.

CHAPTER 46 - PRACTICE THE ANCIENT ART OF FASTING

'If there is one powerful technique to heal anything therapeutically, it is fasting! Fasting is an ancient, most powerful lost approach to healing. By not feeding yourself for some time you help your body break the toxic matter from within & push it out. Fasting may make you diseased initially, as sickness does! However, the big differentiator here is that a disease makes you permanently sick by adding on toxins, whereas, fasting makes you temporarily sick by breaking down & removing toxins from the system!'

Fasting is in for years and still remains to be one of the most fundamental, quickest and oldest methods for health recovery. There are many references in ancient cultures about how people used fasting as a medium to regain their health and wellness.

Fasting refers to abstinence from food and/or drinks for a certain period of time to give body and mind a chance to cleanse from deep within.

In various ancient cultures, fasting has a mention as one of the most important healing remedies. In the Biblical fasting served as a tool to heal the body. Rather, the people of remote Hunza Valley of Northern Pakistan are famous enjoying an exceptionally high life span of 120 to 130 years on an average. However, where no one could figure out their exact reason for such a long survival, some researchers hold a view point that due to lack easy accessibility of the valley, Hunzas had to abstain from food for days and months. On the other side of the globe, the native American Indians realized the benefits of fasting and incorporated it as a ritual in many of their ancient sacred ceremonies. Even in the history of India, fasting enjoys a ceremonial importance and is incorporated in routines at various times of the year. However, the main purpose of fasting during ancient times and in modern times is to provide the body and mind, an apt environment for internal cleansing and toxin removal.

Fasting is known to detox the body organs including kidneys, liver and digestive tract. It purifies and heals our body from within, offers a resting phase to the biological functioning and helps organ activity to slow down. On fasting, our body automatically gets rid of toxic accumulations, diseased body tissues, and excess nutrients. Ayurveda specifically positions fasting as a potent medium for internal cleansing and recommends its practice few times in a year.

However, today fasting has lost its purpose as people are not much aware of the true purpose and benefits of fasting. In many religious cultures, it is practiced as a part of religious ceremonies versus for its true purpose of cleansing.

PREPARING FOR A FAST

Fasting must not be observed randomly, specifically by the people who live by modern standards of diet and lifestyle. Wrong dietary practices and over burdened body state may lead to stronger repercussions as toxins begin to break within.

One must prepare the body for a fast so that the actual purpose of fasting is realized. Before a fast, one must begin the process of reducing food intake and try to be majorly on whole and natural foods. Any foods that may add to body toxicity must be stopped instantly. Even if one plans to practice fasting for one or two days, one must begin consuming more of fruit and vegetable diet few days before fasting. This way the body gets used to lighter and lesser foods and adjusts its functioning to the foods being consumed. It helps greatly to avoid the shock that body may feel if you plan to go on a sudden fast.

So, the best way to prepare for a fast is to begin improving the diet and eating habits few days before going on a fast. Support your diet with more and regular intake of fresh fruits and vegetable juices before fasting. Go slow on a fast. If you are fasting for the first time begins with one day at a time, increasing the frequency of your body feels comfortable. You may go on water-only fast or may substitute water with fruit and vegetable juice fasts frequently through the day. It provides energy and enhances the cleansing action of the fast. You may also keep rotating cleansing drinks through the day rotationally with water, lemon juice, cucumber juice or any other vegetable and fruit juice.

Ayurveda approach to fasting includes the following approaches:

- ❑ Light foods fasting that includes foods such as rice & dal porridge (khichari) and fermented such as fermented steamed rice cakes (idli).
- ❑ Fruits & vegetable foods fasting.
- ❑ Liquid fasting which includes drinking water and other herbal and detoxifying teas through the day.
- ❑ No foods and water fasting where you do not consume anything during the fasting duration.

Ayurveda further suggests that the choice of fast purely depends upon a person's condition and constitution, the internal health state of a person, digestive strength, toxicity level and overall strength to be able to fast. Fast must not deplete one's energy.

It is also important to choose a relaxing time for fasting where you get ample time to rest and relax.

In my personal experience, our bodies today are highly toxic owing to our dietary and lifestyle habits. Going on a sudden fast may come as a shocker for the body. So, it is recommended to go slow on a fast by first eliminating toxic foods from your diet and being on a light food diet. Then slowly moving on to fruits and vegetable diet and juices, further narrowing fast to herbal tears and water and then practicing a total fast by abstaining from foods and drinks.

FASTING DURATION

Our body is intelligent enough to decide how long we must fast. The bottom line here is to keep listening to the body during the fasting period, and anytime if it feels that health is being compromised, the fast must be broken logically, as explained in the next section.

However, a 24 hour fast is good to begin with. Even 1-2 days of fasting can yield immense benefit for our body. Even if the toxins do not get eliminated at such a short duration of fasting, the impact of fasting still continues and toxin elimination process is still on. This may commonly show up physically as diarrhea, skin rashes, fever or any other cleansing action by the body.

Technically, the body communicates on its own when its time to break the fast. When the cleansing action of fasting is at its peak, hunger subsides and the stomach shrinks. Until this stage, the body keeps using its own internal reserves for survival. The appetite is back only when the body runs out of these internal sources to be able to perform its internal functioning efficiently. Few signs to notice include transparent urine, eyes becoming shinier, body odor is gone and the tongue gets back its original pink color. It is an indication that its time to break the fast. However, if you do not break the fast at this stage, there is a high probability that fasting begins to go in a negative direction of starvation leading to severe internal damage and even death.

ART OF BREAKING THE FAST

Like you prepare for a fast, likewise, you must prepare for the breaking of the fast. When you do not consume food for long and if you immediately begin eating heavy, oily or processed foods, it can harm the internal body functioning, as after the fast the body functioning needs to recover from a phase of rest. Also, after fasting the digestive flora in the stomach needs to be replenished to be able to perform digestion optimally. If at this stage you overwhelm stomach with wrong foods or too many foods, it may have an opposite impact causing digestive issues like abdominal pain, gastric issues, headaches, indigestion etc.

So, as it is a good idea to slow down when planning for a fast, similarly, it is highly recommended to break the fast in phases. So you must begin eating slowly after a fast, preferably in the reverse order of how you planned a fast. This means first liquids much be reintroduced, then fruits and vegetable diet and juices and then light foods. Only when the digestion regains its strength after this gradual process, the full diet must be incorporated back again.

HEALING STAGES DURING FASTING

As a ground rule, the more toxic one's diet is the more detox side effects may be experienced by an individual. This is because in the case of major internal toxicity, the breaking up of further toxins will create physical symptoms such as diarrhea, nausea, skin rashes, bad breath, hunger, mood swings, dizziness, frequent urination, anxiety etc. It simply means that the detox action of fasting is working.

In the first stage of internal cleansing, the body begins to use its internal reserves in the absence of foods for its internal processing. These reserves may include excess fat and tissues. The body tries to get rid of toxins, wastes, tumors etc. by eating up the wastes. The elimination organs of the body get activated during this process to eliminate wastes from the bowels, kidneys, lungs and the skin. The digestive system gets a much-needed break at this stage and the rapid healing gets enforced. This is all a normal part of the fasting process and it indicates your fasting is working! The cleansing reaction may cause some external symptoms as discussed earlier. Till this stage the body uses all its efforts to eliminate toxins.

In the second stage of elimination the repair and regeneration of organs takes place. The signs of improvement depend upon how toxic the body is. In the case of high toxicity the positive signs may take some time to appear. Physically and emotionally you begin to feel better, your moods improve, you begin to gain clarity, mental fogginess is gone, your body odor is gone, your skin begins to glow, fatigue is gone and you begin to feel more active and energetic through the day, after this stage.

SPIRITUALITY & FASTING

Perseverance of physical health is just one sided aspect of fasting. However, it is helpful in enhancing one's spiritual experiences. In the absence of foods the energy channels of the body called 'nadis' in Ayurveda open up. In the absence of food, the body absorbs more positive vibrations of life-force from the environment. One can enhance their fasting experience by preferring a natural environment during the fast duration such as walking in amidst nature, swimming in the sea, being out in thefresh air and sunbathing. Probably that is the reason that we see ancient saints, yogis, and monks either eating less and fresh or fasting during specific times of the year.

FASTING BENEFITS

Fasting is the ultimate healing remedy and the results show up as:

- ❑ Enhanced digestive fire that burns toxins rapidly and relieves from gastric issues.
- ❑ Light feeling in the body and sense of overall health and well-being.
- ❑ Mental clarity and increased energy.

CHAPTER 47 - PRANAYAMA

'Slow, deep breaths are elixir of vitality, youthfulness, physical stamina, mental alertness, and calmness. Each new life is naturally gifted with slow, calm, deep breaths. As age progresses, our breaths transform into fast, erratic & shallow breathing patterns. Pranayama is a powerful ancient breathing wisdom that not just provides techniques to stabilize our natural breathing patterns, but also heals us internally by optimizing biological functions with greater intake of oxygen'

We are currently living in times where everything operates fast, including our breaths! We have no time to sit back and eat, drink, relax, sleep and enjoy anything properly, and believe it or not, our body just does not like it and pays for it in the background! The human body is designed to operate in a slow, calm peaceful internal environment. The fast trend has led to a puzzled physical and mental state of the body, and the outcome manifests in the form of physical and emotional health issues. For optimum physiological body functioning, we must breathe slowly, calmly and deeply, because, how much modernized we become, our biological processes will continue to operate in a particular fashion as designed by nature, and no science can change that natural rhythm of our bodies.

Our breathing pattern is a direct interpretation of our state of mind and how we feel in a given moment. For example, when we are angry, our breathing pattern automatically becomes aggressive; when we are stressed out, our breathing pattern automatically becomes hard and breathless, when we feel happy and relaxed, our breathing pattern automatically becomes slow and calm. The way our minds interpret life experiences is the foundation of our breathing pattern. But, what we do not know is, that slow, calm and deep breaths can provide positive direction to our thought process and life experiences. Further, it can add more fulfilling years to our life.

'Pranayama' has survived the tests of time, and is still available as free, potent tool to ward off physical and mental problems. Its origin dates back to the times when people used to observe nature and take clues to devise ways for a happy and healthy living. It was then observed that some of the longest living animal species, such as elephant and tortoise, have a slow, calm and deep breathing patterns.

'Pranayama' is the exclusive science of breath management and stems out from Ayurveda. It has the power to transform & elongate the quality of life. It supports entire biological functioning and promotes deep oxygenation. It helps purify and clean blood and eliminate toxins. It helps control heart rate by promoting slow respiratory rate and deeper breaths, enhances digestion, relaxes blood vessels and releases carbon-di-oxide from the body at a much higher rate than what normal breathing does. Dedicating 20 minutes a day to the practice of 'Pranayama' can help one deal with common problems such as irritability, anger, lack of energy, emotional stress, mental unrest, emotional instability, insomnia and ill health. It can also help one achieve more with focus, concentration, positive drive and zest in one's respective areas of work.

How does Pranayama work within the body and why is it important?

We have various toxin elimination channels within our body such as bladder to process and filter out liquid wastes, colon to process and filter out solid wastes, skin to process and filter out toxin in sweat form and lungs to process toxic gasses in the form of breathing. When we practice pranayama, basically we are trying to eliminate toxic gasses by deep and hard breathing. If done properly and regularly, it can protect you against toxic gasses that reside within our body and need a push to be out.

Breathing is not just an essential biological activity. It also speaks loads about the personality and emotional state of a person. For example, a relaxed breather will always be relaxed and stress-free by nature; a shallow breather will be one who is always tensed and nervous by nature; a fast breather will be someone who is always in a hurry; a deep breather will be happy and healthy; an incomplete breather will always showcase traits of restlessness and fatigue. To an alternate practitioner, knowing a breathing pattern of a person does reveal a lot about a person's behavior, stress levels, health state, organ functioning and emotional state. Alternatively, an alternate health practitioner can help you breathe well for attaining a state of health and wellness. By regulating your breathing pattern, you can become a calm and peaceful person from an angry and impatient person and a healthy and emotionally strong person from a sickly and emotionally weak person.

Though a lot of pranayama techniques have been defined in Ayurveda, one of the most powerful pranayama techniques is explained below:

Alternate Nostril Breathing: It is the technique of alternate breathing through the left and right nostril. Inhaling from the left nostril and exhaling from the right helps to calm a person. Whereas, inhaling from right nostril and exhaling from the left fosters clarity of thought. A technique to perform alternate nostril breathing is as follows:

1. Close the right nostril with the thumb of the right hand and inhale deeply and fully through the left nostril.
2. Now, using your index finger or ring finger of the right hand, close the left nostril and exhale through the right nostril. This completes one cycle of alternate nostril breathing.
3. Complete 8-10 cycles.

CHAPTER 48 - TOUCH & HEAL – MASSAGE THERAPY

'Massage therapy is the art of touch used for relaxation, beautification & stress control. In today's times where stress rules all walks of life & mental relaxation is under the siege of modern lifestyle pressures, massage therapy can be a savior. When practiced regularly, massage therapy has the power to enhance health, serenity, and well-being of an individual. If there is one common healing art among the oldest cultures of the world, it is the 'Massage Therapy'! And, guess what, you can benefit from it for free, it just requires two hands to get started!'

The term 'Massage' originated from the Arabic word 'Mass' meaning to press softly. Massage is a holistic wellness approach that dates back to 3000 years and is known to heal a person at body, mind and soul level.

The concept of massage is not a new one. During ancient times the magical powers of massage have been well documented in various cultures of the world. Where West has now begun to value the importance of body stimulation through massages, almost all ancient cultures of the world have incorporated massage therapy into their healing and beautification practices since ages. Thai massage, Indian Ayurveda massage, Swedish massages are few on the ancient touch & heal techniques that are getting attention in modern times due to their healing capabilities. The touch and heal therapy has got recognition with the opening up of a lot of spas and massage centers across the world. Where Chinese & Indian cultures utilized the benefits of massage to enhance health & longevity; Greek, Roman & Egyptian cultures included various kinds of massages in their bathing rituals for maintaining the timeless beauty and for relaxation purposes.

Massage therapy is a time-tested technique that has the power to soothe, promote general well-being and self-esteem. It works on soft tissues of the body including, muscles, connective tissues, tendons, and ligaments. Massaging tends to stimulate the nerves that transmit a well-being signal through the spinal cord to the brain. Nervous system stimulation through massage also tends to stimulate all nerve-connected areas throughout the body. Equally beneficial effects of massage therapy are its effects on emotional well-being. It is a great way to relieve anxiety and stress and immediately helps one regain a peaceful state of mind. The physically accumulated tension in the muscles can easily be found by an experienced masseur, and just by applying pressure the muscle tension can be released. The benefits may include relief from worry, anxiety, sadness or irritability that are typical traits of unreleased tension. The power of massage is believed to be coming from the magic of touch, which is an absolutely primal and a basic instinct of any human being. A newborn baby rests calmly in the warmth of the physical touch of its mother. Anyone can benefit from a massage therapy and experience a sense of security and strength through the healing touch. Massage therapy also helps to regulate the physiological processes of the body including lowered blood pressure and enhanced brain function. This is probably achieved through the relaxed body and mind using massage therapy. In today's fast paced life, when massage therapy can help one put back to rest, the irony is that this ancient art is losing its identity and is just limited to spas and massage centers. Through such places are great for community service, massage is not a very technical art. It can be practiced by anyone at the comfort of their home; all you need is your hands, an oil and little technical know-how about right massaging strokes!

CHAPTER 49 - SELF CARE

'Simple routinely acts of self-care are an underestimated yet great tool to tune-in into one's own self. Acts of self-care had a special relevance in the ancient cultures. It was believed that self-care bridges the gap between your emotions and others' emotions & help one connect better with oneself & with others.'

The fact is we have been taught to believe that we must be givers always, without giving anything to ourselves!

Ancient Indian, Japanese, Greek, Chinese and French cultures have a deep-rooted history of self-care. Specifically the women of that era, used to spend substantial time of the day just pampering and taking care of themselves.

Today, we are time-pressed and end up struggling each day with aroutine like tasks. We are harsh on ourselves, and the signs of deterioration and aging begin to show up so early in youngsters today. Young people are getting bald in their 30s'. Still, younger generations suffer from gray hair and use hair coloring as a solution to their problem. No one wants to think why they are facing gray hair at such a young age! Rather, baldness is becoming a matter of concern for a lot of women too. Such trend never existed so frequently in the past.

Our generation just knows the following about self-care:

- ❑ Getting hair dyed to keep the young look alive, even if the body is aging faster internally. A lot of youngsters today have artificially dyed hair that may give them a young look, but the truth still remains the same…they are aging faster!
- ❑ Visiting a salon or a spa and getting all latest chemical-laden treatments done all over the body. Many people are salon addicts considering it to be the only source of self-renewal,

without realizing the body is absorbing all the applied chemical products.

- ❑ Getting frequent medical tests done. Now, this is ironical as we work really hard to create our diseases each single day, and for health maintenance we aim to get our yearly medical tests done hoping that everything turns out to be well!
- ❑ Getting medical insurance is our ultimate health goal! In my experience, as a lot of people are just struggling to insure themselves for health without minutest of focus on what is making them diseased. It is like working rapidly towards getting sick and working double-hard to have a bed to lie on when you get sick. Though, medical insurance is a must in modern times, it must not be done with an ultimate thought of relief that the health is insured. Health can only be ensured by taking care of ourselves naturally.
- ❑ Planning going to the gym through the day is another self-care act that we adhere to. While some people abide by limited gym time which makes sense, some people keep gymming for hours as if it is not a body but a machine. Over exercising has a negative impact, one must always keep that in mind.

Though, ourtimes do not give us much liberty to take care of ourselves that elaborately, we can still spare some obvious time like bathing to devote to some self-care routine activities that will help us connect with ourselves better. Basic acts of self-care may begin with ensuring that we do not indulge in wrong foods often, we do not overeat, we keep a check on alcohol consumption, we take enough rest and sleep, we maintain hygiene of ourselves and our surroundings consume health supporting foods often and spare sometime to with ourselves. Elaborate acts of self-care may range from performing yoga and pranayama daily, having good 1-hour bath following the bathing rituals each day. Preparing fresh meals from whole and clean natural foods. It may sound tough considering our daily commitments. However, the rewards that the small acts of self-care carry are plenty. It makes us feel beautiful, bright, fosters self-confidence and self-esteem, makes us feel energetic and helps us maintain a positive outlook. It makes our life more productive, fulfilling and thankful.

Whether it is a basic or elaborate self-care practice, the idea is to choose a few acts and follow them religiously specifically during morning or evening hours. It also helps to keep a check on your mood and energy levels after beginning the acts of self-care. Slowly, more practices can be added when the results begin to show up in our improved health and overall well-being.

INCORPORATING SELF-CARE IN DAILY ROUTINE:

As we exist at the physical, mental and emotional plane, it makes sense to choose the self-care acts for both physical and emotional body. Incorporating a few of these self-care techniques for both body and mind will create a cumulative positive effect on your overall health & well-being.

SELF-CARE ACTS FOR MIND

- ❑ Sort things and activities and organize yourself. If you have plenty of tasks to perform in your daily life, begin with a to-do list and prioritize the to-do tasks.
- ❑ Manage your time well so that you can dedicate time to all areas of life evenly regularly, if not daily.
- ❑ Be thankful for whatever you have. It helps you look at positives of life than cribbing about negatives.
- ❑ Change your perspective to look at things, such as look at disease as a wake-up call to take care of yourself better and transform the anti-nature ways of life for healing & well-being.
- ❑ Spend time in nature, nothing soothes like nature.

- ❑ Spend time with children and elderly people. Real-life peaceful experiences come by spending time with the people of these generations.
- ❑ If traveling to work takes too much time, use that time to even and normalize your breathing than thinking and cribbing about the traffic on the road.
- ❑ Stop worrying about what you cannot change.
- ❑ Work on creating healthy habits one by one.
- ❑ Get out of your comfort zone and create new experiences for yourself.
- ❑ Take time off gadgets and spend alone time with yourself.
- ❑ Connect with yourself, listen to your body & mind and listen to your intuition. Follow the path that your intuition directs, you will be happy always!
- ❑ Be away from stress and anxiety.
- ❑ Invest time in self-affirmation and self-talks.

SLEF-CARE ACTS FOR BODY

- ❑ Move your body without tiring yourself.
- ❑ Perform breathing exercises that oxygenate you fully.
- ❑ For at least 15 minutes each day, analyze yourself head to toe. You will get clues where your problem lies, if any!
- ❑ Be your best expression. If you like to dance, sing, paint, write or have any other creative interest, don't let it die. Don't wait for occasion either, create your opportunities. If you have inhibitions join learning classes in your area of interest.
- ❑ Be in the sun and absorb the vibrancy of sunshine.
- ❑ Smell natural and fragrant.
- ❑ Laugh out hard, crack jokes and don't take life too seriously.
- ❑ Catch-up on power naps, they rejuvenate by putting body functions at some rest temporarily.

- ❑ Stretch in the morning and stretch at night. Stretch yourself, it relaxes you like nothing else.
- ❑ Give your body ten minutes of mindful attention. Use the body scan technique to check in with each part of your body.
- ❑ Eat less, and invest in best quality food products.
- ❑ Connect with your food, cook for yourself!
- ❑ Consume healthy and healing foods to get the vibrant energy right in your kitchen.
- ❑ Activate your toxin elimination channels. Let the physical and emotional toxins flowing through sweating, exercising, rubbing your skin and breathing hard.
- ❑ Love yourself and pamper yourself with natural self-care products. You will see yourself getting younger by the day!

SELF-CARR ACTS FOR THE SOUL

- ❑ Sense a healing touch. In ancient sciences touch is considered to be the food for the soul.
- ❑ Maintain silence for some time each day. It enlivens the energies back.
- ❑ Slow down, you are not going to achieve anything extra by rushing fast. Rather, you will end up tiring yourself in the rushing act.
- ❑ Listen to what your intuition is guiding you towards. Follow your heart.
- ❑ Look for beauty and purpose in everything that you do.
- ❑ Keep a close check on your emotions. If they seem to be slipping, take action immediately. Talk to someone, go out running or simply say 'NO'. Saying no relieves!
- ❑ Be empathetic towards others and help others in need.
- ❑ Make it a habit of using encouraging and positive words in all your conversations. Words are power and create a positive if frequently used in conversations.

- ❑ Talk positive about people, encourage them and lend a listening ear to others.
- ❑ Do not take the burden of everything, learn to delegate and find alogical solution for problems.
- ❑ Need help? Do not hesitate to ask. We are social animals and ego will lead us in self-distress.
- ❑ Go out traveling and connecting with nature and its mysteries.

ANCIENT ACTS OF SELF-CARE

Self-care practices in Ayurveda have a special relevance. The Yogis in ancient times used to follow series of self-care practices in the wee hours of morning religiously. The purpose was to keep the body pure and clean so that the body functions at its peak. This is important for them to reach a high meditative state as a diseased and disturbing body creates pain and discomfort and distracts one from achieving their goals.

Few acts of self-care from ancient practices include:

Watching Breath: Being aware of your breath helps you to breathe right. Most of us are chest breathers and not diaphragm breathers. Relaxation is induced and stress is alleviated when we learn to perform diaphragmatic breathing. Pranayama is a special Ayurveda's modality that teaches to be aware and take control of one's breath. It has the power of bringing one back in the moment.

Energizing Early Morning: One of the easiest and energizing techniques is generating body heat by rubbing palms first thing on waking up and applying it in acircular motion on the face, body joints and whole body. It keeps the joints flexible and acts as an anti-wrinkle treatment for the face. It also enhances the radiance of the face.

Drinking Warm Water Through the Day: Early morning the first thing must be sipping a glass of warm water with a squeeze of lemon juice. Adding aloe vera juice to it will make your bowels running faster. Lemon activates the peristalsis action in the digestive tract making the toxin cleansing action faster in the digestive tract. Peristalsis is a series of wave-like muscle contractions due to which our food moves to diffident compartments of processing. Lemon also alkalizes the body.

Dry Skin Brushing: Dry skin brushing is an excellent technique to activate the toxin removal process through the skin by shedding off the dead cells. It can be performed by rubbing a coarse towel or a coarse loofah on the dry skin surface each day before bathing. It is recommended to begin this activity bottom-up by starting brushing from feet in circular motion and slowly moving on the upper parts of the body.

Jal-Neti (Nasal Irrigation): Also known as 'Neti Kriya' in Ayurveda, it refers to the practice of rinsing the nasal passage with clean or saline water. It is a great Ayurvedic remedy to improve respiratory health and get rid of sinus and other related issues. It washes off all diet, bacteria, and mucus from the nose and helps drain the sinus cavities. Allergies, cold, flu, migraine, mental tension, headaches, cough, sinus and other bronchial issues are well taken care of it jal-neti is performed as a regular practice. It is also beneficial for cleansing the eyes internally. You may get a jal-neti pot from any Ayurvedic store and add lukewarm water and a pinch of salt to it. To use it, tilt the face to look upwards and sidewards and keep breathing through the mouth. Tilt the jal-neti pot to start flowing the water from one nostril until it begins to flow from the other nostril. All though you must maintain mouth breathing. Now, the process must be practiced on the other nostril. On completion, drain the left-over water from the nose. Preferably perform this activity under the guidance of an expert for the first time.

Warm Oil Massage: An Ayurvedic term and concept, it refers to applying anatural oil like sesame, coconut or almond oil on the whole body. It is helpful in nourishing and calming the body. It helps defy aging, improves circulation, calms the nervous system, flushes out toxins, helps you sleep better and maintains the radiance of the skin. It can be practiced before bath.

Walking Barefoot on Grass: Research studies suggest that our connect with Earth helps us draw electrons that drastically improve our health. Earth contains amagnetic field with energy and by walking barefoot on earth or grass we directly get in touch with that magnetic field. Our connect with earth's magnetic field impacts our own electric and magnetic field positively leading to exchange of positive energy of the earth and our negative energy. From physical health perspective, it helps relieve stress, stimulates the reflexology points, benefits eye health and can enhance the brain activity.

Foot Massage: Reflexology is the exclusive science of pressing the acupressure points in feet that can relieve a lot of health conditions. Pressing feet on right pressure points can open up the energy channels of the body thus recreating energy balance. It can relieve eye strain, make you feel fresh, enhance beauty and radiance from within and can even help in curing nerve related and other issues. Feet must be oiled and massaged in the morning and before sleep. An invigorating foot soak with 3 tablespoons of Epsom salt and a peppermint aromatherapy oil help you relax and rejuvenate instantly. After a foot soak, foot massage in circular motions can greatly enhance health & well-being.

CHAPTER 50 - PRACTICE SILENCE

'Silence takes you in the state of stillness where disturbing thoughts, anger, pain & all other negative emotions dissolve automatically, provided you connect with yourself in your silence. In these times of extreme internal & external noise, it is important to connect with ourselves intentionally & there is no bettei way to achieve this than going silent!'

A report released by World Health Organization in 2011, reports that noise pollution is a silent killer and silently escapes attention due to our focus on other types of pollution. It further states, 'there is overwhelming evidence that exposure to environmental noise has adverse effects on the health of the population. '

Our senses are always busy. Throughout the day intentionally or unintentionally we are listening to the radio, television, podcasts, meetings or talking and listening to someone on a cell phone. It is not just external noise that impacts us. Our internal noise in the form of thoughts, racing mind and overwhelming emotions contribute equally towards misbalancing our health proposition. Even during the times of isolation, we intentionally surround ourselves with gadgets or television. We intentionally prefer to ignore ourselves and our body signals, by continuing to surround ourselves to worldly and internal noises.

Let's delve into the world of Buddhism to understand the concept of silence. Lord Buddha believed in the Philosophy that when there is no solution to things or when things are not under your control, its best to keep silent. Silence resolves it all automatically. He believed that if your mind wanders, be silent. When there will be no questions arising in the mind, there will be no answers that you need to look for, the silence and presence in the moment will automatically arrive. In Buddhism silence is considered to be the source of peaceful life and cure for all diseases. Silence is an essential part of Buddhist culture. It is believed that only if you keep silence and calm, you are able to listen to your deep-lying conscious which is our supreme source of guidance in all facets of life including health & well-being.

Interestingly, the Buddhist monks in middle ages lived the vow of silence as their Buddhist practice. Two types of silence is practiced in Buddhist monasteries: Internal & External. Internal silence means keeping silent, meditating to quieten the mind and controlling the mind so that it remains in the present with no questions and no answers. It's the state of stillness. External silence is more of an effort to avoid doing anything that disturbs the inner silence. So, this may mean no outside noises, no radio, no television, newspapers or magazines in the monastery premises. Alternatively, the entire focus is on keeping the focus on natural sounds of the nature including thesound of animals, a whisper of birds, the rustling sound of wind blowing the trees, sound of the flowing river etc. All these natural sounds are considered to be very powerful and referred to as transcendental sounds.

Ok, so we are not trying to get saintly here, though that's the aim of silence, but here we will discuss how maintaining silence consciously each day can help you enhance your health & well-being drastically.

Silence is a great inherent tool that all of us possess and it helps us self-reflect, self-introspect and connect with ourselves. It helps us observe our sensations, listen to ourselves, observe our emotions, our wants, desires, answer ourselves whether or not we are happy and realize out true nature. By intent no human being wants to be sad, aggressive, angry or feel any other negative emotion. Silence helps us realize that by nature we are not meant to be under the grip of these negative emotions and being peaceful, calm, joyous is our actual nature. With a belief and strengthened connect with ourselves, we can better handle ourselves in times of stress. Rather with silence we learn to slowly transform ourselves towards positivity of life and negative influences begin to impact us much lesser.

So, let's intentionally begin practicing silence for some time each day…Does that still sound scary?

Now consider certain natural reactions of humans in different situations. Have you ever noticed that many people become silent when they are angry? Even if they shout a lot in the rage of anger, after a certain while they become silent. An infant cries for a while and restores silence automatically even if no one puts any effort to calm the child. If your spouse is silent you know something is wrong. If someone is sad they become silent. When someone looses their dear ones they become silent. As an act of respect two minutes of silence is observed. When respecting our nation we are supposed to go silent for a few seconds. Rather, if someone is ashamed then also they tend to go silent. When you know that your words will not be listened or respected you go silent. Also, if you are confronted with questions of non-interest, you tend to go silent.

Our body automatically practices silence in its own capacity. So, what is silence doing to us?

Initially, being silent stops the progression of all pain, anxiety, sadness, anger and agony and any other negative emotionto subside slowly on its own automatically. After a while we automatically restore our balance and regain our normal moods. If one practices silence regularly for a longer time few minutes each day, we are able to take a break from the outer noise. As a result, the inner noise automatically begins to subside. And quietness begins to become our nature. That quietness keeps us in the present moment, free of disturbing thoughts, worries, anxieties of past and future. We begin to focus on transcendental sounds of the nature like the chirping of birds. It creates an internal environment for us to listen to ourselves still deeper and connect with ourselves at the deepest level. At this state we realize who we are and what is our ask from life. To summarize, silence grounds individuals and provides serenity and mental clarity. With that clarity taking decisions become easier, following what your heart speaks becomes much easier and may lead to you being yourself and attaining a permanent state of happiness.

SILENCE FOR HEALTH & WELL-BEING

Relieves Stress: The British nurse of the 19th century, Florence Nightingale, once mentioned that unnecessary unnatural noise is the worst form of the absence of care for diseased and sickly. It causes sleep loss, interferes with the healing process of sick people and causes mental distress. From a scientific standpoint, research suggests that loud noise contributes towards the release of the stress hormone cortisol and create an atmosphere of restlessness, stress and tension. However, silence has an opposite effect.

Improves Blood Pressure & Respiration: Research suggests that maintaining 2 minutes of silence is more powerful than any other relaxation technique. That is the reason meditation scores high in stress relief as it fosters silence. Research further suggests that maintaining silence for some time each day showed positive changes in the blood pressure and blood circulation in the brain. It also caused a slow down of respiration leading to deeper and fuller breaths.

Activates Our Mental Energies: The Attention Restoration Theory (ART) focusses that nature can readjust our attention mode even after we work or study for long hours and tire our mind endlessly. It further suggests that natural restorative environments and healing sounds of natural habitats and nature itself has the power to activate back our mental energies. The never-ending attentional needs of the modern era often makes us over-think, plan, make quick decisions and be a problem solver. This exerts a lot of mental pressure leading to inability to focus, fatigued mind and sometimes wrong decisions. Research on a restricted group reported the development of new brain cells responsible for better learning capability and enhanced memory.

Creates Self-Connect: As connection requires listening to someone, similarly, self-connect requires listening to self. In all the worldly noises listening to ourselves takes a backseat leading our disconnect with ourselves. Rather, this is the trend we see in the modern world that is living amidst the internal and external noise and is totally disintegrated with itself. Silence is power even in company. Just try doing something in silence with someone you love or admire and you realize how just silence creates magic. Further, I see a lot of people running from themselves today and surrounding themselves with the noises of all kinds. Silence gives us the courage to face our true selves. It may be overwhelming initially, but if you can face yourself, you can stand for anything weight in the world.

Detoxifies Mind: As we exist at physical, emotional and mental planes, it is important to detoxify at all levels of existence. Due to the lack of awareness, often we end up investing all our energies in detoxifying just our physical plane. Silence helps us to detoxify at other two planes of existence. It helps us slow down and be aware of our thoughts. It works as a universal rule that when you stop putting new stuff inside your body, the body starts to break the resources within. It happens with the mind too. Once you stop feeling your mind with new thoughts, the older and deeper thoughts that are already set in begin to break and clear out.

Increases Awareness: For anything to change awareness is a must. Awareness leads to self-reflection and realization that further fosters change. Silence helps one self-reflect and become aware of the positive and negative traits of one's personality. It helps us enter our emotional zone and tune-in into our emotions. It also helps develop a broader perspective about everything as the focus shifts inward, and we realize that everything is a manifestation of what we think and perceive. It teaches discipline as you realize that a lazy person and the biggest achievers both have 24 hours in a day. It is what we think, plan and perceive that makes a difference. For the ones who get attached to everything easily, silence teaches to let go as it balances thoughts and gives direction to thinking. You can intentionally set apart sometime to be aware of bothering thoughts and letting them dissolve with each breath exhalation.

Directs Attention on Natural Healing Sounds: When observing silence, nature's healing sounds make more sense. Any novice practicing silence may be overwhelmed initially with supreme quietness, but ask a Buddhist monk and they know there is a realm of natural transcendental sounds in the air if you focus on it. Specifically, in the quiet places, mountains, rivers, oceans, the silence is backed by healing sounds of nature.

Fosters Positive Mental Traits: Some important mental and emotional traits develop all by themselves in a state of supreme silence. Faith, perseverance, self-trust, and endurance are a few traits that succeed silence. Try using a silent vow your most powerful tool the next time, when someone doubts you! Silence fosters simplicity when you realize how much peace, happiness, and joy it holds. Ask people who are surrounded by noise each day, whether or not they feel fresh and joyous, and there is great possibility that they do not! A beautiful perspective towards life and simplicity can be attained through the practice of silence regularly.

CHAPTER 51 - MEDITATION

Vipassana is a meditation technique that originated in India during Lord Buddha's era. It is one of the most famous meditation techniques being practiced throughout the world. The essence of Vipassana meditation is to maintain equanimous, that is accepting whatever comes, be it good or bad. It means seeing things in the true light, the way they are, without any interpretations. It involves observing oneself and our interconnect between our body and mind. The technique involves directing attention to the physical sensations and the patterns of changing mind with changing body sensations. It teaches how to be detached to the experiences of life. It is believed that Vipassana dissolves mental impurity and fosters the feelings of love and compassion. It focusses on the fact that neither must one be too attached to the positives happening life nor get distressed by the negativities of life. However, the technique must be learned at Vipassana meditation centers.

However, Vipassana is not the only way to meditation. You can practice meditation anytime each day in your area of comfort. The process may go like this:

1. Decide on a specific time each day to practice silence.
2. Be away from all disturbances during that time including cell phones, radio, computer, laptop etc.
3. To keep your focus on, light a candle and keep your vision set on the flame until the time you practice silence.
4. Focus on your breath and just observe any sensations being felt. Do not react to any thought, just let it come and go.
5. Listen to your silence and set your focus on any natural sounds that you hear. Try to be in the moment.
6. When you end the silence, keep a check on your words and try to keep them positive and motivating.

CHAPTER 52 - STRENGTHEN YOUR BELIEF IN SELF-HEALING

'The little secret about self-healing is that our body knows how to heal, provided we create an environment that is required to heal.'

So, you have just been detected with cancer or diabetes or arthritis or any other lifestyle disorder. Does it seem like an end of the world? Stop that thought then and there, and consider it as an opportunity to live back your life, this time by adopting the right ways of living and eating. Believe me, you will enjoy your new life much more than the previous one!

Self-healing is the natural ability of our body. That's how we heal our burns, cuts and even broken bones. No one joins the broken bone, it joins itself. No one heals a wound, it gets better itself. Similarly, no one can heal your disease but you. So, your next question will be, if self-healing is our natural nature then why are we continuously getting sicker? The logical answer to this is because we are creating barriers for our self-healing. We are also not understanding our diseases well and not considering the roots of their origin. We often get stuck with the symptoms of a disease and do not look any further.

If you want to go about strengthening your belief logically, just think when the western medicine was not born, people still used to heal themselves. Logically, this means that somewhere we have been empowered by the nature to be able to heal ourselves, and the only mandate here is to provide yourself with the right environment that supports healing which happens through right ways of eating, living, and thinking.

Taking about the brilliant design of our body, our pharmacy has been fitted inside our system as our immune system. The intelligence of the highest order has been blessed to us that not even the most advanced supercomputer can beat. Your eyes adjust to the short-sightedness and long-sightedness automatically, it does. not need two different lenses to perform this action. Our body possesses the intuitive power to sense and feel what we cannot see or interpret physically. We automatically adjust to different temperatures unlike an air conditioning system that must be operated all the time to adjust the temperature. Our ability to reproduce and give birth at the apt time without fitting in any timers is the most miraculous system of our body, our structural composition, the bones, provides perfect frame to keep us erect yet so flexible, We do not need a box to store our lifetime precious possessions, our memory, and experiences, our brain stores it all in such a compact space. It is about realizing the intelligence of our design, respecting it and believing in its power. No one can interfere with the healing power of our body, even cancer is a healing act from our body's perspective to prolong our life!

What differentiates healthy people from unhealthy ones is not just a diet plan or a strenuous exercising routine. Healthy people realize and believe in their power to self-heal, they provide the ideal functional environment to the body by not poisoning themselves slowly with drugs, processed and wrong foods, cosmetics, chemicals, artificial sweeteners, personal care products, household cleaning products, meat toxicity. As a result, their immune or defense system is always active, they are clean, natural and free-flowing from within. As a result their innate healing powers are always alive and keep healing them naturally!

Now, how does this idea sound to you, 'Symptoms are body's efforts to heal itself'. This may mean your allergies are good because in its absence the body would give up its optimal functioning capability. Or a high blood pressure is an indication that the blood is thick, dehydrated, unclean and lacks good fats that keep its flow smoothly. Let's explore few symptoms from their roots angle.

FUNCTIONAL EXAMPLES OF BODY'S SELF-HEALING CAPABILITY

Bronchial Issues: Consider how dehydration could be at the root of your bronchial issues. If you are dehydrated or do not consume enough water, consider the intelligence of your body here. It tries to save water internally as it needs it for internal functioning. However, a lot of water in our body gets lost due to our breathing act. Water vapors get released with each breath that we exhale. Now, since you are dehydrated, the body must adopt mechanisms to conserve internal water by all means. So, it constricts the bronchial tubes by developing histamines so that you exhale less water. Histamines are produced as an immune response and cause inflammation. Now, due to inflammation your breathing gets constricted. This state in modern science is called 'asthma'. Though, it is not as easy as it sounds, there are various other factors, situations, the state of your health and other aspects involved before a disease matures. And once a disease matures, it has to be handled from all angles, be it medication of dietary or lifestyle changes. However, the point here is that as simple cause as dehydration may become the root of your bronchial disease, who could think! However, bronchial issues like asthma are a self-healing act by the body to do its best to keep body functioning when the internal resources are insufficient or toxic. It is the root-oriented perception of looking at your bronchial disease. Now, consider, what does your body need here, medication or water to get alleviated? Remedy as simple as hydrating yourself will begin to show some signs of relief here, though medication may be required along with your other efforts as the issues have already birthed and may have caused some other issue. But as the body will stop conserving water and will ease the pressure on bronchial tubes, the bronchial symptoms may begin to ease. Self-healing here will be initiated automatically by providing the root of the problem the ideal environment that it needs.

Blood pressure: As another example consider the case of high blood pressure. Blood is a liquid element within our body and is very much dependent on water for its formation. In the case of dehydration or due to too much toxic stuff mixed in the blood, the blood tends to become thick. The thickness of the blood obviously hampers its smooth flow through the small capillaries. Now like a pumping action where more pressure is required for more pumping, our heart being the pump to supply and push blood, it has to work harder to push the thick blood to circulate well through the body. And thus, a blood pressure is born. Now blood pressure may look like a disease in modern medicine, but it is so in order to make sure good circulation is taking place. The heart has to pump harder, thereby raising the blood pressure. This is body's way of making sure that thick blood reaches all the cells throughout the body. Now, looked from self-healing perspective, high blood pressure is your body's way of performing a self-healing act so that the blood reaches all parts of the body despite of being thick. Now, consider what does your body need here, medication or freely flowing blood to ease your blood pressure symptom? Obviously more water, live nutrients through plant foods and right nourishment in the form of right fatty acids (more omega-3s in particular), so that the heart does not work as hard to pump thick toxic blood throughout a lifetime. It also betters circulation as the free flowing blood reaches all nook and corners of your body.

TIPS TO STRENGTHEN SELF-HEALING BELIEFS

'Quite logically, if you continue to follow disease creating lifestyles, you will get diseased only...Health & healing cannot emerge from a disease causing environment! There is no short cut to health & well-being. The only right way to health is to look at it from the right perspective & focus on self-change!'

The first most important step towards your health and healing begins with strengthening self-belief about self-healing. Whether it is cancer, diabetes, heart disease or any other disease, everything heals. It is important to change our perspective about our diseases.

Believe it or not, our body is performing a healing act all the time. That is its primary function, or else our life would have been at threat! Disease is nothing but an effort from our body's side to get rid of the high toxicity that it carries and recreate the balance.

Tips to strengthen belief in self-healing:

- ❑ Realize that self-healing was always a part of human life even when the medical systems were not there.
- ❑ Look at a disease as an opportunity to connect with yourself and realize the actual requirements of your body.
- ❑ Listen to what your ancestors talk about their own times. Most of the health secrets are hidden in that conversation.
- ❑ Believe that your choices and decision are all yours and build you physically, emotionally and mentally.
- ❑ Accept the change that is bound to give you health, happiness, and wellness.
- ❑ Ask yourself thought-provoking questions such as, What made me sick? What can I do to make myself well? Is medication the only solution for me? Is there any safer, natural alternative that I could explore?
- ❑ Seek convenience only till it does not impact your health adversely. If convenience is what nature would have intended for us, early man would have been born with a car, and air conditioner, a mobile phone and a laptop!
- ❑ Listen to your body signals. If you think positive they do not survive for long. If you think negative, you give them a vent to survive and grow within you.
- ❑ Change your mindset towards your diseases. Consider them as a wake-up call to get back to the right ways of eating and living.
- ❑ The human body is highly intelligent. It knows what time it is tired, it knows what time it needs its fuel, it knows when is the time to expel. Since it operates on its own where you do not have control, help it heal by providing it what it requires.

- ❑ Healing is automatic, you do not have to be after your wound to heal. It heals itself automatically.
- ❑ Be stress-free, when you do not have control on the happenings of the body and nature, there is no point stressing. Rather, stressing creates a vicious circle by worsening your illnesses which creates further stress, and it becomes a vicious circle. Rather being light-hearted will fast-forward your healing, research suggests.

CHAPTER 53 - FAQS

Q: I am a foodie and don't want to give up my favorite foods. But I also want my health to improve. What should I do?

A: 'You shall reap what you sow!' If you want to stick to your current ways of eating & living and supposedly they are wrong ways, then toxin accumulation is going to happen and your body is going to accumulate toxins. That toxin is bound to spread if not eliminated and is bound to create diseases. If you begin to transform yourself through right ways of living and eating, the toxicity is bound to break, reduce and get eliminated making you get and feel better.

So, to answer this question, it is about getting on to the right ways as much as possible. It can be planned in a way that maximum time you live upon healthy ways of diet and lifestyle and maintain a balance between fun and health. The problem in today's times is that we majorly are eating ready-made stuff that burdens the body. Further, we are hooked to gadgets throughout the day, live indoor lives, have a sedentary life, are stressed and have become aggressive in our thinking. The net effect is a compromised state of health.

Q: I sometimes feel that I get sicker when I begin to change my diet for better? Why is that so?

A: The havoc that you have created for your body over the years will not leave you without troubling you! This is nature's way of healing. Sickness may precede healing because the toxicity that you have accumulated over the years is deposited in all nook and corners of your body. When you begin the toxin removal process through your changed dietary and lifestyle efforts, the accumulated toxin begins to break and mixes in your blood for removal through elimination channels such as bowels, skin, lungs and kidneys. So, initially this broken toxin in abundance from everywhere gets mixed with your blood and overwhelms your body with toxicity. It is this overwhelming response that makes you feel sick temporarily until the toxin gets eliminated. Once it is done, you emerge as cleaner, healthier and radiant you with better functioning body processes that show up everywhere in your physical, mental and emotional health. Consider this like cleaning a house that seems clean otherwise, but if you begin deep cleaning a lot of accumulated dust is gathered from everywhere from all nook and corners of the house. The symptoms of elimination that you may experience include nausea, diarrhea, enhanced aches and pains, cold, cough, flatulence and ageneral feeling of sickness. But these temporary symptoms are for good!

Q: Can I detox whenever I want?

A: Detox is an art! So, when you plan to detox, your body must already be strong enough internally to be able to deal with the cleansing process. This means that any burden on liver must be removed, kidneys must be well-flushed, lungs must ideally be strengthened. This can be achieved by stopping the consumption of foods that weaken liver such as highly processed foods, commercially sweet foods, and alcohol. Kidneys can be kept in best shape by hydrating yourself properly and lungs can be strengthened by focusing on deep breathing techniques. So, before going on a detox, it is suggested to begin the first level cleaning by altering diet towards whole and natural foods. You must begin eliminating toxic foods and that's how you help your internal organs gain strength. After a certain period of being on a clean diet, you must then incorporate specific foods that are meant to cleanse the body. The detox must end subtly before you move on to your regular ways of living and eating. The end must not be abrupt so that your body is not burdened after a detox.

Q: Is alternate holistic treatment a generalized treatment?

A: Yes and No. Yes because we as human beings belong to the same universe. And so the roots of all our maladies broadly are the same; wrong diets, wrong lifestyles, no exercise, sedentary life, indoor environment etc. And so the route to healing for all is the same, which is going back to the roots.

No, because each individual's condition and the constitution is different. And so the health solutions of holistic healing are unique and specific to each person, even though they may belong to the set of generalized healing therapies. For example, a Diabetic patient is not allowed to consume foods that give sudden rise to blood-sugar levels, but the same foods may prove to be health building for someone else.

Q: What is the difference between a holistic whole and natural foods nutritionist and a clinical nutritionist?

A: Holistic Whole and Natural Foods Nutritionist: A holistic whole and natural foods nutritionist understands the vital life-force of foods. She understands what foods to consume or eliminate when you feel low in moods, or when you suffer from cancer or any other physical or emotional state to promote internal healing. She has been trained to understand that foods not only contain nutrients and enzymes but also an unseen spark called vital life-force that makes them grow and absorb the energy of the universe. She has studied the functioning of the human body in relation to nature and its connect with the nature and can guide an individual towards the path of reversing the condition that they have created over the years.

Further, she believes that foods coming from the nature are made complete by the nature in nutrition and nutritional combinations, and we need not process or create man-made products with added nutrients to fulfill our fuel requirements. For example, she considers green leafy vegetables as a source of vibrant energy apart from the goodness of their inherent nutrients. Alternatively, she understands that fried foods may make you feel full and impart lethargy. Most importantly, she does not believe in exchanging nutritional components for energy requirements, such as she does not believe that protein diet is good enough to replace body's energy requirements, as, the primary energy fuel for the body is carbohydrates. She believes that each kind of nutrition and specific energy existing in natural foods is equally important and must not be exchanged to meet the body needs that some other nutritional element must provide, otherwise imbalances are bound to occur. A holistic nutritionist plans you diet based around clean, fresh, whole, natural and live plant foods. She further understands that human health is holistic and cannot sustain just upon best diet. It must be balanced with various other important aspects of life including rest, exercise, relationships, social connect, and most importantly a sense of purpose in life and counsels and guides the client on all these important aspects of life.

Clinical Nutritionist: A clinical nutritionist works on the modern concept of nutrition that does not consider food energy as an important component of natural foods. She works on a standard dietary system that is research based and understands foods in terms of their calorific values. The purpose of clinical nutritionist primarily is to balance your calorie intake, irrespective of what foods the calories are derived from. She believes that an individual must consume a defined standard set of calories as per their height and weight, irrespective of their body type or health condition. She just caters to your diet plan and ensures that you consume sufficient calories to meet your specific health goals. The diet plan from a clinical nutritionist may contain all combinations of foods such as fruits, vegetables, cereals, healthy commercial products, dairy or chemical-laden foods. This is because the entire focus is calorie adjustment and types of foods being chosen for calorie adjustment are secondary. She looks at nutritional elements individually and not in combined form, and so, it is ok of your energy requirements are being met by a protein diet versus a balance of carbohydrate and protein diet. The food theory used by clinical nutritionist does provide you with a deeper understating of foods, yet the way this theory complicates food consumption for many people due to its associated numeric value, may make people count numbers all the time! Further, it simply generalizes diets, which is one of the major causes of diet failure among many people. Thought logically, calorie counting is a complicated system that our body does not relate to. What it understands is its requirements of specific nutritional and energy elements that must be fulfilled through right foods and help the body grow, perform internal functions, keep it clean and heal itself.

A classic example of the difference between the approach of two nutritionists is, aclinical nutritionist may recommend a slice or multi-grain bread or a bowl of sprouts of similar calorific value for your breakfast. However, a holistic nutritionist will avoid recommending bread because the vital life-force quotient of bread is nil even if it provides the same amount of calories as sprouts. She believes that bread is a dead food while sprouts is a living food where all its nutrients are tightly coupled naturally and it provides nourishment as well as a subtle flow of positive energy that supports the biological functioning of body and mind. However, a holistic nutritionist's viewpoint on multi-grain bread is negative as it is a dampening food that creates a damp environment inside our digestive tract to support bacteria and virus activities leading to ill health. Additionally, she believes that additives in bread is an overhead that our body must deal with!

Q: I am used to a certain diet and lifestyle since ages and I feel ok. Why Should I change it?

A: To answer that question simply, the entire world is living by their own ways of diet and lifestyle since ages, and we see the entire world is falling sicker by the day. Our physical, emotional and mental health is deteriorating overtime. The energy levels and strength that our ancestors had, we are not even half-way near to that health state. Our children are beginning to get diseased at tender ages. Emotional issues today grip the children more than any adults. Emotional issues and mental health conditions are on the rise.

So, it may seem useless to change your regular diet and lifestyle patterns initially, but if you look at the health trends, I am sure you would not want to fall prey of any diseases later in life. Prevention is the keyword to keep your disease-free in modern times, and it can only be achieved by adopting the right diet and lifestyle and positive mental make-ups. The way we choose to live our life, and our foods have a direct impact on how healthy we are and we feel, how quickly we age and what we achieve in life. Everything is influenced by a healing diet and natural lifestyle, including our health, wellness, emotions, aspirations, capabilities, thought-process and ability to achieve! So, if you seek for internal health, well-being and internal healing in its true sense, there is no other route but to transform yourself!

Q: My goal is weight loss. What is the right approach?

A: Now, as explained earlier our body works in a holistic fashion and it cannot interpret the term 'Only Weight-Loss'. There is nothing like exclusive weight loss from your body's perspective. And so you see that many-a-times when people go on a weight loss plan, they lose their charm and glow. For any weight-loss efforts that you go ahead with, there are some other related bodily functions happening inside your body. Though your weight-loss efforts may show up as weight-loss at the physical level, but internally a lot of other parameters get adjusted. If you have adopted a healthy way of weight loss, not just internal fat melts but your generic health condition may also improve. Your body may get cleansed of toxins, your digestive health may improve, your cholesterol levels may come down, your moods may begin to improve, your immunity may get better etc. However, if you opt for quick or wrong ways of losing weight such as being on a high protein diet for long and depriving your body of foods by fasting frequently, you may still achieve your goal of losing weight, but may end up with other deficiencies.

Healthy ways of losing weight and their impact:

- ❑ Following aholistic approach to weight loss by correcting dietary and lifestyle areas.
- ❑ A good diet containing a lot of fruits, vegetables, and fermented foods.
- ❑ Elimination of foods that weaken our body functioning.
- ❑ Leads to nutritionally balanced body state.
- ❑ Regular exercise that does not tire you preferably done in the morning versus evening hours.
- ❑ Not stressing much.
- ❑ Leads to Improved digestive health.
- ❑ Leads to healthy weight loss with areduction in weight numbers and inch loss.
- ❑ Leads to the improved, glowing and radiant skin, lustrous hair and shiny nails.
- ❑ Leads to a disease-free body and reversing health conditions.
- ❑ Leads to happy, healthy and joyous mind

Unhealthy ways of losing weight and their impact:

- ❑ Following quick-fix, one-sided approach to weight loss that may include artificial, surgical and machine based weight-loss mechanisms.
- ❑ Fasting, following quick-fix fad-diets.
- ❑ Consuming a lot of processed foods as a part of dietplan leading to nutritionally deficient body and compromises the digestive health.
- ❑ Irregular or highly aggressive exercise routine at the wrong hours of the day may tire you more than helping you lose weight.
- ❑ Too much stress making you prone to emotional eating and continuous weight gain despite of all your efforts.
- ❑ Leads to unhealthy weight loss dull skin and lifeless skin, thinning hair and non-lustrous nails.

- ❑ May not guarantee a disease-free body.
- ❑ May lead to irritability and severe mood swings.

Q: If 5 days a week I follow a healthy diet and 2 days I enjoy all kinds of foods, is my lifestyle ok from health maintenance perspective?

A: To answer this simply, will it be ok if you fuel your car with the best quality petrol 5 days a week and rest 2 days you fuel your car with water? As we have learned in the above chapters that human body works holistically. Whatever you consume must be processed by your body equally. So, if 5 days a week you follow a healthy diet and 2 days you enjoy all kinds of foods, it does not give any leverage to your body to discount the wrong foods consumed over the 2 days. Your body still will have to process those foods once they enter your body, it will still have to deal with the toxins that go in, it will still have the same negative impact of wrong foods, as consumed on any other days!

However, we live in a quick and convenience-loving world, and so it may not always be possible to eat healthily. The bottom line here is to try to strive as much dietary and lifestyle balance as we can and provide our body the ideal environment where it is able to perform its operations optimally without breaking down. And this happens with efforts in all directions and not just by consuming healthy 5 days a week.

Q: Can I become highly alkaline and are there any negative implications to that?

A: This is a very hypothetical situation and it's the rarest of the rare case to get too alkaline. However, if at all you get alkaline, there will be as many implications as in the case of an acidic state. This is because we thrive on balance and our body's ideal functional state is 'slightly' alkaline and not 'highly' alkaline. If the balance is disturbed on either side, we are sure to bear the consequences. High alkaline state leads you to weakened digestive power, compromised metabolism of nutrients, blood lacking oxygen and compromised hydration.

Our diets and lifestyles are all highly acidic today and there is a bleak chance of getting highly alkaline because:

- ❑ Modern diet and lifestyle are highly toxic and acidic.
- ❑ Lifestyle disorders known to humans today have one common foundational factor – Acidic body state.
- ❑ Stress is the predominant factor in modern lifestyles and stress always leads to acidic body state.

Q: Is there any relation between modern lifestyle disorders and acid-alkaline imbalance?

A: There is a strong link between acid-alkaline (pH) imbalance & lifestyle disorders. Before any disease becomes mature and surfaces in its worst form, there is something that begins to happen at the foundational level. This foundational level of a disease is the changing body chemistry of the body where we start to become acidic internally and our alkaline balance begins to get disturbed. Too much acid inside the body begins to destroy the body cells and making them weak in their functioning. The weakened functioning of body cells leads to weakened immune system where we get prone to getting sick frequently and our body begins to age rapidly. This rapid aging shows up physically in the form of aging skin, thinning hair, metabolic problems leading to weight gain, allergic reactions, body's inability to absorb nutrients, accumulation of body toxins, blocked arteries, cholesterol issues and vitamin and mineral deficiencies. Sadly, this is the health state of all of us today. And believe it or not our high acidic body state makes us highly prone to uninvited lifestyle disorders!

Further, the research has proven that a disease, be it a cold or cancer, cannot survive in an alkaline body state. It is only in the acidic and non-oxygenated state that bacteria, viruses, mold, fungus, mold, and cancer cells thrive. We create the acidic state within our body due to acid-forming modern diets, lack of self-care cleansing techniques, breathing in a polluted and indoor environment, living a sedentary life and not stimulating our body to release toxins, lack of exercise, compromised lung capacity, using too much chemical-laden products, wearing synthetic clothes that do not let our skin breathe, emotional and mental stress, accumulating toxins from various sources, keeping ourselves dehydrated and by consuming high protein diet. Lifestyle disorders including osteoporosis, heart diseases, arthritis, and cancer are an outcome of acidic body state breeding within us for years.

Q: How can I ensure that how I maintain right acid-alkaline balance?

A: Maintaining a healthy acid-alkaline balance requires you to work in various areas of your life. A good beginning may be to focus on:

- ❑ An alkaline rich diet consisting of lotsof colorful fruits and vegetables consumed each day.
- ❑ Eliminating foods that may be making your internal environment acidic such as processed foods, junk foods, artificially colored foods and chemically altered foods to suit your taste buds.
- ❑ Strengthening body's elimination channels including lungs, bowels, lymphatic system, liver skin, and kidneys through right dietary and lifestyle practices.
- ❑ Improving lung function by practicing deep breathing exercises.
- ❑ Cleansing the skin regularly and enhancing perspiration to eliminate toxic acid in sweat form.

Q: How do I decide when do I need a symptomatic treatment and when I can just go ahead with holistic healing practices?

A: Firstly, holistic healing practices are nothing but your ways of living and eating right to be incorporated into your routine. It is more of a lifestyle versus quick-fix for a disease. Having said that, holistic practices or routines are irrespective and independent of any treatments that you may be seeking. Rather the purpose of both varies entirely. Look at it in this sense. Due to wrong dietary and lifestyle habits when you started accumulating a lot of toxins inside your body, it converted into a disease years later. Now when you got diagnosed with a disease you had no choice but to seek medical help as the damage is already done within. So, medical intervention is not a choice but a necessity here. However, if you continue to live by your current dietary and lifestyle principles that caused you the disease, there is a high probability that you will never be healed completely, though the progression of your disease will be arrested to some extent due to medical treatments. This is because what caused you a disease is very much a part of your living style even after treatments. Here, if you manage to practice holistic modalities along with treatments, the chances of your recovery at body and mind level are very bright, while you save cost of treatments, you skip the pains and perils of your disease and treatment side-effects and most importantly you gain back your happy, healthy and joyous self by changing your sick body chemistry to a healthier one. This is in the case of chronic diseases. However, for the ones who are enroute to disease progression, body weaknesses and imbalances that show up in routine nagging body issues, if you adopt right ways of living and eating and help your body cleanse itself routinely, you may avert any big surprises that may be seeding within you slowly and steadily.

Q: Why is it important to focus on the individual who has a disease versus focusing on a disease?

A: Focus on a disease takes the path of localized treatment of a disease only while leaving the sufferer's feelings, thoughts and emotions behind. However, focus on an individual takes the path of holistic healing where not just the disease, but its root cause, the person who has the disease, person's thoughts, emotions and feelings all are taken into consideration. Research suggests that a disease-centric mindset cures a disease but fails to improve the quality of life if an individual. It is important to understand that human body is not mechanical to be only fixed through a series of diagnosis and treatments. Though the treatments do make a person better 'mechanically' and 'functionally' , it does not really help a person to improve upon their self-worth and be aware of the importance of right ways of living so that the problem does not resurface. After the treatment the patients succumb to their old ways of living and eating, this creating a probability for the problem to resurface.

Q: What is gluten intolerance?

A: Gluten intolerance is a relatively modern term to define sensitivity towards specific foods. Gluten is a kind of protein that exists in high concentrations hybrid and genetically modified varieties of wheat, rye, barley and other grains. It is a known fact that gluten can irritate the digestive tract of sensitive individuals. The prominent signs of gluten intolerance show up as bloating, dizziness, headaches, pain in the digestive tract and irritable and low moods, specifically after consuming wheat or other gluten grains.

An alternate school of thought does not consider only gluten-containing foods as the primary cause of gluten intolerance. It focusses that gluten intolerance is a consequence of poor and underlying digestive issues. It believes that we can become sensitive to certain foods not because the foods are the culprits, but because our digestion is weak enough to handle specific foods. Though, a caveat here is that the genetically modified foods or the use of pesticides artificial fertilizers is altering the chemical bond of our natural foods, and the altered chemical chemistry does not match with our body chemistry. The result shows up as gluten intolerance!

The thought is further verified by the fact that it is the only handful of people that are diagnosed with gluten intolerance, whereas the entire world is consuming the same foods. Having said that, there have been cases where people have been able to heal their digestive tract and the underlying digestive problems by adopting the techniques to healing gut based upon Ayurveda and Traditional Chinese Medicine techniques. Such people have reported to be able to digest gluten-containing foods without any gluten intolerance signs after healing their gut. Though, the exceptions here has been the Celiac disease as it is one of the most dangerous form of gluten intolerance case where gluten irritate the digestive tract to dangerous levels. However, generically, if one focusses on improving their digestive health, consume organic foods in moderation and stay away from the processed food world, there is a high probability that one can improve their digestive health drastically and thus their food sensitivities.

Q: What are digestive enzymes and probiotics and why are they important for digestion?

A: There are a lot of biochemical forces behind a smooth digestion. The two important forces include: 'Digestive enzymes' and 'Gut bacteria'. Digestive enzymes and gut bacteria are live biochemical elements that facilitate digestion process. In the absence of digestive enzymes and gut bacteria, our foods do not digest well, leading to impartial digestion. The leftover food in the digestive tract proliferates and gives rise to dampness and further creates a bed for bad bacteria to thrive upon. We experience the result of this in the form of digestive issues ranging from flatulence, gastric issues, acidity issues etc. Our modern cooking techniques destroy the digestive enzymes and modern processed foods destroy the gut bacteria. Sources of digestive enzymes include fresh, raw vegetables and fruits. Sources of gut bacteria include fermented foods such as probiotics.

Q: What are dead foods and living foods?

A: Dead foods refer to foods that are devoid of vital life force, though they may have some nutritional elements. Examples of dead foods include a host of processed and refined foods such as fortified bread or commercial cereals that do have the nutritional elements but have their power to regrow. Dead foods do provide us nutrition but do not lend us the live energy as the foods we consume are dead and devoid of live energy. Dead foods stress our internal organs including liver, gallbladder, and pancreas by making them produce additional digestive enzymes, which should ideally be consumed from foods itself. At the digestion level, the dead foods create a havoc leading to poor digestive function and ultimately poor nutrient absorption. The consequences of dead foods thus show up as dullness, broken skin, frequently ill health, dull hair, broken nails, weak immunity, frequent cold and cough, allergies, mood swings, fatigue, headache, constipation, unknown sadness and anxiety issues. Probably this is the reason that people are more diseased today despite of consuming best foods and following rigorous diet plans.

Living foods are recognized as foods that have the ability to grow such as plant foods, sprouts, seeds etc. Such foods are complete in balanced nutrition as our body needs and contain the vital life-force that makes them grow and absorb the vital energy of the universe. Apart from nutrition, living foods impart bright, radiant and live energy to our body cells which shows up in the form of radiant health, strong immune system, shiny skin, hair and nails, light moods, joy, happiness and disease free body state. Living foods are a complete package that comes with freshness, nutritional elements and digestive enzymes. They aid the digestive process in breaking and absorbing nutrients.

However, modern science does not validate these terms as it does not believe in the concept of life force. Modern science just relates to the term 'Nutritional Foods' irrespective of its source from either dead foods or living foods. Whereas ancient holistic sciences consider the concept of 'Dead foods' and 'Living foods' as the most important theory behind the liveliness of an individual at all levels of existence.

TRANSFORMATIONS – PEOPLE SPEAK THEIR STORIES!

LAVANYA IYENGAR

'Deepti empowered me to take right dietary and lifestyle decisions. Apart from consultation, she imparted valuable knowledge that will help me avoid dietary & lifestyle disasters for life. I contacted Deepti in a hope to get clean & clear skin, as I suffered from severe acne problem. I saw a direct connect behind my issues and my diet and lifestyle disasters after following her recommendations. On correcting my dietary & lifestyle patterns, based on Deepti's recommendations, my issues started to revert!' – Lavanya Iyengar, Bangalore

GARIMA RASTOGI

'I am really blessed that I met Deepti as my eczema was getting bad to worse. My healing and transformation of a decade old skin allergy has been phenomenal after following Deepti's diet and lifestyle recommendation. Within 2 months of consultation, my decade old problem, which no medication could cure, got 80% better without any medication. The solutions given by her helped me adopt a better, healthier lifestyle!!! It's not just about recipes, ingredients, way of cooking but about a total holistic experience of health and well-being! Today I enjoy a much more smooth, soft and supple skin. And I am too happy as my skin now has an even tone, glows, and is more radiant. I must acknowledge that my problem was gone in a couple of months but the lifestyle change which happened then will remain forever…Thank you so much Deepti, it wouldn't have been possible without you. ' – Garima Rastogi, NCR

ANURAG SEHGAL

"Deepti guided me through a path of holistic diet that reversed my sinus problem that existed since childhood. In last 3years, I have transformed from a sickly man to a healthy individual. I reversed my acute sinus problem, lost 12 kgs and feel at the peak of my health. Thanks Deepti for making me experience health and wellness which I never experienced ever before!" – Anurag Sehgal, NCR

GINNY MAHANT

'I started a Macrobiotic diet with Deepti a few months back. Her dietary and lifestyle offer a bundle of benefits. I have seen remarkable changes after consultation with Deepti! Within the first month of starting diet, I felt reduced fatigue, increased stamina and more energetic feeling throughout the day, my PMS has reduced; facial swelling & my body bloating was gone and I experience better immunity with lesser incidences of falling sick. Love the diet! Today, this healing approach of hers makes perfect sense to me. Changes in my body and mind make me realize how all principles about health and food just fall in place when I keep the guidelines in mind. Thanks a ton Deepti for showing me a better way to good health. This changes the way I look at food & health. ' – Ginny Mahant, Bangalore

SUNALINI BHATIA

'After my phenomenal transformation, I truly begin to believe that the doctors in future will no longer treat the human frame with drugs, rather will cure and help prevent diseases with nutrition and correct lifestyles. This wellness diet and lifestyle is a natural state of my body and directly corrects the root of the problems…By cleansing your body on a regular basis and eliminating toxins from your environment and your body, I realize that body does heal itself, and it is remarkable to see that happening! You can easily prevent diseases and become stronger and more resilient than you ever thought of, by adopting the dietary and lifestyle changes!" – Sunaini Bhatia, NCR

CAPTAIN PRAVIR SAHAY

'Deepti is my food, diet & lifestyle doctor, That's how I address her! I was totally unclear about the basics of diet, health, and wellness until I followed Deepti's recommendations. Now, I feel much lighter, leathery look on my skin is all gone, I feel very light which I haven't experienced in years, I weigh less now for the first time in my life, and most importantly at my age, I still feel active and full of energy! By the way, I am year young captain! Deepti's recommendations also made me believe that health and diet is an art and must not be approached based upon one single factor, as we mostly do…Read something in a magazine and newspapers and start following any health remedy blindly…I know my body is responding excellently to Deepti's diet and other recommendations internally, and the results are already visible! Deepti's belief in ancient ways of healing has made me believe in ancient food wisdom and importance of right lifestyle!!" – Captain Pravir Sahay, NCR

SANDY CHUGH

'I was bloated, overweight, suffered from hypothyroidism, had very less stamina, felt fatigued and used to fall ill every season or in apolluted environment. Today, I look half of what I used to look like, I feel better double times of what I used to feel, I have lost 8 kgs within 2 months of being on this holistic diet and lifestyle. Most importantly, I feel positive and clear-headed which is just unbelievable. But yes, right diet and lifestyle can alter your thinking and phycology for a happier, healthier and peaceful you! I have personally experienced this journey of transformation!!' – Sandy Chugh, Canada

SHAGUN KHARE

'I consulted Deepti for general well-being and weight loss. She has given me a thorough consultation and has set realistic targets for me. Her knowledge in the field of nutrition is exceptionally good. It has only been a month but I can see the difference. I am very excited that I fit into my pre-pregnancy jeans & my skin definitely shines through…I look forward to more pleasant surprises. '– Shagun Khare, London

BIBLIOGRAPHY

Lousie Hay, *You Can Heal Your Life* (Faber, 2008)

Robert O Young, *The pH Miracle* (Warner Books, 2002)

Steve Gagne, *The Energetics of Food* (Healing Arts Press; 3 edition; 5 November 2008)

Carl Ferre, *Acid Alkaline Companion* (George Ohsawa Macrobiotic Foundation, 2009)

Michio Kushi, *Your Body Never Lies* (Square One Publishers, 2007)

Bateson, Gregory, *Mind and Nature* (Bantam, 1979)

Ted J. Kaptchuk, *The Web That Has No Weaver* (McGraw-Hill, 2000)

Michio Kushi, *Your Face Never Lies* (Avery, 1983)

Dr Daniel Keown, *The Spark in the Machine* (Singning Dragon, 2014)

Robert Becker, *The Body Electric* (William Marrow, 1985)

Zhang Jiaofei & Wang Jing, *The Body Clock Guide* (Shanghai Press and Publishing Development Company, 2015)

Lori Deschene, *Tiny Buddha* (Manjul Publishing House, 2012)

Shanti Gowans, *Ayurveda for Health & Well-being* (Jaico, 2015)

Dr Deepak Chopra, *Perfect Health* (Bantam Books, 1993)

Vasant Lad, *The Science of Self Healing* (Lotuc Press, 1985)

ABOUT THE AUTHOR

'Lost wisdom to live right, eat right, sleep right, think right and work right; disintegrated body, mind and soul; unawareness about our own self…

…Primarily, these are the core foundations of all pain, disease, agony and frustration in the world today; From a holistic standpoint, Diabetes, Depression, Cancer, Arthritis, Osteoporosis, and any other lifestyle disorders are all the manifestations emerging out of this unawareness, lost wisdom, and disintegration of body, mind and soul!'

– Deepti Sehgal

I am a registered Doctor of Oriental Medicine, internationally certified Macrobiotic Health Consultant, Acid-Alkaline (pH) Health Coach, Detox Specialist, Holistic Whole & Natural Foods Nutritionist, Raw Food Nutritionist, Holistic Health & Wellness Educator & Trainer, Holistic Meal Planner & Whole & Natural Foods Chef Instructor. My holistic knowledge is based on the ancient health & wellness concepts from Macrobiotics, Traditional Chinese Medicine & Ayurveda.

Before transforming into a holistic health & wellness practitioner, I have spent 11 years in Information Technology (IT) industry as a software documentation writer. In my IT career for a decade, I gained success but lost my path to health, achieved laurels but forgot my path to contentment, enjoyed recognition and fame but forgot the real charm to live and feel alive. Somewhere, I had forgotten to listen to myself and work on myself, the way we all do each single day!

A few years back, I suffered from frequent allergies & sinus infection. Unexplained aches and pains had nested within me forever. Having undergone two C-sections, my weight ultimately bargained with me and stopped at 76 kgs leaving me totally out-of-shape, fatigued, irritated. I lacked even the basic energy to carry on my day to day tasks. I suffered from extreme anxiety and nervousness. I longed for a slim frame which looked like adistant dream. I suffered from gastritis and was bloated to the extent of looking five months pregnant at any point in time. I was a conscious healthy eater only to realize that I had developed high uric acid levels that caused pains in my joints even with the slightest movement. And, I learned at that time that even healthy diet cannot ensure health, or there was something wrong with my way and understanding of health. Despite of eating very healthy, I had a blotched face, uneven skin tone & dry flaky skin. My moods were under the siege of emotional lows frequently, and my face cut was hidden under layers of fat. I did everything from using cosmetics to seeking medical help for my skin condition, and to gain a better appearance. And at some point I gave up because it never turned out to be a permanent solution. I longed for health, beauty, energy, radiance, vitality, happiness and well-being inside out rather than quick fixes. And this was my story until 3 years back!

Today, I weigh 58 kilos, uric acid levels have gone down without medication, I look & feel younger, live in a healthy body, have a good digestion, have clear skin, have high energy levels, sleep deep and feel light. Most importantly, my transformation happened both at physical & emotional level. My body and mind changed for better & my thoughts gained balance. I follow what I have imbibed over the years as a part of my holistic health education. I live by my dreams and beliefs and have completely changed my diet and lifestyle; alternatively, all by itself, what else changed was my body at the biological level, my appearance, my thought process and my attitude towards life. My cooking techniques are now more oriented towards creating healing health recipes. I have consciously learned to focus on my breathing patterns, and have given up on cosmetics and chemical-laden beauty products. I try to live completely in sync with nature and try to utilize items directly made from natural products. Today, I eat better, live better, breathe better, sleep better & work & enjoy better. I wake up with enthusiasm each day to learn more and serve more. Now, I live each day to the fullest, and definitely not with a thought that it is my last!

As a health & wellness consultant, my practice begins with empowering people to understand themselves first, and then using right dietary & lifestyle practices to achieve health goals. I impart ancient health & wellness trainings & workshops in schools, colleges & corporates.

My vision is to change the way people perceive health in modern times. Through my workshops & training sessions I pass a strong message that health & wellness was much better understood in the ancient times of Traditional Chinese Medicine & Ayurveda. Through my consultations, workshops, writings, training sessions & cookery classes, I intend to bridge the gap between age-old ancient health & healing practices & modern lifestyles. My education & knowledge in ancient healing therapies has made me believe that anyone can achieve amazing results by eating right, by consuming whole & natural foods, by breathing right, by focusing on internal health, by living a natural lifestyle, by keeping meal timings right, by tuning activities with nature's patterns & by natural self-care techniques.

Dr. Deepti Sehgal – Founder of Macrobiotic Wellness

Website: www. macrobioticwellness. com

Email: deeptimacrobioticpractice@gmail.com